CREATE THE LIFE YOU DESIRE
UNLOCK YOUR GREATEST POTENTIAL

Frank Di Genova

Allow Right Now Publishing
Toronto, Canada

Copyright © 2019

By Frank Di Genova

Cover, Graphics, and Interior Design

By Frank Di Genova

Editing and Book Development Provided By

The Awakened Press

www.theawakenedpress.com

Allow Right Now Publishing

www.frankdigenova.com

Allow Right Now
PUBLISHING

The author of this book does not dispense medical advice or prescribe the use of any technique or form of treatment for physical or medical problems without the advice of a physician, either directly or indirectly. The intent of the author is only to offer information of general nature to help you in your quest for spiritual and emotional well-being. In the event that you use any of the information in this book for yourself, the author and publisher assume no responsibility for your actions. All written material is soley the opinion of the author.

No part of this publication may be reproduced, stored in a retrieval system, or transmitted in any form or by any means, electronic, mechanical, recording or otherwise, without the prior written permission of the authors, except by a reviewer who wishes to quote brief passages in connection with a review written for inclusion in a print or online medium, magazine, newspaper, periodical, or broadcast.

First edition.

ISBN: 978-0-9951596-5-5

This book is dedicated to all those who have the courage to look within themselves and make the changes needed to become the best possible version they can be.

Contents

An Important Message and Disclaimer.................................... *vii*
Chapter 0: The Zero Point... 1
Chapter 1: Who Are You?...13
Chapter 2: Spiritual Amnesia and Separation Anxiety............25
Chapter 3: Forgiveness and Taking Responsibility................45
Chapter 4: Fear, Self-Sabotage, and Pleasure.......................53
Chapter 5: Self-Care..75
Chapter 6: The Body: Part 1..91
Chapter 7: Chemistry, Sleep, and Exercise: Part 2.............109
Chapter 8: Guts and Bolts: The Aliens Among Us.............133
Chapter 9: Food Myths and Toxins That Can Kill.............155
Chapter 10: Food..173
Chapter 11: Back to Nature...195
Chapter 12: Energy Life Force...209
Chapter 13: Controlling and Directing Energy..................225
Chapter 14: Energy Flow..241
Chapter 15: Beliefs..255
Chapter 16: What Do You Want?....................................285
Chapter 17: Putting It All Together..................................303
Chapter 18: The End of the Beginning.............................309

In Gratitude:

I would like to thank Luke Di Genova, Theresa Marcotte—Spiritual & Energy Intuitive, and Dr. Ljudmilla Miranovich (Belarus) for your love, wisdom and support

Gracias to my lifelong friend Felipe Luis Martiniello for your knowledge and experience that you've shared with me over the years.

Thank you Lindsay R. Allison for your editing, and insight. I'm grateful for the growth that this adventure has afforded us.

An Important Message and Disclaimer

Before we start on this transformational journey, we should address an ongoing and often neglected accord. This agreement is unique and you'll never guess who it's from. I suggest you read it thoroughly and agree to its terms. Accepting will be for your greatest benefit.

Due to the spiritual nature of me, your Highest Self, it may be possible that you will be unable to manifest everything that you want. My Divine purpose may prevent you from attaining all of your desires. This is due to reasons which may not be conductive to your awakening here on Earth. Your life's experience may contain elements that have been mutually decided upon pre-incarnation, which may be affected by and not limited to: karmic debts, and other contracts and agreements which may be required to be paid in full.

All agreements are not final and are subject to change at any time. Nothing is guaranteed, however, all circumstances and events that may occur are the result of my deepest love for you. All that may arise comes from my desire for our Soul to awaken in physical form.

Deepest Love,
Your Soul

Your signature here
And So It Is

THE PLAN

Before we *came in*, we had a plan and goals that we set out to achieve. We anticipated certain obstacles and challenges from which we could learn from.

The biggest misconception is that our Soul is in need of healing or saving—it is not. Our Soul is whole and complete and waiting for us to awaken to this realization on a physical level. This is what the Game of Life is about.

We may be bound by Soul contracts, agreements, and vibrational debt (karma). However, the journey is to work through and dissolve these entanglements. We can't even begin to understand the complex web of karma and how it works. So there is no use in trying to fathom *why* things happen the way they do. I feel that it's best just to trust the process and allow it all to unfold.

We also have to accept the fact that we may never get everything we desire. What fun would that be, anyway? Although there are powerful tools presented here, we have to be aware that maybe not everything we want is the best thing for us. One thing is for sure: *what is for you, won't pass you by.* You will get exactly what you need at the right time. Somehow, things always seem to have a way of working themselves out. Our Soul has our back and can see things we couldn't even imagine. Even though we may not realize it at the time, everything that happens is for our benefit. All is well... All in Divine time.

Welcome to *Create The Life You Desire*. I want to thank you for choosing this book and for investing in yourself. There is a reason why you're reading this now. The journey is finding out why. My intention, and your desire have crossed paths. On some level, you have asked to receive what I am offering. Most importantly, thank yourself for having the courage to follow through. One book, class or course will not give you all the answers. In fact, they should lead you to ask more questions. Generally, the more you learn in life, the better you can remedy and satisfy them. I encourage you to keep inquiring, just like a curious child does who is full of wonder. Don't believe anything anyone tells you until you can prove it with your own experience and research. My desire is to help lead you on your path to self-discovery, and to answer the queries you may have at this point in time.

In any case, this material may not resonate with you. There may be many reasons for this. When we hear something new that challenges our current belief system, we may react in a few ways—with acceptance, indifference, or with resistance. The German philosopher Arthur Schopenhauer once said, "All truth passes through three stages: first, it is ridiculed, then it is violently opposed, and finally, it is accepted as being self-evident." If what you read in these pages resonates with you, I am grateful. If they challenge your personal views in any way, I invite you to do one of two things: simply reject them and carry on, or perhaps take a look at what you are resisting against. If your way of thinking isn't threatened, there will be no need to defend it. If anger or other fearful emotions arise, then perhaps there is something to further examine within.

We are born to do great things. Within us we have unrealized potential waiting to flourish. This feeling is inherent inside us all. The tragedy is that we're committing the worst possible offence by neglecting the expression of this creativity. Unfortunately, when unused, these unique gifts and talents turn into a toxic and destructive poison. This act of repression leads us to unhealthy behaviours, the core of which is self-sabotage. We have been taught to suppress our power and to stop trusting our innate intelligence and natural instincts. We are kept powerless by the burden that is imposed upon us (debt), and its effect on reducing the time we have to enjoy life.

Attaining success isn't easy, or else everyone would have achieved it by now. The knife only gets sharp against the friction of the grinding stone. The only difference between a diamond and a piece of coal is how much pressure it undergoes. You've already been through enough compression and resistance; now it's time to leverage it and use it to sparkle with brilliance.

There is safety and ease in following the collective norm. If we have been told a lie enough times, eventually it becomes a part of our reality—whether it's true or not, it's no longer questioned. Whoever challenges it may undoubtedly encounter resistance. Furthermore, many of us don't want to pull back the layers of our ignorance.

This means taking responsibility for our actions and facing our fears. It means that we may have to drastically change what we presently believe. We often avoid cutting to the bone because we know it will be painful. Even though we know following the status quo may be wrong, we still continue with the madness. Instead, we self-medicate to avoid facing it all.

We are kept numb and distracted from facing the demons dancing in our head. If we really wanted to heal, we would give up all that made us sick in the first place. Conversely, we may even trick ourselves by following pseudo-spirituality and false *New Age* "teachers" that fluff over the root causes of our struggle. All avoid facing our shadow, or unconscious self.

The antidote to our suffering is through the pain. The very thing we are avoiding is what will heal us, set us free.

> "The wound is the place where the Light enters you."
> —Rumi

Many of us desire freedom. Instead, we've settled for false liberty. Collectively, by mass hypnosis we've allowed and partake in the dumbing down of our society. Eventually, the time comes when we can no longer accept how things are. In time, the pleasure we feel from our negligence becomes our bane. Our deepest urge is to love, be loved and live authentically. We want more—a way out of the fear and darkness. When you ask different questions, you'll get new answers. How many of us live our life without realizing how powerful we really are? Most often, our short time here is wasted. This is tragic, but it doesn't have to be this way. I'm inviting you to rise into your magnificence. My desire is to share all that I've learned with you. I do so with as much clarity as possible. I offer you all the tools that you'll need to *Create The Life You Desire*.

0

THE ZERO POINT

In numerology, the numerals one through nine each represent distinctive attributes. The number zero, however, has no attributes. Instead, it's a blank page of unlimited potential—the nothingness. Metaphysically, zero contains the potentiality of all the numbers and all the elements of the Universe. She is the empty womb, and the giver of all life who can unite both spirit and matter. Her circle is not fixed, she can change in size, grow or shrink. She is the holder of Yin and Yang. Zero is the creator, expander and the destroyer.

She enhances all the numbers that are placed before her. The number two increases its vibration to twenty, five quintuples to fifty, and so on. When any number is divided or multiplied by zero, it is either dissolved to nothing, or is destroyed altogether.

She rejuvenates and transforms. Everything we desire sits in her hollow circumference, waiting to be born.

HOW TO GET THE MOST OUT OF THIS BOOK

I've put my heart and soul into this with the intent that it assists you in fully realizing your highest potential. You can peruse these pages like a leisurely stroll alongside the edge of the Amazon Rainforest. Or, you can make it the most rewarding adventure by making your way deep into the ancient woods. Doing so, you start understanding the balance and subtle communication between every living organism in its ecosystem. Similarly, you can play it safe and continue snorkelling through life as you splash on the surface. Or, you can put on your oxygen tank and dive deep into the unknown—experience with excitement the magical wonders that await. The greater your investment, the greater the reward.

THE BUFFET

Many of us have a tendency and desire to learn everything we can all in one go. This causes us to rush through things. This book is designed for you to experience, absorb and integrate the lessons presented. Each section and chapter leads into the next, building off one another to paint the full story. Cherry picking, or skimming through these pages won't lead you to the magic bullet. In truth, the secret kernel lies within the process of integrating its contents.

We can understand, or overstand a concept, but unless it's fully integrated, we won't. *Innerstanding* is when the cells of our body know. When something is learned rapidly most often it's not fully absorbed, and is quickly forgotten. *This excludes an intense experience or trauma.* Although we may convince ourselves that we'll be able to remember something, most times we won't. A sudden distraction, or a powerful emotion, and all bets are off. When we are in fight-or-flight mode, our ability to think rationally takes a back seat to our instincts. When knowledge is anchored experientially, it integrates within our unconscious mind, body, cells and nervous system.

The challenge with learning is maintaining the discipline required to fully integrate the subject matter before trying to consume more. This is like eating at an all-you-can-eat buffet. There is so much food available that we tend to overeat, which usually leads to bloating and indigestion. We are so seduced by the bounty of food, that we fail to fully savour it before filling our mouths up again—unlike fine dining, where each morsel is savoured. Eating consciously leads to greater enjoyment, and in the process, refines one's taste. I strongly suggest you complete the exercises that are presented before starting the following ones. Take a few days in between to allow for their integration. Practice what you learn before taking a bite out of the next lesson.

BEAT THE ODDS

Studies show that most people who attend workshops or take online courses don't follow through to the very end. Do you know that more than ninety percent of you will not fully read, or apply what's in this book? Those who achieve success are those under the ten percent range. Successful people take action and follow through. They also know that information alone is not power. If you ask any truly successful person for advice, they usually have no problem giving it, unlike the unsuccessful who tend to guard and hoard what little they know. Access to the Internet is available to the majority of this planet. Knowledge is readily accessible to everyone. There isn't anything that you can't learn on your own. We should all be accomplished geniuses by now. Most of us are too busy, or lazy to apply ourselves. Many look for the quick fix, and want it easy. They don't want to do the work needed for success, and give up when results aren't attained quickly. Instead, they focus on why something is not happening, complain and make excuses.

Success is afforded to those who are willing to put in the work. Those ten percent are willing to do what it takes to realize their goals. Free, quick and easy are what entice the masses. When something is free, it's not valued as if it was paid for. Investment creates perceived worth. When something is valued there's a stronger inclination to follow through. An unripe fruit is bitter and doesn't taste good; when it ripens, it becomes sweet and it tastes wonderful. If the fruit is left sitting on the stem for too long it starts rotting. We need to keep growing, or we, too, will rot. We can pick the easy low hanging fruit, or climb and get the most coveted. Success requires the motivation to climb up the tree. Something earned creates gratitude and appreciation. There are talkers and there are doers. There are know-it-alls who hide behind basic knowledge, or masked biased opinions. These are the same people who have failed and given up—who were either too afraid or lazy to try. They are also the first ones who will discourage you from following your dreams. You can't make them look bad.

Gym goers exercise and workout to achieve better health. Some are more diligent as they work their core, upper, and lower body. Missing leg day is common for some, and for others, it's always jaw day. You can tell how successful a person is not by what they say, but by what they have accomplished in their life. Seek advice from the doers, not the talkers. Find someone you can model who has achieved what you want. Ask them how they did it. Watch another's behaviour: they will show you how they approach everything in life. How they do the little things is how they do everything.

My challenge to you is to become the rare ten percent who cross the finish line.

WORK SMARTER, NOT HARDER

There is an easy way and a hard way to do something. Unfortunately, most of us do the latter. Is this because of human nature? Or, is it a lack of education? I believe that success has a formula, one which can be reproduced and applied to achieve a desired result. Life has many contradictions and success is no different. We've been conditioned to believe that success is achieved by struggling like the salmon that swims against the current of the river. We feel that nothing of value is earned easily. Working smarter—not harder—means that things should not be extremely difficult, nor complicated. It's best they flow. You can try lifting a heavy rock with your bare hands. But if it's too large to lift, no amount of blood, sweat or tears will be enough to hoist it. We need leverage, not only mathematically, but mentally and biologically.

The best example that I can give is by my personal experience of losing weight. I've tried every diet in the world and they all produced the same result: although some helped me lose weight faster than others, in the end I gained it all back, and always a bit more. It was a constant struggle; I felt like a yo-yo. I expended more discipline and willpower than was necessary. Yet I still failed. How do others lose weight so easily? The fact was, I approached it the wrong way. I was trying to lift a rock five times my size. You see, the first three letters in diet are *die*, and that's what I was doing. I was dying of starvation and was ready to eat the hands off my arms. The moment I learned how to eat properly the weight came off effortlessly. I stopped dieting and chose instead to live a different lifestyle.

When I was doing it wrong, no amount of willpower or discipline could offset my body's natural instinct for self-preservation. It always won. That was until I learned how to hack my body's compulsion to survive and use it to shed tons of fat. It was so easy that the only thing hard was not falling into the psychology of needing to eat. My past conditioning strived to convince me that I was hungry when I really wasn't. At first I couldn't believe it; aside from the initial four day adaptation phase, it was a piece of cake. Well, not exactly cake, it was more like fat. You may be thinking, "Wait, Frank lost fat by eating fat?" Actually, you would be absolutely correct. My body instinctively held on to fat so it could survive, but I wasn't giving it what it wanted. I restricted it from my diet. Instead, I was eating everything low in fat, all of which was making me just what I was trying to avoid. Stay tuned.

When you know how to attain something the right way, you'll stop struggling. You will begin having great success. Less effort—greater results. This applies to every aspect of your life. This is how CEOs make three hundred times more money than the average worker. Work smarter, not harder.

MOTIVATIONAL HYPE AND POSITIVE THINKING DON'T WORK

I'm not here to con you, nor to momentarily hype you up. How many of you are put off by the so-called "gurus" that promise you how to get rich and live the life of your dreams? They use short-lived approaches like motivational and positive thinking. These guys know how to psych you up, and have you believe that it's all a matter of following their program. This strategy keeps us powerless while giving us false hope. It's not about just staying motivated; I offer you the opportunity for true change. We both know that motivation comes and goes. There needs to be a solid foundation established beforehand—one that will help sustain the necessary momentum.

Who remembers the TV evangelists of the early 80s? One character claimed to heal people, got them to quit smoking, and persuaded them to get out of their wheelchairs. "Throw your canes and cigarettes on stage, you are healed!" They knew how to pump people up with adrenaline. This example of hype isn't motivation, it's a con job. When we are artificially jacked up, we're ready to tackle any challenge. Yet, it's unnatural and impossible to be totally motivated all the time. Have you ever experienced a carb crash? That's exactly what it is: an ultimate carbohydrate crash. When we eat too much sugar, our blood glucose skyrockets, and we shake with energy. Someone has to peel us off of the ceiling like a cat—*meow!* Motivational speeches, seminars and workshops do just that. They pump you up like tires, only there is a leak in them. In that moment you can lead a revolution. Then, before you know it, psss… you are deflated and can't even get out of bed.

Motivation stimulated by external means supplied from gurus, conferences, and powwows is no different than taking drugs that raise dopamine. You'll experience the same addiction and withdrawal symptoms because you haven't addressed the root of what makes you feel powerless. True motivation starts off as a *desire*, but most desires aren't strong enough to turn in to the proverbial carrot. Initially, we are full of piss and vinegar, but before we know, we start self-sabotaging ourselves back into our safe zone. We all want to make more money, lose weight and get healthy. But how many times of promising yourself, "I'll start on Monday," does it take before you actually follow through?

POSITIVE THINKING

What about positive thinking? This is another Ponzi mind game. Seriously, what is the use of positive thinking if you're a pessimist? Most of the time we don't even believe what we are saying as we mechanically repeat meaningless words. When we are told an affirmation, it's another's statement which usually doesn't mean anything to us. How and what we say something also matters. When you affirm, "I want more money," what you're really saying is, "I have no money." I want it because I don't have it. This keeps us in a wanting state energetically. How can positive thinking work if you say a few feel good affirmations but think negative ones for the rest of the day? What does positive thinking mean to you? Is it an attitude of anticipating the best outcome? Does it mean looking on the bright side of things? We shouldn't send out negative thoughts to the Universe because our words do affect how life responds to us. However, positive thinking alone doesn't change a thing. Jumping off a cliff while chanting, "I will have a soft landing," won't stop you from splattering all over the ground below. There are still natural laws to abide by. Was I being a bit dramatic and unrealistic?

Imagine that I give you a combination lock. I would like for you to open this lock. Now all you have to do is focus on it, open it using only positive thinking. I know you can do it. So, think good and hard… I'll wait… OK, maybe that wasn't fair.

How can you open it without knowing the correct number combination, right? Even if I gave you the numbers, you will still have a hard time opening it. You'd be closer, no doubt, and with enough effort you'd eventually find a way to unlock it. But why go through all that frustration? You could always use a crowbar, or shoot it open. To open the lock effectively, you not only need the numbers, but you must know their proper sequence. You have to know when to turn clockwise and counterclockwise.

TRUE MOTIVATION

Motivation can be explained simply by stating, "The desire to do things." There are basic motivators that override all others. Most of us want to stay alive, so we're motivated to breathe. Hunger stimulates us to eat, and thirst pushes us to drink. If we want to live, then it's pretty much guaranteed that we'll follow through. Other motivators don't always command the same respect. If we don't have to do something, many of us won't. If your doctor advises you to stop eating french fries and drinking soda you may or may not. If, however, you had a heart attack, I'm guessing you would.

The level of fear, or severity of a situation influences our motivation.

Conversely, many of us have a mentality of invincibility, especially when we're young. We believe we won't get cancer if we continue smoking. Or maybe we do and are secretly punishing ourselves. Most often, we try to convince ourselves that we'll stop before anything bad happens. If it does, then it's not today and we'll deal with it then. When desire exceeds the pain of not doing—change happens. Anyone can say "yes" when they are jacked up in the moment. The character of success is built when that excitement has passed. Have you noticed that the ones who are first on the wagon are usually the first to jump off? Usually when we make a decision to change, life has a way of testing us to see how committed we really are.

Inside each and every one of us burns a flame. Sometimes it's just a glow, a pilot light, or it can be an inferno. Often, we douse this fire by apathy and doubt. Let your blaze burn so intensely that nothing can douse it. How do we set fire to what is behind us so it will propel us forward? We need a compelling enough reason to create and sustain momentum. Motivation starts off as a desire, but most of them aren't strong enough to keep us going. We quickly burn away the paper and never get to the logs that keep the fire going. Where do our desires come from? Are they preloaded, or do they arise as new options are offered? Have you noticed that the more choice we have, the harder it is to make a decision? What we don't know about we can't crave. The more we experience, the more we seem to want. You may say, "I don't have any motivation in my life." I say, "You're just bored and don't have anything that excites you!" How many times do you forget someone's name? The truth is, that most of the time, you didn't really care about them. Of course you'd forget. What if you met someone who you were very attracted to? I'm guessing that you would immediately become a memory expert. When something is important to you, it will motivate you and you'll make it a priority in your life.

A lack of motivation is a result of not being aligned with your purpose.

This leads to boredom and laziness, a toxic brew that festers into a self-destructive behaviour. Perhaps it's not a lack of passion or purpose. What if you're discouraged because you've tried and failed too many times in the past? Instead of giving up and thinking, "What's the use?" consider it an invitation to direct your energy in a totally different way. We tend to settle for things by convincing ourselves that what we currently have is better than not having it at all—even if it's not what we want. "It's good enough," you say—but is it? When we are devoted to something we stick with it even if it looks bleak. We believe in it, knowing the benefits will outweigh the detriments. Results are what keep us interested, the momentum that turns the wheel. Focus on what inspires you and keep feeding it with your attention. This will get you feeling good, and when you feel good, awesome stuff starts happening. Those good feelings stack on one another. Play and fun are very strong motivators for sustained behavioural change. If there is pressure to do something, we won't be as driven to do it. Focus on the benefits, and not on the work that is ahead of you. Just as exercise can never work off a bad diet, motivation and positive thinking can never overcome limiting beliefs. Enthusiasm cannot be inspired by negative thinking.

1

WHO ARE YOU?

Knowing who we are is essential in understanding how we interact with the world. Understanding our biography affects our ideology, and our biology. Self-knowledge helps in uncovering all that may be blocking us from creating and enjoying the life we want to experience. Do you know who you are?

I will ask you to get a pen, a sheet of lined paper, and an envelope. We are going to do a little exercise. I'm going to ask you some questions below. Since you don't have them written down, you may want to answer them by using the question in your reply. An example is, "What is your full name?" "My name is Frank Di Genova, I was born on…etc." This is not necessary, however it will help when reviewing your answers.

What is your full name? What is the date of your birth? Where were you born? Are you male, or female? How old are you now? What is your mother's name? What is your father's name? What nationality are your parents? Which religion do you believe in? Are you an atheist, or agnostic? What is your occupation? What is your favourite food? Who was your first crush? Who was your first heartbreak? Which is your favourite sport? What are your favourite hobbies? Are you a chocolate or vanilla person? Do you prefer beer or wine? Do you even drink at all? Which political party best represents your views? Are you enjoying filling out this questionnaire?

Fold and place your sheet of answers inside the envelope but don't seal it. Set it aside for now.

IDENTITY

A good actor can play different roles without becoming them. They can immerse themselves into a character without being affected or changed in any way. The actor remains who they are. Method actors take it a little bit further: they become the character, sometimes for months even before filming. Occasionally they may lose themselves in the role and have a difficult time coming back. There are some who believe that the actor Heath Ledger succumbed to his death because of how he prepared for his incredible performance in a *Batman* movie. Did he really become the sociopathic, cold-blooded and mass-killing clown in his own mind? Having said that, I believe there was more going on inside Heath's mind that caused his fatal end. Have you ever noticed how much you change when you put on a costume?

Have you ever been to a masquerade party? Have you ever acted in a school play?

Life is a stage, and we are the actors. We play different roles, and each one is important to carry out the story. At the end of a play, the curtain falls, the hero and villain both hold hands and bow to the crowd. In sport, the players shake hands after the match. Life is the same: it's a show. Unfortunately, we have taken the production a bit too seriously. Actors get cast for different roles, and sometimes they don't get the ones they audition for. The lead role may go to another, or they can get a callback and play a supporting role. Either way, the actors do their job and the production ends. The performers may change, but the show goes on. Eventually the bright lights fade, but sometimes actors can't step out of the spotlight. Some cling to the character that made them famous—they are unable to detach from it. Others, subsequently, don't want to have anything to do with it. The weight of this anchor can sink them fast. There are those that understand this process and are able to reinvent themselves—or can choose a whole new career. Sadly, some start on the proverbial downward spiral of depression, substance abuse, and sometimes suicide.

What about the roles we play in our own life? Do we have the leading role? Are we the supporting actor? Or, are we only an extra who's barely seen in the background? What happens when the lights dim on us? Who are we without our career, money and possessions? What if you lost a limb, or lost your sight? Who are you without your story—your emotional pain? Do you play the victim? If so, do you use it as leverage? Why won't you give it up? Nothing will change until you drop the act.

All things come and go, and are in constant change. These are all temporary conditions. If we attach our happiness and our sense of identity to them we are in for a rude awakening. We are all wearing a costume, acting and hiding behind masks and personas. We've become the character who we believe we are, defending and protecting it. We play the role of father, mother, husband wife, brother, sister, and so on. Most of us are following a script: one in which is often not written by us, but by others. The plot of life doesn't have lines to be memorized—although some of us do abide by rehearsed and practiced routines. What would happen if we stepped outside of ourselves and watched the performance from the seats? We'd undoubtedly have a greater perspective and see the bigger picture. We would see that our life was only a story. How daunting would that be? Can you look beyond what you've been made to believe you are? Can you imagine yourself without a name, career and status?

Perhaps it's time to go backstage, remove the makeup and take the costume off. Maybe the time is nigh to remember our true identity, and to awaken into this new awareness.

EXIT STAGE LEFT

In theatrical scripts, "Exit Stage Left" instructs the actor portraying the character to disappear from the stage.

Get out your envelope from the first exercise and take out your sheet. Review what you've written down. Now, mentally affirm, "I am not these experiences! I am not the thoughts I think, the choices I make, or the emotions I feel!" Whatever you wrote down or believe about yourself is not your true identity. Nor does any of it define you. You've been given a name, a race and a religion to follow. You could have been from any culture, and spoke any language. There is no exclusivity. You are pure, unlimited awareness who is passing through situations and experiences in life. The past is only memories which you've chosen to invest in. Some have left deeper imprints than others, while some have been forgotten altogether. Indelible scars are actually subsidized memories of an experience. I'm not suggesting for you to wipe the slate clean, or ignore or discredit who you are. Nor am I asking you to trivialize whatever has happened to you. We all have a role to play, and we're all part of the production. Neither should you file a grievance, or go on strike against the actors union—just step back a bit, sit down and watch from a chair.

It doesn't matter what has happened to you thus far. Life is simply a journey, an experience. Celebrate your victories, and also your losses. Realize that on a spiritual level you have chosen your story so you could learn from it. Everything that happens to you has been designed by your Higher Self to teach what it is you need to learn. Things don't happen *to us*, they happen *for us*. Our Soul is all-knowing, but our conditioned human self isn't. Every experience is designed to help reveal this innate deep awareness. Events guide us along the path, they help us navigate through obstacles. We are travelling on the river of life toward the threshold of our Highest Self. Like religion and beliefs, an experience takes us to where we need to go next. This process is a lot like the function of a boat. After we reach the destination we no longer need it. The problem is, we hang on to these events and the story. We make it our identity. Why would you need to drag your boat behind you when you begin climbing a hill? Wouldn't mountain gear be more efficient?

It matters not what our circumstances are, it's how we react to them. The same boiling water that softens the hard potato hardens the soft egg. In your story, does your character play the victim, or the victor? True freedom is the ability to move through an experience without labeling or judging it. It's not allowing previous memories to influence your interpretation of an arising event—liberation means not being triggered. True freedom is also when you have the awareness to choose how you want to react to an experience.

Unfortunately, we keep reinvesting in our story, this is what keeps it real.

If we realized our true nature, this wouldn't happen. If the current narrative of your life is not what you want it to be, you can change it by the same way it was created. Be mindful, however—*it's not about replacing one story with a different one, because it's still a story.* My intention is to inspire you to innerstand, and to move through an experience as a witness. Play your character well, but don't become it. Experience each moment for what it is, allow it to unfold—be the observer.

Life is about enjoying its different aromas, textures, sounds and delicacies. *Create the life you desire*, not the one that was imposed on you. You are pure energy with unlimited potential. We are human beings who have failed to remember that we are both—humans and beings. I agree that looking beyond this can be quite challenging. How can one believe in something that can't physically be seen? You have a body made of flesh, you feel pain and pleasure, and so on. But behold, listen to the whispers, the gut feelings, inspirations, dreams, and synchronicities that beckon from beyond. These invite us to seek the truth that we are so much more than we perceive. Science is quickly catching up and proving that there is more behind the veil of this physical world.

Place your exercise sheet back in to the envelope and save it for later. Don't seal it yet.

WHO HAVE WE BECOME?

Your parents and all those who have helped rear you have contributed to building your narrative. You've learned from your tribe, adapted to their story, their belief systems, their fears, behaviours, and general outlook on life. Your personal experiences have shaped you; many of these have been decoded not solely by you, but by the filters of your caregivers. We have learned to accept others' distorted interpretations of us.

Typically, when we follow the script, we are rewarded. When we don't, we are not. Some souls come in with such a strong sense of Self that they don't resonate to the chronicles of their birth family. They are sometimes called the problem child, or the black sheep. Sadly, the majority yield and assimilate as not to rock the proverbial boat. As children grow, they explore the world and take in more information. As a result, their belief system recalibrates, and they seek greater independence as an individual. Society too has a script, and is built on a system that rewards compliance, and punishes defiance. In our early years, we quickly learned that if we expressed ourselves without inhibition, we'd likely experience rejection. Consequently, we edited our behaviour and betrayed ourselves by the act of people pleasing, and approval seeking. We didn't want to appear vulnerable and risk feeling pain. It's much easier to follow the rules, be normal and fit in. We police ourselves by colouring within the lines. Those who choose not to usually encounter resistance. It takes courage to stand against the crowd and call its bullshit.

We pattern what we see others do, and what's on television. The desire for social acceptance is much stronger than refusing the illusion that society upholds. Not many are able to walk against the herd that's headed for the cliff. One shepherd, and one sheepdog are only capable of herding around a hundred sheep. Imagine the potential chaos if a bunch of sheep decided to break free of the pack. There are not as many leaders as there are followers.

In fact, those that lead and control the global masses consist of less than one percent. Are we following true leaders, or misleaders? We follow the scripts laid out by our parents, culture, religion, the legal system, and government. These storylines have been passed down through generations by word of mouth, fairy tales, stories and myth. They are repeated over and over until they are ingrained into the fabric of our being—encoded into our DNA. Yet, none of them are questioned or challenged. We buy them as fact and assume they are for our benefit. But are they? Who put these narratives in place, and why?

Question everything with an open mind and heart. Are things really as they seem? We are living in a time where so many things don't make any sense. I'm sure you feel it. The world seems like it's upside down, and instead most of us decide to ignore it. As long as we are kept distracted, pacified, ignorant and fearful, nothing is scrutinized.

"Just look at us. Everything is backwards, everything is upside down. Doctors destroy health, lawyers destroy justice, psychiatrists destroy minds, scientists destroy truth, major media destroys information, religions destroy spirituality and governments destroy freedom."
—Michael Ellner

ARE WE SLAVES?

Could we be unaware slaves to a system that's been designed to keep us from realizing our truest potential?

For most of the week, we go to school and leave our parental guidance behind for seven or more hours. The level of our success is dependent on how obediently we follow the rules. We are shaped by a pre-written curriculum that the educator recites—governed by the ringing Pavlovian bell. The teacher asks us to turn to page six in the book—we obey. We learn the lesson, and graded on our ability to memorize and regurgitate it back. Basically, we're rewarded for our ability to comply and memorize. If we don't fit into this structure we are penalized. Some students don't respond well to this process. They may have different learning patterns, become bored, or simply call bullshit and resist. They get labeled with an attention disorder or a type of cognitive problem. The solution is typically to subdue them by medication.

The educational system, culture and society in general hold us to a standard. We are evaluated by a similar model. Not everyone is the same, and not everyone is happy about being homogenized and put into a box. This reward and punishment game continues on until we ascend to higher levels. The more we yield, the more letters we get after our name. Incidentally, the more money we are rewarded with. Unfortunately as it is, more student debt is incurred. This burden will have to be paid off. What better way is there to indoctrinate a person into a system than to bind them to it with a financial obligation? Disobeying means no candy, no more toys, or living the good life. Debt is a great motivator and can challenge a person's integrity. Incidentally, creativity and thinking outside the box is stifled. The poets, artists, and freethinkers aren't compensated the same way—they're discouraged. Who wants to be a starving artist? This indoctrination works wonderfully to create obedient workers. It doesn't matter whether it's in a factory, an office, or any medical or government institution. If you refuse, there is always another waiting to take your place. Did you know that the origin of the word "*gradu-*

ation" comes from the words *gradual* and *indoctrination*? Are we being educated, or indoctrinated?

United we stand, divided we fall. The family unit seems to be under attack.

Have you noticed that most children's stories show one or both parents either killed, or not around? With the rise of feminism, mothers are becoming career women no longer rearing their children. The system parents and educates the children of today. Who is creating the curriculum? Media promotes the glorification of sex, promiscuity, adultery, and the sexual exploitation of young women. Before you know, this all becomes "normal", being just static noise in the background. We are divided by religion, culture, race, language, social cliques and financial class, sports teams, war, fabricated enemies, borders, and even backyard fences. The desire to compete arises from the mind's belief that it is separate from the whole. This division keeps us from uniting, and encourages fighting with one another. We want more money, a bigger house, a fancier car—it never ends. We are drunk with a "winner takes all" mentality. This is all an illusion.

Slavery still exists, and is more dangerous now because we don't see it. We think we are free, but we are not. There is no better way to create a slave than to burdened them with the debt of imaginary money, with a controlled interest rate. Furthermore, we are fined for not obeying the rules, we are overpaying for insurance, petty traffic violations, and utilities. We are literally taxed to death. We are given the false sense that we have choice. Pick the blue pill or the red one, Conservative or Liberals, drink Coke or Pepsi. The list goes on and on. We don't choose, we pick from what we are given—red or blue. You may vote for the left or right, but it's the same bird, different wing. Our real freedoms are being taken from us, and replaced by useless free-dumbs. We can choose to identify with any gender, smoke, drink or partake in any drug of choice. We can bury our heads by binge watching our favourite tell-lie-vision programs, which further indoctrinate us.

> "Seek the truth or hide your head in the sand. Both require digging."—Andrew Nolan

The insanity is that we are policing ourselves and don't even know it. If anyone questions the system they are called out. Freedom of speech has been muted by political correctness. Questioning labels you a denier, or an anti-this or anti-that. We are ridiculed and shamed simply for challenging the status quo. In extreme cases, we can be jailed or killed for telling the truth.

The equality agenda amalgamates the strong with the weak, the doers with the non—we're all given medals of participation. This is how nations crumble. We're afraid, or too numb to stand up. Deep down we may know something is wrong, but because we feel powerless we do absolutely nothing about it. We don't have to save the world, we need to save ourselves. Stop waiting for a saviour that promises you salvation tomorrow. This trick is as old as time itself. Just because deception is being sold, doesn't mean we have to buy it. The answers lie within you, they always have. Tap those ruby slippers.

> "We can accept God becoming Man to save Man, but not Man becoming God to save himself."
> —Vernon Linwood Howard

2

SPIRITUAL AMNESIA ~ SEPARATION ANXIETY

Amnesia is the state of partial or total memory loss. Aside from injury to the brain and other medical happenings, memory loss can occur due to psychological amnesia, or dissociative amnesia. Emotional shock such as trauma, sexual violence, and other harrowing events can cause amnesia. Have you ever lost your train of thought while talking with someone? Ever gone into another room and forgot why you did? You were probably distracted and offset by a strong memory, or emotion. In conversation, you may have been cut off in mid-sentence, or have had the subject abruptly changed. Have you ever been in a heated argument and forgot what started it in the first place?

The moment we were born we forget our true nature. Imagine being transported to another planet. You're placed into a strange body that resembles an eight-legged spider. You're angry at being confined, and bound within a strange body. You feel restricted. You're not only unaware of how to move, but unable to communicate with the other inhabitants. You can't speak, or express yourself. All you can do is make strange sounds. In addition, around this planet is a dense energetic field (a firewall) that starts to dissolve your memory. You begin forgetting everything, losing all of your previous memories. Slowly, you learn how to move this new body. You learn how to make the sounds you hear others use to communicate. After a while a comfort level develops and you feel somewhat more secure in this new world.

There are safe and accepted behavioural patterns that you abide by. Avoid the others. Soon, you integrate and find your place in this alien civilization. You learn the ways. You may even begin to enjoy this new life. Deep down, however, burns the imprint of what you once were. Sometimes whispering, at other times gnawing at you. Although you may thrive in this new world there is a yearning for something else. A distant memory, a knowing perpetually beckons you. The time comes when your body dies off and you have to come back. But you fight and cling on, not wanting to leave. This world, our body and its five senses distract us. We've been hijacked and forced to believe that we're only the body and the conditions surrounding it. Our physical senses can only sense a small fraction of the colossal spectrum of energy that exists around us. We've convinced ourselves that what we can't see doesn't exist. We are suffering from spiritual amnesia.

Every expression of consciousness—whether it's human, animal, or insect—is subjected to some degree of conditioning. We identify as our body, and our social environment shapes who we think we are. The Japanese are known for their Bonsai trees. These are very small trees that have been cultivated to appear full in size. The concept of this delicate art form has also been applied—albeit crudely—to create square watermelons. Space is limited in Japan, and new techniques are always being developed to maximize limited real estate. Young watermelons which are still growing are inserted into square boxes made from tempered glass. This creates melons that can be stacked, and fit perfectly inside refrigerators. Likewise, fish will only grow in portion to the size of tank they are kept in. Do we live in a world that is designed to keep us believing that we are no more than our corporeal experience and environment? Many of us think that we are just human beings trying to become more spiritual. When in fact we are spiritual beings having a human experience. This sense of being separated causes us to feel disconnected from our connection to Source. This leaves us feeling powerless, fearful and alone. Remember, we are both the body and the Spirit residing within it. There is no separation. We are always plugged in to our Highest Self.

Our human aspect is just the tip of the iceberg. We are so much greater than we can envision. Knowing this changes everything. Not only is this a game changer—it's a life changer! We are all suffering from separation anxiety on the grandest scale. We have been conditioned to believe that we are powerless. Nonetheless, we are on the verge of a mass awakening. There is a tear in the veil and more are noticing the glitches in the program. The system is failing. I invite you to rouse from the dream, become

Douglas Quaid and Neo from the movies *Total Recall* and *The Matrix*. Both these characters are eventually awakened from their false programming, and learned their true nature. This is also our journey! Remember who you are, not what you have been or told.

EARLY TRAUMA AND INFANT PTSD

The first ten days to a few weeks of a newborn's life is so utterly critical for their development. In order for the baby to grow and establish itself into a healthy adult, it needs a favourable start. Unfortunately, many of us haven't been given that. Instead, we've been traumatized to varying degrees. Most of us suffer with some form of infant PTSD (Post Traumatic Stress Disorder) and not even know it.

We talk about PTSD as something that only happens to young adults, soldiers and First Responders. No one talks about it as a result of having a traumatic birth experience. Imagine being thrust out into a harsh environment after spending nine months in a warm, safe one. The trauma of that alone can affect us in many areas of our lives. After that harrowing event, we are left helpless, relying heavily on our caregivers. We have no defence mechanisms. Newborns need a loving touch, eye contact, and a heart connection with their mother. Many are denied this, especially being breastfed. A failure to bond and intercommunicate with their mother can cause the infant to withdraw. Do you know any baby that smiles at its birth? They cry because the air is cold, and the sounds are loud. They want back in, and out of the hostile environment. You may think that this is par for the course, and no big deal, right? Let's explore a bit deeper.

Whether you came into this world via C-section, prematurely, in an incubator, with umbilical cord restriction (or related issues), induced, or by forceps, you may be suffering from PTSD. Some studies conclude that an unborn baby can feel the emotions of their mother. Incidentally, they are connected by the same nervous system. What if a mother didn't want to have her child? What if she suffered from depression, or was addicted to drugs or alcohol? Furthermore, what if her relationship with the father was that of emotional and physical abuse? There is no telling how extensive the adverse effects can be.

Now, to expose the most denied trauma prevalent in our society today: male circumcision. Wait, what? Ask yourself why does the act of FGM (female genital mutilation) turn your (and for most Westerners) stomach inside out, yet not the disfiguring of a male's penis? One is abhorred, the other is celebrated and accepted as perfectly normal.

There seems to be a bias and shaming toward uncircumcised men. Why is there a double standard on this? The hygiene excuse is weak and averting. The sand in the dessert alibi is even more preposterous. Have we all stopped bathing? This is like saying, "Don't wash your feet, if they stink, just cut them off." There is no difference between foreskin and a woman's hood covering and retracting over her clitoris—similar smegma is produced which can also lead to foul odour due to lack of hygiene. Did you know the rate of circumcision in Finland has been only 1 in 16,667 over the last few decades, and that many hospitals have stopped doing this procedure altogether?

What are the psychological effects caused by these ancient blood rituals? Imagine the betrayal of a child's trust for the mother who is supposed to protect them—the Matriarchal Protector giving their children away to get mutilated. Does the repression of the female via FGM have a similar effect as the emasculation of the male by circumcision? Imagine the anger, and sadness over having genitals altered without anaesthetic, or consent. I'd say this can lead to mistrust of the opposite sex, depression and intimacy issues. It is the ultimate betrayal. Cutting off the foreskin of a male's penis removes over twenty-thousand nerve endings. This reduces up to seventy-five percent of sensation a man can feel during intercourse. A woman's clitoris in contrast has eight-thousand nerve endings. This dramatically reduces oxytocin levels a man can feel during intimacy, and prevents him from forging an intimate bond with his partner. The head of a circumcised penis loses its ability to feel due to the callused skin caused by constant contact and rubbing. Could this be why many genitally-mutilated men experience erectile dysfunction, and semi-hard erections later on in life? Could this be the cause of toxic masculinity? Is this why porn and emotionally detached sex is glorified? Does this explain why Viagra sales have skyrocketed in populations where circumcision is commonly practised? All the aforementioned birthing experiences can and do affect the brain and its development. The greater the trauma, the more it impacts the psyche. Evidence suggests that intense distress hardwires the brain to seek safety and security at all costs. This can lead to short-sighted choices, and risky behaviour—long-term consequences aren't considered as being significant. *Even worse, these early traumas are what set the stage for our early indoctrination.* They keep us obedient, and feeling powerless to resist authority. Trauma can and does happen at any age, yet the most damaging is when the person afflicted hasn't established the coping skills necessary to deal with it at the time. There is a common assumption and misconception that the child doesn't remember these intense pains and traumas. This isn't true; the brain is greatly altered by intense cortisol release caused by trauma. Mostly all surgical procedures leave a mark, not only on skin, but within the fascia, cell memory and in the psyche. *The mind may not remember, but the body does.*

EARLY CHILDHOOD NEEDS

In addition to the first ten days of a child's life, the first five to seven years are just as crucial. Events experienced during this time profoundly affect how they learn and are shaped as an adult. Within this timeframe, a child's brain develops faster than any other time in their life. Solid foundations are laid down. The clay is still pliable until it hardens—the tree will grow as the twig is bent.

"Give me a child until he is seven, and I will show you the man."
—Aristotle

Hitler's version was more sinister, "Give me a child until he's seven, and he's mine forever." As children we need nourishment beyond our physical needs. If these aren't met, or we have been traumatized, these feelings of incompleteness and invisible wounds are brought into our relationships and adult life. As babies, we had to rely heavily on our parents to keep us safe and nourished. If our early emotional requirements aren't met, later we tend to seek their fulfillment through other means—mostly through our interactions and relationships with other people, such as friends and lovers. The deeper the intimacy, the more vulnerability is potentially exposed. Unfortunately, our parents and those we encounter may suffer from the same trauma, anxiety and spiritual amnesia that we have been subjected to. They, too, were programmed by the ones before them, and on it goes. The stark truth is that almost everyone we seek support from will eventually let us down. Why? Because they are not equipped to help us. They have their own issues they're struggling with. The blind can't lead the blind. By the same token, we shouldn't expect another to save us. That responsibly shouldn't be imposed on anyone, ever. Seeking outside of yourself for any type of salvation is codependency. It doesn't matter if it's from a parent, teacher, politician, priest or a prophet—there is a finite time before we have to wean off. Mentors will help us get to where we need to go, but the time comes when they can no longer help us.

Over time, letdowns and failed rescues can cause us to lose faith in people altogether. This can lead to us becoming jaded and pessimistic—to build the preverbal wall—to protect our emotional vulnerabilities. Sometimes we may turn to material fulfillments to feed and heal our sense of incompleteness, and emotional wounds. We may self-medicate by eating, drinking, doing drugs, having promiscuous sex, taking risks, and gambling. Whichever is the case, it's all the same. These are painkillers that also provide a rush of adrenaline, ways to avoid facing our pain. Most addictions are the result of unprocessed wounds and traumas largely experienced during childhood. At this time, we didn't have the resources or the know-how to cope. Subsequently, we found ways to numb these experiences which often lead to dependency on them.

Unlike addiction, compulsive behaviour is a repeated action which is not motivated by a pleasure or reward; there isn't a rational motivator. Compulsive behaviour is driven by the need to reduce anxiety.

It's hard to find fault with ourselves, and much easier to blame another. How can we take responsibility when we are playing the victim, or the bully? When we use manipulating behaviour, it's an attempt to control a person or situation we feel powerless to. There is no denying that we all feel the craving to connect with something more—it's human. Whether it's with a person, our Higher Self, or with God, loneliness leads to unhealthy behaviour.

Nonetheless, we have largely stopped trusting our inner guidance. Instead, we place the responsibility onto others for validation, acceptance and to love us. How different would it be if we were born into a family that nurtured and taught us that we are extensions of Divine Source Energy?

PLANTS

Just as a plant needs the proper care and nutrients for it to thrive, so does our mental and emotional sense of self. Talking to plants in a caring voice and playing uplifting music around them has been proven to help them grow with more vitality. Neglected plants that endure harsher environments don't do as well. They become weak, prone to disease and are susceptible to predatory attacks from insects. Too much of a good thing isn't always best, either, as coddling may lead to weak and unhealthy plants. Seedlings need to be hardened off before being planted outdoors. This way they are able to endure fluctuating weather conditions. Plants move toward the sun so their leaves can absorb its energy. Their roots grow deeper in the soil in search of moisture and missing nutrients. Likewise, when we lack emotional nourishment, we search for those who can feed us the missing pieces. We do so by unconsciously drawing toward us similar archetypes and experiences so we can heal and integrate them within ourselves. This pattern repeats until we finally address the matter.

Each year and stage of a child's growing life is crucial for them to develop into a healthy and mature adult. These aspects are composed of many facets that together form the totality of a thriving adult. If any are fractured, then complete integration may not be fully realized. Trauma—both physically and emotionally—can occur at any stage or year, and it's important to identify it. These affect the learning stages we need to evolve into healthy adults. They affect our ability to safely communicate and express ourselves mentally, emotionally and creatively. This also applies to our physical security. We learned how to relate with others by how we interpreted our parental model, if we even had one. The first day of school is critical in the development of our independence and ability to get along with others. The older we get, the more we question our place and purpose in this world. Eventually we learn responsibility and how to get things done by our own efforts. To truly heal we need to investigate the history of our nurturing. We have to ask ourselves if we lacked support and nourishment on any emotional level; and additionally, if and how this may have affected the consolidation of our psychological sense of our identity.

A moving pendulum with high tension usually swings too far to one side before it settles and finds its balance. Helicopter parenting, social justice, passing grades and winning trophies without the deservedness has been known to produce children who are unable to cope with life's challenges. Likewise, the "tough it up and don't be a pussy" mindset of years past has led to unreported concussions and injuries. Boys were told not to cry, or to show emotion. We are told that it's weak to ask for help, or to appear vulnerable. This is false—in fact, it takes courage to do so. In order to still the unbalanced see-saw of emotional pain-reaction, we need to uncover what's fuelling it.

MISSING PARTS

We need to identify what emotional needs were unaddressed in our formative years, and how these unconnected fragments are affecting our psychological sense of identity. This section will help you gain clarity on what they are. Delve as deep as you are comfortable going. The more you uncover, the greater the benefit. You'll need your pen, and a fresh sheet of paper. Write down everything you can think of. If you are stuck I have written down a few questions to ponder that may help you.

How did Mom and Dad treat each other? Was there physical or emotional abuse? Were you encouraged and supported? Did you feel loved? How many times were you told, "No?" Were you ever teased and told you were too soft, or stupid? Were you shown and given enough love? Were you or your feelings ever rejected? Did you feel that you were listened to—were you heard? Have you ever felt judged, criticized and ridiculed? Were you allowed to express yourself physically and creatively? Were you ever told to shut up? Have you ever felt betrayed by a parent? Has this led to issues with trust? Have you ever felt manipulated by any of your parents? Were your parents too strict, or too lax? Did they follow through on their warnings? Has Mom or Dad ever cheated on each other? Did Mom or Dad leave? Has this caused abandonment issues? Did they get a divorce? Do you think it was your fault? Did they show up? Did you ever feel that you let your parents down? Have they ever let you down? Were you ever made to feel not good enough? Can you trust your family members? Did they ever lie to you? Did they pay attention to you or were you ignored? Have you endured a traumatic event in your life that caused you to feel unsafe physically or emotionally? Were you ever touched, or violated inappropriately or sexually? Were any personal boundaries crossed?

Before we move on, please take some time to contemplate your answers and notice what feelings arise. Remember, whatever has happened or how you feel about it has nothing to do with who you really are. They are only experiences. I'm not asking you to trivialize any trauma or pain you may have undergone. Nor am I asking you to relive them. I'm simply inviting you to be objective by witnessing whatever wants to surface. If you feel anger, sadness, or indifference, allow it to unfold. No holds barred. Reflect on what arises.

Place the sheet into an envelope and set it aside. Read the following on emotions. Learning which emotions have been associated to these experiences will help navigate and interpret your responses.

LEARNING HOW TO COMMUNICATE THROUGH YOUR EMOTIONS

A thought on its own isn't charged. There is no investment or story built around it. This can be an advantage for accountants, judges and surgeons. This is also a great benefit for self-inquiry. When a thought is fuelled by a feeling, it creates an emotion. This can lead to bias thinking in one's thought process. A toy is just a gadget until memories are attached to it. Then it may become a favourite toy. The more investment in a thing, the harder it is to let it go. Emotions can trigger intense responses in some. There are those so sensitive that they cry at everything—others can get angry in an instant and only know how to use violence to express it. The cold-hearted sociopath and the emotionally volatile mess both reside on extreme ends of the same emotive spectrum, each represent an imbalance.

We have become a collection of our thoughts and emotions. These are stored as memories in our brain, and in our biology. They can be triggered to ignite fear and anxiety—both can lead the mind into neurosis. Emotional wounds are simply unprocessed life experiences which are trapped within our cells and nervous system. We experience pain because our body is living in the past and won't let go. They become our identity, and we wear them like a badge. Some are proud to share their traumas; they become the victim—others hide it and suffer alone. Often, we won't know of a dormant wound until a situation triggers it. Many haven't developed the proper skill sets to communicate their emotional needs. Our parents had a major role in this area of development. We may have gotten away with temper tantrums, or by withdrawing—perhaps it was safer not expressing our feelings. We can become addicted to our emotions much like a drug addict is to drugs—both release dopamine and endorphins. Some love falling in love, others crave the chaos of conflict and drama. There are those who easily get bored and kick the cat to stir up some excitement. Others are perfectly content with safe and predictable. Some grow fearful when everything is going too well. Like with any drug, we may begin to develop resistance—needing more intensity for a reaction. We can become numb and stop feeling.

Emotions can be used for communication, or for manipulation. We have to decipher how we're directing them. Learning how to decode and communicate our feelings and needs not only with others but with ourselves is important to emotional maturation.

We have to know what we are feeling first before we can impart them to others. This is how we honour ourselves and prevent anyone from crossing our boundaries—it also stops us from biting their heads off.

EMOTIONAL MATURITY

We've all heard of the term IQ—the measure of how smart someone is. I'm sure people with a high IQ prefer to call it Intelligence Quotient. IQ is the score derived from one of many standardized tests designed to assess an individual's intelligence. Have you ever heard of EQ? Emotional Intelligence, or the proper term EQ (Emotional Quotient) is defined as an individual's ability to identify, evaluate, control, and express their emotions. This means that an individual can identify and manage their emotions without being affected by the emotive responses of others. A basic example of this is when you can express your displeasure calmly toward an other instead of wanting to punch them in the face. This also means having the capacity to empathize with another—the ability to calm or cheer someone up. It's one thing to have a high intelligence, it's another to be able to hold it together and not allow destructive feelings get the best of you. Emotional Intelligence can be impeded by the lack of emotional support experienced during our early years. How can you tell if you have a high EQ?

Do you have the ability to identify an emotion as it arises and filter your reaction? Can you assert your personal boundaries unruffled and without confrontation? Are you calm, with little stress and anxiety? Can you diffuse a situation without creating a fight or making enemies? Are you kind and empathetic? Are you aware in advance that certain reactions may have certain consequences? Do you think things through? Are you inclined to make quick opinions and assumptions? Do you learn from your mistakes, or do you hang on to them? Do you hold grudges? If you don't display any of these characteristics, you may display signs of having a lower EQ. Do you instead fail to understand how you come across? Do you feel that you're often misunderstood? Are you quick to anger? Do you feel like slapping someone's head for not being able to understand your point of view? Are you afraid to show how mad you really feel? Do you instead pretend that you're happy? Can you take responsibility for your own feelings without blaming them on others?

Emotionally intelligent people can communicate their feelings with stability, instead of erratically. They aren't easily offended and can even poke fun of themselves because they are comfortable in their own skin. We can be adults, yet still suffer with a low emotional capacity, similar to that of a whiny six-year-old child. I'm sure you know of a few. Mature people can listen to what someone is saying with appreciation and without being swayed. They don't interrupt, talk over, or neglect what has been said. Do you ever get the impression that some just wait for you to stop talking so they can say whatever they wanted to regardless? I've noticed that behaviour can almost be anticipated by a person's EQ level. Those who are stubborn, closed off, give the silent treatment, are easily offended and attack don't usually possess a high EQ or maturity. Conversely, emotions need to be expressed, and repressing them is unhealthy. We all have a different internal language to interpreting and communicating our ideas and feelings. Many lack the essential tools to cope and impart our needs to others. They didn't learn how to properly communicate beyond being the victim or the victimizer.

THERE ARE NO BAD EMOTIONS
We just don't understand them

Fear is considered the mother of all lower vibrating feelings. I believe there are no bad emotions. Yes, there are higher serving ones than there are others. The feelings of happy and sad are self-evident. But what about those that are more ambiguous—ones we can't decode as easily? As mentioned before, fire can be either destructive or transformative. The same is true for emotions such as anger and frustration—both can destroy us, or propel us forward to make positive changes. Sadness can help you pay attention to the details you may be overlooking. Pessimism can help prepare you for potential obstacles. Feeling guilt can help you upgrade your moral compass. Anxiety can help you solve problems. Jealousy can be a motivator to make you work harder, and so on.

You can see that emotions are simply indicators and great barometers that help us navigate through life. They are also critical fuses that protect our biological control panel, our energy pathways and nervous system. An overload of pent up energy may cause a trip in the circuit breaker. Unfortunately, we have let our feelings run amok and have allowed them to hold us hostage. So what do we do next time we have been held captive by an intense emotion? When one arises, simply allow it to unfold. Look at it objectively. Take a deep breath, step back and don't react. Try seeing the bigger picture. Ask yourself questions that will help identify what has triggered it. "Why did this happen? What is the message here?" We may not always know what triggered the emotion, but there is always a root cause.

Most times, it's better to express a feeling rather than to let it fester by suppressing it. If you need to let anger out, find a healthy outlet. Punch a pillow, listen to heavy metal, lift some weights, or yell at the top of your lungs. Eventually you will find a more empowering solution to express it.

When sadness arises ask, "Why am I sad?" When you feel anxiety, "What am I nervous about?" When anger erupts ask, "What didn't happen the way I wanted it to?" Each emotion is arising because its trying to show us something. We live in a dual reality, there are two sides to every thing. *Sadness* can be interpreted as a feeling of loss or failure. Or, it can show that you care and have depth. *Anxiety* signals *what if* thoughts about the future or any threat that may happen. Or, it can invite you wake up to right now and be present. It can show that you're stuck in the past, or living in fear of the future. This is also true about feeling *resentment*. *Bitterness* shows you where you need to heal, and where you're holding on to judgements. *Anger* can represent *should thoughts*, and injustices. Or, it can show what you're passionate about, where your boundaries are, and what you believe needs to change. You can let guilt eat away at you because you felt you went against your morals. Or, instead of feeling responsible for another's negative outcome, you can realize that you're still living in an other's expectations. Do you feel *shame* at the thought of being judged? Are you internalizing others' beliefs about who you should be? If so, maybe you need to reconnect with yourself.

In a romantic relationship, there are differences within the realms of caring, jealousy, control, and dependency. To care is to have feelings of concern, responsibility or love for someone. Is caring feeling anxious about one's spouse going out to a singles bar without you? Or is it showing fear and a lack of trust? Compassion literally means to suffer together, and can be defined as the feeling that arises when you're confronted with another's suffering. You feel motivated to relieve their suffering. Compassion is not the same as empathy or altruism, though the concepts are related. Those who feel less so typically dwell in their head, those who are emotionally sensitive are governed more by their hearts. Some say thinkers are leaner, and feelers are heavier in weight. Is this true for you? Did you know that when people feel emotional pain, the same areas of the brain get activated as when experiencing physical pain? Remember, our identity is not the thoughts we think or the emotions we feel. We are pure Spirit.

WRITING THE LETTER

Review your list on needs, and modify anything you feel that requires it.

I invite you to write a letter to your parents, or whoever were your caregivers. Imagine that they are sitting across from you listening intently. Tell them what you needed from them, and what they failed to provide you. An example may be, "Mom, you were too smothering, I felt that I couldn't breathe. You didn't show up when I needed you emotionally. Dad, you were too strict and never gave me compliments." Write whatever comes to you and stop when there is nothing more to pour out. Identify what you feel is lacking—and note, this isn't about blaming anyone. There is no need to show anyone this letter. This process is for you only. Keep this letter in a safe place for the next chapter. If you know anyone you can trust to help walk you through this, it can be very beneficial.

3

FORGIVENESS AND TAKING RESPONSIBILITY

If you haven't completed writing your letter, I strongly suggest you consider doing so. You won't fully benefit from this next and very important step.

In order to grow healthy and vibrant plants, toxins must first be cleared from the soil. Likewise, we need to clear the poisons that affect and limit our growth. There is a reason why the past is called history; it's only a story. His story (the past) is simply a place of reference, it's not one of residence.

Did you know that if someone stole Sally's lollipop when she was eight and she hasn't let it go, it will still affect her to this day? The past is gone, never to return, unless one decides to repeat it.

In order for us to grow and emotionally mature, we need to heal from all the injustices we believe have been done to us. This is accomplished by forgiving those who we feel are responsible for causing our pain, rightly or wrongly so. Forgiving is hard to do, especially when you feel they don't deserve any of it.

What you see and how you react to the outside world are merely reflections of what you have inside. Two individuals can experience the same event, yet can react very differently. Our involvement with the past most often governs our behaviour in the present. Negative emotions are just reactions to unpleasant experiences which represent untended wounds. The relationships we have with others are designed to reveal what they are, so we may tend to them. Everything we experience, we're perceiving inside our mind. Since they are observed as happening outside of us, we feel that we're not responsible for creating them. When in fact, we're responsible for everything we allow into our awareness—this includes all our thoughts and emotions. This is a hard one to grasp; however, when it's realized we stop blaming and start taking responsibility. We are able to finally set ourselves free by letting it go. The most powerful action we can do is *forgiveness*.

To forgive another is not a sign of weakness, nor is it a way to let another off the hook. Forgiveness is a higher form of love; it's seeing ourselves in another person. Absolving all who have trespassed against us frees us from our entanglement with them, and from our past. Exonerating another is not for their benefit, it's for ours. No one is perfect, we all screw up and are on Earth practising to get better. Whether something is done against us in spite or not, it doesn't matter as it all comes from pain. This wound and attack pattern must be stopped and be healed, not perpetuated. Do you think that if you knew of a better way to respond to a situation that you would? How hard is it for you to change even a small behaviour in yourself—let alone expect another to? We are all doing the best we can with the knowledge we have at the time. When we forgive another we are actually forgiving ourselves. Compassion heals. Meet others on their level and honour where they are at.

There are many techniques available on forgiveness. One of the most powerful is the Ho'oponopono prayer. This technique is an ancient Hawaiian practice, and it means to make right through reconciliation. Some call it The Hawaiian Code of Forgiveness. If you have ever heard anyone say, "They come from a good family," or, "That family is messed up,"—or if any of you have watched *Game Of Thrones* you'll understand the terms *lineage* and the *sins of the father*. Many traditions around the world honour their ancestors and draw upon their wisdom. The family name carries with it honour, or the lack of it. Good or bad, these family patterns are passed down through the generations. They are encoded within our genes. This is why it's important that we clear up our ancestry, our DNA legacies, and the karmic entanglements within all of our relationships, friends, family, and so on. This means to make right with the ancestors, and with the people with whom you have relationships with. Dr. Ihaleakala Hew Len, a Hawaiian therapist, cured an entire ward of criminally insane patients without ever meeting any of them. He did so by using the Ho'oponopono prayer of forgiveness. He reviewed each of the patients' files, and then healed them by healing himself. Sounds impossible, right? If something angers you about another's behaviour, they are merely mirroring an unresolved aspect within your own unconscious that makes you angry. Healing it by forgiveness frees both the mirror and the one that sees the reflection.

There are four simple steps to this method, and the order is not that important. They consist of four amazingly powerful forces: Repentance, Forgiveness, Gratitude and Love. We empower ourselves when *we name our sins*. This is the true meaning behind confession in the church.

I'M SORRY

At first, it's hard to apologize and accept that we're responsible for matters occurring "outside of ourselves". Practicing this method of forgiveness will eventually allow you to understand this concept and how we're all interconnected. Choose something to *say sorry to* that you know you've caused for yourself. This is not a self-punishing exercise, so don't be hard on yourself. Acknowledge that you did the best you could at the time—there is no blame. Are you overweight, addicted to nicotine, or alcohol? Start with small things then later, move on to others. You can say, "I realize that I am responsible for causing X in my life, I am deeply sorry." In addition to this, you can do the organ emotional release presented in my book *The Ultimate Journey*. You can learn to apply this to anything that upsets and irritates you.

PLEASE FORGIVE ME
After you've addressed all of your apologies, ask to be forgiven for each of them.

THANK YOU
The next step is to say, "Thank you." You can thank your body for all it does for you. Thank yourself for being the best you can be. Thank the God of your understanding; thank the Universe; thank whatever it was that just forgave you. Just keep saying thank you.

I LOVE YOU
You can extend saying, "I love you" to your body, to God, to the air you breathe, to the house that shelters you. You can even say, "I LOVE YOU" to all of your challenges in life. Say it over and over. Mean it. Feel it. There is nothing more powerful than Love.

You can practice Ho'oponopono anytime, even when you feel resistance coming from a stranger. There is no need to speak out loud, you can do it mentally. The power is in the feeling and in the willingness to forgive. From a place of love and compassion silently express the following phrase, "I love you... I'm sorry... Please forgive me... Thank you."

EXERCISES

Take out the letter you wrote and do the forgiveness prayer for each entry that you want healed. You may not want to forgive anyone, but you owe it to yourself. Remember, it doesn't matter who's fault you think it is. The intent is for absolution and letting go, so that you can heal on all levels. Take this opportunity to forgive and release any birth trauma, or PTSD you may have. Remember, the greater the emotional investment—the more real it appears—the more it affects us. Sometimes the wounds run too deep and are too painful to address. If this is the case, layers have to be peeled back slowly. When peeling off the layers of the artichoke, eventually you will get to the heart of it. You can watch painful events happening to you as if you're seeing them seated in a movie theatre. This is a great way to detach, then you can slowly delve deeper as you feel more comfortable. If you'd like to explore a powerful technique that can help you release trauma and manage physical pain, please refer to "Spicy Chocolate" in *The Ultimate Journey*.

After having completed forgiving and releasing, it is time to begin nourishing yourself. You are the only one who can truly do this. Knowing that you are already Pure Spirit and complete makes this much easier. You lack nothing: draw from the well of your eternal and abundant Spirit. This means giving yourself the love, trust, and acceptance that you mistakenly seek outward. This will start the process of dissolving the wounds, and empower yourself. You'll realize that you were never dependent on anyone for your sense of fulfillment and completeness. This will be covered deeper in the chapters on Self-Love and the succeeding ones on food and the body.

RITUAL

> "Step into the fire of self-discovery. This fire will not burn you, it will only burn what you are not."
> —Mooji

Fire is transformative. It has a cleansing and purifying effect. In nature, it burns away disease and harmful microbes—symbolically, it burns away the old. The Phoenix rises anew from the ashes of the old. Fire can be destructive, as well; however, whatever it consumes it leaves behind fertile ash for new growth to occur. Fire may take life, but it generates it as well. Fire-killed trees attract scores of insects that flourish in the wood beneath the charred bark, and in the new foliage. Numerous bird species specifically search for the temporary riches of these burn-induced ecosystems. The birds feast on the bounty, thereby preventing an over-abundance of the insects. As a result, this attracts other species that flourish and gives birth to a new ecosystem.

To end this chapter, you are going to perform a ritual to symbolically transform your energy—to allegorically burn your old story. This is a symbolic process of releasing the illusion that shrouds your true identity. The fire will destroy the old perception of your self so that you can embrace a new and vital ecosystem of growth and abundance within yourself.

Take out all of your envelopes: Who you are, Needs, and Forgiveness. If you desire to reread what you've written beforehand, please feel free to do so. Seal the envelope(s). In a kitchen pot, fireplace, or in a covered barbecue, place the letters inside. Light an edge (or two) of the envelopes and let it burn away to ash. If you desire, prior to this ritual you can light a candle and meditate on it. You can set intentions or say a prayer. If you want to add any personalized intention I encourage you to do so. Meditate on this desire with your eyes closed in front of the candle—set fire to your past. You can use the flame to ignite the paper. Please observe caution and safety when you do this. Have water on hand and a lid for the pot.

Suggestions for meditation and setting intentions: "I am not these stories. They are not my identity, they are only my experiences. They have helped shape my sense of self in my human form. I am grateful for every lesson that each experience has given me. I have no regrets. I forgive everyone. It is my intent that this Divine fire which also burns in me transmute all perceived injustices and sense of unworthiness done unto me. It is my intent that the ashes of this fire represent the fertile substrate that will nourish my expanded and renewed self. Every day I awaken into my true nature."

"I Am Enough, I Am Safe."

4

FEAR, SELF-SABOTAGE AND PLEASURE

The strongest enemy is the one you can't see. Once you know your opponent, the battle is over halfway won. Internal and external conditioning play a huge part in shaping who we become. Psychiatrist and psychoanalyst Carl Jung coined a theory called "the shadow", or "the dark side". This refers to an unconscious aspect of one's personality that the ego doesn't identify itself with. Typically, we are not conscious of our shadow, yet it governs many of our thoughts, beliefs, and actions. Carl Jung also said that when an inner situation is not made conscious, it happens outside as fate. This is inevitable, because if you ignore your shadow side and focus only on its other half, there is conflict. This tension must be resolved or balanced, as in Yin and Yang.

Although we are responsible for everything that we perceive, others are accountable for creating fear and limitation during our formative years. Eventually we have to face our shadow self and liberate all that impedes us. Sadly, we'd rather not, but instead deny it altogether. We tend to project this resistance onto others, often playing the victim which defers our responsibility. New Agers and Spiritualists are often guilty of perpetuating this problem by encouraging us to wear rose coloured glasses. Peace, love and sugar will not heal a wound that is denied and neglected.

Our early programming drives our behavioural tendencies. Some of which can be either constructive or destructive—or in other words, limiting and empowering. I truly believe that our cultural and social collectives subconsciously perpetuate fear-based ways of thinking. I am convinced that these disempowering notions are a result of a deeper global agenda. There seems to be an insidious hand behind this narrative—a self-serving motive that limits the masses yet benefits the select few. If the circus elephant really knew its own strength, it would break free from the rope and the illusion that it was powerless. Similarity, we are kept from realizing our greatness.

Collectively, we give our power away to those who promise they'll take care of and save us—usually not today, but surely in the future. We are given hope, divided, and played against each other. Likewise, we battle a similar war within ourselves. The enemy is fear, and our ignorance to our true power. We fight against ourselves by employing the weapons of low confidence, self-hate and sabotage, all of which keep us feeling inadequate. We are slaves to our residual habits and patterns. We've become prisoners by our thirst for pleasure and material comforts. We are led to believe that we're solely our body and its limited sensory faculties. I invite you to wake up and reclaim your magnificence.

FEAR

From a spiritual perspective, it's observed that there is only one true emotion: Love. Not the conditional kind that has to be validated by an action or a desired state; but one that is independent of all conditions. The absence or disconnection from our awareness that were are all one and powerful is what causes us to become fearful. This sense of separation is what creates fear and all of the other so-called negative emotions—which are tendrils growing from the same root. An acronym for FEAR is False Emotions Appearing Real. I am not discrediting that fear doesn't exist. The fear of falling, loud noises, and when your life is threatened appears very real. Aside from these protective responses, all other fears are simply learned beliefs. They are triggered when similar traumatic experiences arise from our past.

Fear comes to us in many forms such as: anxiety, an intense rush of adrenaline, a palpitating heart, immobility, and the little voice. Externally, it usually manifests as self-sabotage. Fear is what stops us from getting what we want. It keeps us in our comfort zone. The more we feel disconnected from our true self, the greater the fear we experience. Emotions are indicators that tell us what to pay attention to. The best lessons aren't always taught, they are experienced. Putting your hand in the fire will burn your hand. This is a great reference for the next time you decide to play with it. But being afraid of fire and avoiding it altogether is ludicrous. What's insane, however, is perpetually putting your hand in the flames and complaining that it keeps cooking your flesh. Sometimes listening to the little voice inside is wise. Mostly though, it's a scared little child terrified of the imagined bogeyman hiding inside the closet. How do we know the difference? Is it our friend or our foe?

THE LITTLE VOICE

We often hear the narrative of a parent, spouse, sibling, educator, or another telling us that we aren't good enough, or smart enough. That we'll never become successful, or that we're not worthy and deserving. "Who are you to think that you can do that?" Who's voice is muttering these words? Somehow, we've let these voices become encoded in our psyche, and set on auto-replay. Do yours whisper, or yell at you?

Evolution has developed our subconscious mind to keep us safe. This state of being is often referred to as our "comfort zone". Our subconscious will do whatever it takes to keep us there. The little voice is the obedient servant. It does a great job by drawing on its collection of past memories. Our subconscious also anticipates what may or may not happen in the future. How many of you overthink and analyze every potential action? This keeps one immobilized. The little voice knows every trick in the book. We need to discern if it's simply masquerading as our intuition, or if it's just afraid. Does it really have our best interests at heart? Speaking of which, the best way to interpret this is by the level of fear that is felt. "Listen to your heart."

What words does your little voice say to you? "You can't do that! You're stupid. What's the use, it's too hard, it will never work. What will other people think? Why go through that pain and aggravation? You don't deserve it, anyway. You haven't suffered enough. Wait until something guaranteed presents itself. Don't take the risk. Don't be selfish. They are way out of your league. You can't afford that. You're too old. You're ugly. You've run out of time. What makes you think it's gonna work this time? You're better off staying where you are."

EXCUSES

The little voice uses excuses to keep us disempowered. We blame our parents, God, the government, our teachers or coaches. Some even accuse karma and astrology for their woes. We'd rather hide behind our excuses, suffer and complain than to find a solution. It's much easier to feel sorry for one's self, procrastinate and wait for a miracle. Instead, we whine and wonder why our life doesn't change; yet do nothing or very little about it. It's all about priorities. We will do everything else except for what works. We'll buy the next miracle pill, cutting edge product, and hire professional trainers. This way when we fail, we can blame everyone else. This is a cunning way to mask our self-punishment. We tend to lay the blame on others so it deflects the responsibility away from us. "It's not our problem so we don't have to deal with it." Well, it's usually always our problem, if you want to call it one. We are under the impression that if we complain about something long enough, somehow it will get fixed. Or, if we ignore it, it will go away. Does it ever? No, it grows teeth and comes back even stronger. Speaking of teeth, if you ignore them they will go away.

Often, what we worry about doesn't happen. The truth is, if we really want something we'd go after it, no excuses. Some of us suffer from an extreme laziness and procrastination. Have you noticed that those who complain the most are the least successful? It's almost as if they enjoy the misery. What would happen if they had nothing left to bitch about?

Which excuses are you familiar with? "It will be too hard. I don't know what I truly want. I'm too comfortable where I am. I worry about what other people may think. No one in my life has inspiring goals. All good things come to those who wait so I'm waiting for something to show up."

Are you waiting or hiding? "I'm not smart enough. I'm expecting too much. I'm too ambitious. I'm too old. I don't have enough time. I'm afraid of failing and won't take unnecessary risks. It didn't work before, so why would it work now?"

STANDING UP TO THE BULLY

Before political correctness took over, the way to deal with a bully was to give them a taste of their own medicine. When you stood up to them they either cowered, fought back, or they became your best friend. Either way, a bully is usually the result of being the victim of bullying. What a thug really needs is a hug. The next time your inner bully decides to challenge you, give it a long, tight embrace. Tell it, "Thank you for trying to help me." Make friends with it, and soon it will become an inner voice you can trust. The tormentor becomes your mentor. This approach is much more constructive. You will begin to have a better innerstanding behind the origin of your inner dialogue.

FEAR OF SUCCESS

You may be like most people who are afraid to fail. But what if you are actually afraid of *success*? You may ask, "Why would anyone be afraid to succeed?" There are many reasons. Do you fear that you won't be able to perform at the level necessary to maintain your position? There is a term called *impostor's syndrome*, which is the fear of being exposed as a fraud. Maybe you feel that others foolishly have convinced themselves that you're an authority, and will eventually call you out. This worry may increase as your success continues. This is normal and afflicts many successful people, especially spiritual seekers. There are many reasons to fear success, and these include: the fear of letting people down, being unable to deliver when it matters, losing your free time, it will change you, achieving success won't fulfill you, that you are undeserving of praise and accolades, that you will outshine family and friends, or that the pressure of the spotlight would be too much to handle.

We may not consciously be aware that we are afraid. In fact, we may be in denial.

There may not be any evidence of this on the surface, but we might be tricking ourselves into complacency. We may feel that everything is fine as is, and there isn't any need to be so ambitious. Many of us live life day to day preoccupied by what we'll eat for our next meal. We count the days of the work week so we can enjoy the weekend (weakened) and plan for our next vacation. A great deal of us engage in activities primarily to kill time, reach for the next dopamine rush and be entertained. We're robotically going through the motions. Have you ever considered questioning why you seem unhappy and unfulfilled? What your purpose is? Why are you here? Self-inquiry is essential for personal growth and success, yet instead we decide to distract ourselves.

There are questions we can ask to help us uncover why we are not progressing. "Am I a know-it-all with an answer for everything? Am I the all-talk and no-action person? Do I feel that I'm doing better than my friends, family and coworkers so there is no need to try any harder? Am I already working hard enough? Do I secretly compete with lesser people? Am I the big fish in the small pond? Do I associate with others who are less successful and attractive so I look better? Am I overcompensating by being the alpha in my circle or group? Do I feel that I have to keep suffering so that I can earn the right to be successful?" All these justifications keep us locked and unable to progress.

SELF-SABOTAGE

Judgment is one of the biggest human fears.

"The greatest prison people live in is the fear of what other people think."
—David Icke

Spiritually, we are literally dying to fit in. What do you think of when you hear the words "self-sabotage"? This is a touchy subject as is with anything that challenges "our story". We are betraying ourselves when we fail to succeed due to our fear. Society in general doesn't seem to acknowledge this act of personal punishment. In fact, it is subtly glorified and encouraged. Some may even get offended and attack those who say that they're performing such an act. Don't believe me? Self-sabotage is not designated to those injecting needles and inflicting personal harm.

In truth, this entire chapter is about self-abuse. Previously, I mentioned that if we experienced any type of trauma in our formative years that it will most often rewire our brain. Like any type of PTSD, it causes us to emotionally withdraw and numb out. This leads to the avoidance of any situation which may be a reminder or a trigger of that trauma. We seek safety and security when anything takes us out of our comfort zone. We police ourselves and make sure we don't shine too bright. I believe that every addiction, distraction, unhealthy behaviour, and excuses are all forms of painkillers and coping mechanisms.

Those who have experienced a tragic event like a finger being chopped off, or a bear attack, can attest that pain isn't initially experienced. When enduring an intense event such as any of the aforementioned, adrenaline is pumped throughout our nervous system. Evolution has gifted us a reprieve from feeling excruciating pain. Whether it's a junkie high on drugs, or our body supplying the numbing agent, eventually it wears off. When it does, the nervous system comes back online. This is when the agony reveals itself. Usually, we turn to pills, medication and other means to numb ourselves. In order to remove the painkiller, we first need to address and nurture the pain that it's anaesthetizing. Trauma can be caused not only physically, but also by emotional attacks. By burying these negative emotions, impressions and associations, we defer our ability to process them. These unprocessed experiences are pushed deep down into our subconscious. Silently, they govern our self-sabotaging behaviour. They stockpile, which creates more suppressed pain, more denial and avoidance. We become addicted to the numbness, and avoid facing the affliction and its trigger. Pain is the teacher that allows us to move through the trauma (experience).

How to tell if you are committing self-sabotage? Well, besides the obvious smoking of cigarettes and doing drugs, there are many not so obvious signs to look for. Do you abuse food in any way? Do you engage in punishing cardio or exercise to compensate for your guilt of unhealthy overeating? Do you feel the need to drink alcohol? Are you afraid of being intimate in relationships? Do you break up before your partner does first? Are you afraid, or submissive of authority? Do you suffer from depression? Are you too nice and fearful to offend others? (Sometimes it's the super nice people who are the ones who commit suicide.) Are you generally angry? Do you pose as being tougher than you really are? Are your clothes a reflection of this? Is your skin inked and patterned with skulls, or badass images? Do you raise vicious dogs? Are you a gambler, or promiscuous? Do you indulge in porn? Are you addicted to sex? Did you know that one of the biggest painkillers is an orgasm? Most times, self-sabotage is not so obvious. The next time you find yourself destroying anything that appears too good to be true, ask yourself why you think you don't deserve it.

PATTERNS AND HABITS

Continuous thought patterns trigger neurons which create neurological networks and pathways. These neurological grooves are etched into our brain and create a path, much like one in a wooded forest. Once a pathway is established, it becomes the easiest passage offering the least resistance. Nature has designed our minds to work this way to become more efficient. As a result, this is also responsible for locking us into bad habits and patterns that can limit our growth. Additionally, an intense traumatic experience also creates a deep neurological channel in the brain. This process is important to understand that early childhood and infant traumas do imprint into our cells and neurology. These scarring memories become hardwired which as previously mentioned, cause us to avoid similar triggers. Most of our unconscious actions and reactions are governed by our past experiences.

If any of you have ever lost a pet or dog you will know how lingering patterns can still remain. When the doorbell rings, the usual barking that accompanied it isn't there. The lid of the toilet bowl doesn't need to be down because they are not around to drink from it. These incidental routines are no longer a secondary afterthought, they become a primary awareness. This phenomena surfaces with each change in habitual routines. The absence may affect us, however the residual imprint that lingers often does more so. Even though our physiological dependence on something may be released, we can still remain psychologically enslaved to it. Changing a habit or pattern is not easy. Old movies and experiences are going to pop up. There is no stopping this. What we can do however, is learn not to react to them. Like I mentioned at the end of chapter three, imagine yourself sitting in a movie theatre watching events play out as a spectator. Let them pass. They are only as powerful as you make them out to be.

CHANGING THE GROOVE

Aren't memories simply a recording of an experience? If so, we can use this to our advantage. It can take years and sometimes lifetimes to undo our programming. Or it can be done in just five minutes. Wouldn't it be cool if we could overwrite an old program with a new one? Richard Bandler, co-developer of NLP (Neuro-Linguistic Programming) believes this is possible. The process is to simply dump the old content and change the execution. This works by interrupting the current pattern (program) and replacing it with a new neurological association. It's like changing the wiring of a keyboard of either a computer or piano. The button which is responsible for the key of C respectively can be reconfigured to signal a different note or letter. You can imagine scratching a song on a record or CD so that it skips over the part you don't want to hear. Unfortunately, we let the needle keep bouncing back over the groove so that it replays the undesired track.

I'm not suggesting for you to ignore any intense or limiting experiences. I'm a firm believer that if we ignore something, it will keep occurring exponentially until we confront it. Healing from any pain requires meeting it head on and allowing it to express itself. Making peace with our pain is how to fully let it go. However, sometimes a memory is so strong that we can't stop replaying it over and over internally. Once a healing does take place, there may be lingering expressions of the old patterns. The following techniques will help you diminish them until they have fully dissolved. Some of us are visual people, others may be auditory, or feelers. This means different approaches work better for some than others.

When a soundtrack or movie clip from your past arises, you can mentally edit and remix it just like a Hollywood producer does. If you don't like what you hear, simply change the track. If you can't, play it back at a high speed, or slow it down. You can add marching band music over it to drown it out. Turn it into a song and change the lyrics like "Weird Al" Yankovic. Overdub it with your favourite cartoon character's voice like Goofy. You could always imagine the speakers have blown and you no longer hear anything. Try these techniques on your little voice. We can apply similar techniques to all mental movies and pictures. Simply manipulate what you are seeing. You can add any effect to it, explode the screen into pieces, change the characters into funny Oompa Loompas, and so on. What about a feeling or sensation? Begin by identifying it. What colour and shape is it? Where do you feel it in your body? Move it around, shrink it, and change its colour. Visualize your heart as a powerful Sun. Move the object or feeling into it and melt it away. You can invent and apply any technique you want. There is no right or wrong way to do this. The sky's the limit. Using a combination of all three visual, auditory and sensation is even more potent. Experiment with what works best for you.

PLEASURE SLAVES

Many of you who are reading this book are fortunate enough to be living in the modern world. You are able to enjoy the physical comforts it affords. We live in a dwelling that protects us from the elements, and have adequate heating and cooling systems. We have a bed, hot water, a fridge and a freezer to keep our food from spoiling quickly. Not a bad gig. This is a wonderful example of having abundance in our lives. There is a downside to all of this. We've become pampered by this lavish way of living. Compared to our ancestors, we've become soft. As our basic needs have been met, we've become slaves to our senses. Consider for a moment having to live off of the land without power or running water—needing to chop wood to cook, bathe and keep warm. Water would be scarce and laborious to fetch.

Thankfully most of us don't have to do this. Enduring these conditions develops tolerance; they toughen us up. They're also major motivators. We have become so accustomed to living in comfort that we forget how fortunate we really are.

All conditions change, nothing stays inert. This is true for every physical and emotional sensation. Each arise, peak, and eventually recede. The only change is the duration of each stage and cycle. After some time a hot shower becomes uncomfortable, a soothing massage grows irritating. Anger and happiness arise and subside. An orgasm can only last so long. The trouble starts when we try to hang on to any of these states. When our intellect gets hijacked by the pursuit of pleasure we become unconscious slaves. We need control over our mind, emotions and our bodily senses. We are seduced by the brilliance and ease of modern comforts such is the moth to the flame. Seeking pleasure is not always the problem—it's also trying to avoid discomfort.

COMFORT ZONE

What we have obtained is within our *comfort zone*. What we desire waits for us outside of it. Our nature as humans is to move toward experiences that give us pleasure, and to avoid the ones that give us pain. Avoiding pain is usually the stronger motivator; so we tend to take the easier path that leads toward pleasure. Often the perception of pain and pleasure is stronger than the reality of them. Unless you are a Vulcan, emotion almost always bypasses logic. The marketing world knows this concept very well—make them feel good the easiest way possible. Those addicted to pleasure tend to seek serotonin and dopamine rushes artificially. It's much easier to drink and take drugs than it is to exercise and earn it naturally. In the end, one strategy has a lasting reward, the other doesn't.

Human nature causes us to procrastinate until something gets serious enough that we have to address it. Only until the condition can no longer be tolerated is when we take action. I often hear from many government workers that they hate their job, but it pays well and the pension is even better. They stay yet feel trapped, their minds aren't stimulated, the work is monotonous and mundane. It is slowly killing them. How many of us are slowing dying by the insidious hands of our job and lifestyle?

GROWTH ZONE

If we were to use circles to represent our awareness regarding our growth zone, we'd see that the comfort zone is where it's the safest. This is where the majority of the human population resides. In most cases this is a benefit by being stable and secure. There is a dark side to this which is boredom, lack of growth, mediocrity, and non challenging yourself; it means settling. At the very rim of this zone is where things start getting scary and begin to threaten our safety and comfort. This is also where the magic starts; where opportunity and abundance await—the fulfillment of dreams. It takes courage to push through, but when you do, a world of exploration and self-discovery is waiting to meet you.

Here is where you will feel alive with excitement, ignite your passion, gain confidence, and challenge yourself to be greater. You will get closer to knowing your purpose. This means taking a risk and feeling your heart pump as you press against the membrane of your comfort zone. This is the sweet spot. Each new breakthrough is like a birth, from the comforting womb to a new world. Only twenty percent of the world's population thrives here. Now if you go too far you will puncture the edge and enter the *panic zone*. Here is where intense fear and a loss of control will consume you.

The objective is to get used to the feeling of being slightly uncomfortable until it becomes comfortable. This is how we expand from our current zone and move toward the perimeter of the next one. When the comfort zone becomes an old hat, it should inspire us to reach to the growth zone. Feel the fear, allow it to integrate until it becomes comfortable—repeat.

HACKING THE PAIN/PLEASURE PARADIGM

Generally, our perception is that feeling pleasure will give us a sense of completeness. We pursue instant gratification in order to avoid pain. In our attempts to avoid short-term pain, we end up experiencing long-term pain instead. We crave instant reward over long-term reward. We want to feel good now regardless of the consequences. This is a major cause for procrastination. Initially when we eat that tub of chocolate ice cream we feel pleasure. We are consumed by the bliss of the sugar and dopamine rush—then we crash and feel like crap. Not only did we fail to offset the emotional reason for indulging, we have to battle the guilt and regret of the extra calories that found refuge in our body. So to feel better, we eat more ice cream, further beating ourselves up. It's a vicious cycle.

How do we get off this crazy train? The way off is to be mindful.

When you feel down and reach for something to feel better ask yourself, "Will this short-lived indulgence bring me long-term pleasure or long-term pain?" Look at the bigger picture. Focus on the long-term benefits. This happens when people drink to get drunk. For some, the hangovers stop being worth the price to pay for being numb and artificially happy. Half the time there is no memory recall to enjoy, only the guilt and the alcohol itself. Once we change our motivator, we can convince ourselves that enduring the short-term pain is more worthwhile than the short-term pleasure. Imagine how good it would feel to be lean, have energy, and be able to tie your shoes without losing your breath. Or would you rather eat the bag of chips and drink the bottle of wine?

Enduring initial discomfort by discipline allows us to experience sustained long-term happiness. *Delaying gratification* is the secret to achieving this. Early reward keeps us satisfied, sense bound, comfortable and addicted. This applies to everything whether it's eating to satiate perceived hunger, drinking to numb the pain of stress, or seeking the next hit of dopamine through "Likes" on social media. How do you reward yourself sooner than you should? How are you keeping yourself satiated? Which forms of pleasure do you seek?

PLEASURE AND HAPPINESS ARE NOT THE SAME

We have been taught to believe that pleasure and happiness are the same—they are not. Pleasure is caused by dopamine release, and happiness by serotonin. Gratification is a big business, and is sold to us. As consumers, we are led to believe that more money buys more pleasure. Since happiness is free and non-addictive, an economy cannot be built on it. Happiness is long lasting and is realized when we feel gratitude and a connection to others. Pleasure is short-lived, and based on wanting more things that release adrenaline. Sadly, more pleasure results in less happiness because dopamine reduces serotonin levels. We've become addicted and slaves to feeling pleasure.

In order to bypass pleasure you need to force yourself to take action. You will never feel like doing it, so don't wait for the urge to come—it won't. There is only a few second window from your first impulse (or inspiration) to taking action before you get sucked back into your comfort zone. You have to force yourself to undergo the discomfort in order to break through it—this won't last long. A frog placed in boiling water will immediately jump out. If, however, that same frog is put into the pot with tepid water and is gradually raised to boiling, it won't notice. Eventually, when it realizes that the water is boiling, it's too late. The frog becomes too weak to jump out, and it will die. Every time we reach for our next dopamine hit, or stay in our comfort zone, the same happens to us.

BYPASSING PLEASURE

The next time you feel the need to pick up your cell phone and surf social media, have a coffee, drink, smoke up, have sex or masturbate to distract or numb yourself from the pain you're trying to avoid…STOP! Instead, feel the discomfort—it's through the pain that we heal. If we keep ignoring something, it will get louder exponentially until we pay attention to it. It's like a child vying for their parents' attention when they are talking with others. Pain just wants to say, "Listen to me, there is something I need to tell you." So, meet it, let it arise. When we do this, it will begin to release. Ironically, those who live alone or isolated feel their pain with more intensity, and this leads to a greater need to numb and distract.

Practice delaying pleasure. Start small and stop indulging in things like having a snack or dessert. Pull back on that extra ten minutes of sleep. Reduce the heat of the water in the shower. You can build up to skipping a meal for a day, then two. Instead of watching mind-numbing TV, read a mind-expanding book. Practice mental toughness, it's all in the mind. Build new neurological responses instead of being a slave to the old ones. To stop procrastinating, plan ahead so you can outwit your future self-saboteur. If you want to lose weight and start exercising, clean out all the junk food in your kitchen and lay your workout clothes out the night before. If you're really bad, wear them to bed so all you have to do is put on your shoes.

Are you a serial snooze button pusher? Move your alarm clock away from your bed so you have to get out of it. Do something new every day. Take a different route to work. Write with your opposite hand. Stop indulging in sense gratification, delay it. Be mindful of how you are rewiring your brain's synaptic pathways. Make empowerment second nature. Try something that scares the shit out of you every day. Embrace the feeling, feel the fear and its exhilaration. The experience doesn't define you, nor will it kill you—unless you jump off a cliff. The feeling will pass and you will adapt to it. This expands your comfort zone.

Mantra: "Discomfort is only temporary, I am feeling better every day."

5

SELF-CARE

Most of us have had many years of education, yet no one has taught us how to love ourselves. We are versed to admire and acquire things externally, materially and to pursue mental constructs. We don't know how to love ourselves unconditionally.

Self-care is essentially the essence of this entire book. Self-Love is the opposite of self-sabotage.

When we love ourselves, we have everything. We have confidence, self-worth and respect. We're in alignment with our core beliefs and values, no matter what. It doesn't mean compromising our integrity, ever. We take responsibility for our own happiness and live our life with transparency. Self-care means we understand and help others who struggle without letting them deplete us, or cross our boundaries. In order to truly love who you are, you can't hate the people and experiences that have shaped you. Without Self-Love, there is no self-care. If we can't love our Self, how can we love someone else, or allow them to love us? Many fall into the trap of needing our value validated by another's approval of us—we outsource it. Unfortunately, we can't get from others what they don't have in themselves to give. Even if they could, we would question their motives and sincerity. Either way, insecurity is a toxic friend.

Self-Love is all-inclusive; there is no need to seek it beyond your being. This means there is no need for self-punishment, or anesthetizing emotional pain. We don't need to abuse our body with unhealthy behaviour, food or substances. This selfish behaviour masks our personal self-hatred as we try to convince ourselves that everything is great. Do you know anyone who are hard core exercisers that smoke, drink and overindulge in unhealthy habits? To someone who loves themselves, this doesn't make sense. Why would anyone want to destroy their car by having one foot on the brake and the other on the gas pedal? This is the same with a diabetic who can control their blood sugar by diet, yet rather take insulin so they can overindulge in eating crap. This is Self-Love? How often have you heard, "Life is too short, enjoy it now? You only live once?" The truth is, barring reincarnation, "We die once, but live every day." What matters more to you, how long you live, or the quality of it that you enjoy living? We are all going to die someday, this is inevitable. Living a full life is not about buying more time. It's not about hedging your bets, or bargaining. Two wrongs don't make a right. You can't live by truth and a lie at the same time.

How do you want to live your life? Sedated and numbed out until you're dead? Or, taking care of your body, optimally knowing that you've lived life on your terms, your rules, and with no regrets?

SELF-LOVE ISN'T A COMPETITION

Self-Love is not about being perfect. It's not about comparing ourselves with those we think are better. There is no such thing; it's not a beauty pageant. Our social programming tells us to seek perfection which causes us to lose our Self in the process. Similarly, commercially grown fruit is made to look perfect, but in nature it grows in odd shapes and sizes. Homogenization by genetic interference and unnatural manipulation are used to produce perfect-looking fruit. As a result, flavour and character are lost, producing bland and tasteless fruit. We live in a world of duplication, with a need to fit in. Unfortunately, uniqueness and subtlety gets lost in the repetition of it all. We have lost our ability to value diversity. In nature it's said that every snowflake is created differently. The Universe never duplicates itself. So why do we strive to do so? What's wrong with sticking out like a sore thumb? Each one of us are important and unique pieces in the mosaic puzzle of life.

Human nature compels us to try to fix externally what we see on the outside. We often neglect to address the cause from the inside. How can the ugliness of low self-worth and hate ever see the beauty projected in the mirror? Pick up any magazine and look at how everyone is portrayed to look perfect. Most times what is seen is a freakishly unrealistic perception of what beauty should look like. Photoshop, pills, plastic surgeons and beauty products are the weapons used to manipulate and destroy the ability to love your body. They are deceptive procedures which promise to fix so-called imperfections of how you look. In the end everyone looks the same. Clone-slaves lost in the madness of a society that fabricates inauthentic suppositions—selling out for a false sense of safety. How can anyone find authentic people when the bait they use is counterfeit? Then they complain why they're attracting the selfish and shallow.

We are told how to dress, what to eat and what to drive. If we don't, we're not cool, not included. If you want to fit in, you have to sell out. Nobody wins this human-race. What better way not to be judged than by being the same as everyone else? "Leave me alone, I'm playing the game." In this contest you are admired if you're the top of your class. If you play within the rules and win, you are rewarded. If you buck the trend, you're attacked and ridiculed.

This game is a contradiction: by playing it correctly and outdoing others, you'll be admired and envied. Sadly, if you seek approval from people who value these rules, you will eventually be invalidated. How can you expect fair play from an insane and volatile society that has no backbone? Like with any sporting match, the rules that work for you will be the same ones that can be used against you. You can keep score of your success this way. Or, you can keep score by how happy and peaceful you are. This is true freedom. Which do you choose?

Whether it's a board game or a funeral casket, at the end of this game of life all the pieces go back into the box. This applies to everyone. Have the balls to be unique, not just to be different. Be you and make no apologies. We waste so much time, energy and money engaging in these theatrics that we become spiritually snuffed out. We lose ourselves.

STOP CARING WHAT OTHERS THINK

If you asked a blind person how you look, and believed what they said, who's more insane? One of the biggest causes of our lack of confidence is worrying about what others think of us. Why do we even care? This stems from not wanting to be an outcast from our social circles. Way back when, rejection meant isolation from our tribe, which could eventually lead to starvation and death. Is this simply a matter of how important someone is to our survival, and to a lesser extent social status? Nowadays, does it really matter? You can tell a lot about a person's character by how they treat people they regard with a lower status than themselves. Similarly, those who have no benefit to them directly. Those who respect people lower in status depicts good character.

Would your behaviour be the same in front of a homeless person as when in the presence of your favourite actor or rockstar? Hopefully you answered yes. A lot can be said about a person by how they treat their waiter.

We can't control what others think of us, but we can control our reactions. If others get upset, we shouldn't feel bad if our best intentions are interpreted wrongly. We're often held hostage by the obligations and expectations of others that are imposed on us. This is only true if we accept them, and applies to the thoughts and emotions of how we feel toward ourselves. They are not facts, but ambiguous interpretations. Why do we give our power away and allow others to influence our confidence?

CONFIDENCE

Wouldn't it be great if we could bottle up confidence and take it like a super vitamin whenever we needed it? One day we have it, and the next we don't. Why is it so fleeting? Real confidence is having absolute certainty about something. It's knowing that something is true no matter what. It collapses if it's built on doubt or uncertainty. How do we stabilize and sustain the feeling of self-assurance? Many of us attempt to lose weight, have cosmetic surgery, make more money and raise our status to achieve this. These pursuits rarely work because they are attempts to address our shallow self-esteem by external means. Even if genuine praise was given and the proof was there, it would still be insufficient. Most of us are incapable of receiving a compliment because we don't love ourselves enough. That's why we can have five million "Likes" on our perfect selfie and still feel like crap. The truth is, we only need one like: our own. Press the love button on yourself. Confidence comes from the inside, from believing and knowing absolutely what we are. Regardless of the conditions, we are extensions of Absolute Love Source Energy.

How would you act if you knew this? What achievements would you pursue if you knew you could never fail?

Do you know what the two most common human beliefs are? "I don't deserve to be happy," and, "I deserve to be punished." Whatever the reason for these beliefs, we have to undo them regardless. Having confidence means not having to compare yourself with anyone, it means not having to pretend, nor to overcompensate. When we know our self-worth, we won't ever settle for less. We won't allow anyone—including ourselves—to treat us below our value. No longer will we give away our power, or dim our light to gain anyone's approval. This doesn't mean we have to go around like sociopaths bullying and demanding respect from others. It's not about control.

Stop relying on others to care for you. This absolutely excludes caregivers, family, medical and personal support workers who tend to those mentally and physically unable to do so for themselves. Yet, at the end of the day they cannot give us the Self-Love and care we need. Only we can do that. The best gift you can give anyone you hold dear is the gift of independence. Can your spouse, child, or work staff thrive without you? Do you need them to need you?

STOP BEING A KISS ASS

Many of us tend to and care for others while neglecting our own needs. This is how we compensate for failing to nurture ourselves. We are no good to others if we are not good to ourselves.

We all know of the proverbial airline speech telling us to put the oxygen mask on over our mouth before our kids. The sick cannot heal the sick, nor can the blind lead the blind. We wear ourselves thin when we try to mend others, and we can't even help ourselves. Our tank is empty.

What is the cost of neglecting yourself? What is the result for trying to be everything to everyone? Have you realized by now that you can't make everyone happy? Have you put your dreams on hold to help others?

Do you feel like you're holding up the world for everyone else except for yourself? Do you feel that there is never enough time for you? Do you feel unappreciated and undervalued? Does it seem like no one understands you?

How often do you wear your, "I'm OK" face to hide the broken person behind the mask? How many times do you fake that you have it together, but really are on the verge of breaking down? Do you find yourself crying when there is no one around?

Be a bit more selfish. Somewhere along the way we were reprimanded for something we did. We were told that we didn't deserve something, or that we were selfish for wanting it. Many of us have been raised by guilt and are still governed by it. Do you feel wrong asking for what is rightly yours? Whoever was responsible for this isn't here now, and frankly didn't have the right to tell you otherwise. Who is anyone to lay their ego trip on an other? We've got to allow people to do what they need to make themselves happy. Likewise, we should be allowed to do what makes us happy, too. Why do we have to make an other's business our own? If you want to help someone, then be an inspiration and an example. People will be encouraged by your actions and what you've accomplished. No one wants to be lectured, judged or compared. If they want help, they will ask. If they want help but are afraid to ask, they need to learn how to do so.

Isn't it selfish to take care of number one? Heaven forbid you look like a bad mother, father, family member, or friend. Why do you have to be the white knight, or the fixer? Is it to validate something lacking in you, or to prove that you're worth something? You are not fixing anything, you're actually perpetuating the problem, and enabling codependency. Eventually, you will hate being the good guy. You will forever be taken advantage of by others—the ones who you secretly call "selfish" under your breath. Not everyone is like you. Just because you're being nice doesn't guarantee it will be appreciated and reciprocated. Once we wake up to this and accept it, we will stop overcompensating. Don't allow assholes to turn you into one. Being nice to a snake doesn't guarantee that it won't bite you. Treat others as they are.

Many years of self-loathing and believing the lies we've been given have destroyed our confidence. Low self-worth leads to all types of unhealthy behaviour. We seek attention from others, even if it's negative—it's still attention. A woman once said, "I was promiscuous just for the attention." As she learned to love herself, she stopped whoring for approval. Similarly, when we begin to Self-Love, we are no longer affected by others' opinions. We stop buying into consumerism, or stay in abusive or toxic relationships. We don't allow anyone, or any institution to keep us small.

TURN ON YOUR LIGHT!

As humans, we are social people and want to feel like we're a part of something. We don't need to be duped in conforming, to buy or believing in what we are told. We are powerful beings, and no one has the authority to tell us otherwise. Start being kind to yourself, give yourself love and acceptance. Remove all the toxic conditions and people from your life. They won't change no matter how hard you try. Stop wasting your time giving away your power to those who will never appreciate it. Start looking for those who will, and have the capacity to receive it. Some people are energy vampires and will suck you dry. There will be those who will have you feeling recharged and full of love. Begin creating a more positive environment by eliminating negativity from your life now. These include chronic complainers who complain about the same shit over and over—victims that seek your sympathy—venters who don't want to hear solutions—those who are locked in victimhood with no desire to surrender that identity. If you feel drained and disempowered from anything or anyone, dump them from your life ASAP.

Stop dimming your light. Haters are going to hate no matter what. You are not doing yourself or anyone a favour by hiding your passion and purpose. Keeping small not to offend others is betraying them, and yourself. Shine and soar as bright and as high as you can. Those who are genuine will be able to handle your luminosity, and appreciate you. When you do, you will inspire your children, friends and family. Those that judge and ridicule you are the ones who are too afraid to be their best versions.

We will experience withdrawal symptoms as we attempt to overcome our self-sabotage. Like with any substance leaving our body, the memories of our pain will leave our cells and cause chaos. As our identity of victimhood begins to collapse, we will resist and look for our favourite painkillers. Society as a whole has stopped feeling (caring), needing more stimulation and more distraction. We lose ourselves when we follow the crowd, and we lose the crowd when we follow our Soul. Those who belong to our Spirit Family will begin to appear and support us. The challenge is enduring the solitude and judgement until this process completes.

Self-worth is the sense of your own value and worth as a person.

There is a false belief that if we value ourselves too much, we'll be viewed as narcissists. There is a big difference between self-confidence and narcissism. Narcissistic people seek dominance and are arrogant. Those with true self-esteem value equality, and humility. Don't get duped into believing otherwise. Be the spark that ignites in an other their purpose and passion. Become your own motivational coach, your own cheerleader. You don't need anyone's permission or approval. Bend your knee to no one, surrender only to the Source Energy. Be love, not fear. Your life is yours, own it and love it unconditionally. Go supernova and shine. You'll either be someone's lighthouse, or a scorching blaze they won't be able to tolerate. Without Light, there is no Life, only darkness.

SMOKING BABY

Before you partake in any action ask yourself, "Would I give this to a four-year-old baby?" Any half-decent parent would never expose their children to anything that could jeopardize their health and well-being. Would you let your baby eat junk food, drink alcohol, or allow them to be hit by an abusive babysitter? Why are we any different? If you really love someone, you would never want to hurt them intentionally. We'd only want to harm another if we didn't like them, or if we wanted to punish them for something they may have done. If you find yourself engaging in negative and harmful behaviour, ask, "Why am I punishing myself? What makes me undeserving?" The road toward Self-Love begins by Self-nurturing, not looking for others to do it for you. Once we realize that we're not in love with ourselves, we can see why we are practicing self-torture. No more excuses.

PRACTICE LOVING YOURSELF

Magic mirror on the wall, who is the most lovable of them all? Well, don't ask the mirror, or the scale for that matter. The observer looking in the reflection has to love what it sees. Most cannot accept the image that is cast back. There will always be someone better looking than you, and also less so.

In truth, it's only an interpretation, as beauty is in the eye of the beholder. You are not your body, it will soon decay. Lines will appear to mark the passage of time, which passes quickly—life here is very short. Be grateful for the body that moves you around and allows you to enjoy all the sounds, tastes, aromas and textures that life offers. One of the hardest things for most people to do is look in the mirror, gaze deep into their eyes and say, "I love you." Can you do it and say it like you mean it? Go ahead, give it a try. Yes, put this book down right now and give it a shot. I'll wait...

Well, how did it go? Weird, wasn't it? Was it hard to do? Let's try something even crazier. Go back to the mirror, but this time I want you to do it naked. Find something that you love about yourself. Loving your eyes doesn't count. Start by looking at a body part that you feel is your best asset. Remember no one is perfect so be easy on yourself. If this is hard to do, just accept it as it is and be grateful. I suggest looking at your entire body loving its totality without isolating any part. Say, "I love you exactly as you are. You're beautiful. Thank you for all that you do for me." Say this every day, before or after you take your shower. As you wash each body part, gently caress it as you would with a lover. Let your body know you love it unconditionally. When you're comfortable with this process, move on to the next step. You may feel uneasy about doing this, but again it's about unconditionally loving yourself—make love to your body. The purpose is not to simply get your rocks off, it's about experiencing personal intimacy.

When we allow others to assess the value of our beauty, we become powerless, and dependent on their validation. We are controlled by imaginary expectations which we believe others have on us. In some cases we do extreme things to procure that. Notice how a flower simply is. No matter what, it doesn't compete with others for attention. Similarly, be the same.

In Japanese, wabi-sabi means perfectly imperfect. The word denotes living with the acceptance of the transience and imperfection of all things. Nobody's body is perfect. The object is to love and accept all of your perceived imperfections. True beauty is imperfect, impermanent and incomplete.

SELF-LOVE

As you've gathered by now, if you don't love yourself first, no one will. Practice giving yourself the love and attention you currently seek from others. Give yourself encouragement through self-talk. Be mindful of your thoughts. Give yourself time to relax and meditate. Honour your feelings, they matter. Take responsibility for them, understand what they are trying to say. Take care of yourself emotionally, intellectually and physically. Consider adding homeopathic and holistic modalities to your allopathic portfolio. Visit an osteopath, naturopath, massage therapist and chiropractor, to name a few. Go for a spa day, get into nature, go for walks by the water or forest. Take note of how you feel around certain people. Do you feel drained, insecure or confident? Do they empower you or leave you feeling confused or unsure of yourself? Don't simply cut them off, they could be mirroring back unaddressed aspects within yourself. Feel your gut—your body knows, energy doesn't lie. Move toward feelings of love, and away from anything that causes fear.

Be what you were meant to be before the world told you what you were supposed to be. Children are masters at playing. Get to know yourself again through the eyes of your inner child. Start colouring again, jump in puddles, be in awe and wonder of how a child sees. Go to the park and hit the swings, play in a sandbox. When children talk to you, bend down, face them and pay attention to what they are saying—listen. You will sense their innocence and wonderment.

Do something you enjoy, start a hobby. Remove yourself from any and every thing that doesn't inspire, or nourish you. Let go of the past. Stop being so hard on yourself and trying to be perfect. Many of us fall into the trap of taking things too seriously. This is how we get old quickly. Laugh and play more. Love yourself unconditionally, at the same time raise your standards. Pursue your passions, stop people pleasing, establish your boundaries. Give back to the community. Hang out with new friends, those that are positive and successful. Interact with those who inspire you. Remove and stop feeding energy vampires who complain and have no intention of helping themselves, and who find a problem for every solution. Stop gossiping. Find those who challenge you to be the best you can be. Be kind to yourself during this process, because as you expand to a newer version, you are in foreign territory. You've never been this rendition of yourself before. Growth may be uncomfortable, but it can be fun and exciting, too.

The following chapters will expand on self-care. When we understand how the body works, we can better give it what it needs.

Affirmation: "I give myself permission to love my Self. I do not allow others to dictate this for me." Add whatever you want to this affirmation.

6

THE BODY: PART 1

Becoming the best you can be would be a lot easier if it was just a matter of undoing our programming. There is still a major hurdle in achieving and maintaining success in life. Ultimately, we have to deal with a complex bio-organic machine. Will power alone can accomplish many things, but it's usually not enough. We may be headstrong, but if our body's chemistry and rhythms are off, mental discipline on its own is inadequate. Understanding how our body works and what it needs greatly helps us take control of it. It's one thing to be able to abstain from a drug like cocaine, and another to be able to curb an addiction to one that's eight times more addictive that's in almost every food we buy.

In this chapter we will learn how our body clock works, and how our posture and breathing affects us. The next chapter covers hormones, neurotransmitters, sleep and exercise. All these factors are super important to our health and well-being. Aligning with our physiology is critical for being able to attract and manifest what we want. How can we get to where we are going if we are constantly distracted by pain, poor health, and mental fog?

THE FERRARI AND THE SHITBOX

Have you ever driven a supercar such as the Ferrari? If you have, you'd know how well the car was built and calibrated to perform at top levels. They way it accelerates, takes corners and brakes is literally a dream. This type of car is refined and built to the highest of standards, and it's super fun to drive. Have you ever driven a shitbox? Would you pray that it started, and that it wouldn't leave you stranded far from home? Was there always something rattling and knocking around inside the engine? Putting status and personal taste aside, I'm sure if given the choice, you'd rather drive a car that was reliable and fun to drive.

Have you considered that your body is such a car? It moves you around and lets you experience life's terrain. Wouldn't you want your body to perform like a supercar, rather than like a shitbox? Many of us treat our car way better than we treat our body. We use premium gasoline, change the oil, rotate the tires, and follow a proper maintenance program. Similarly, we buy nice clothes, get our hair and nails done, and make ourselves up. Some of us look so amazing on the outside, but on the inside is an unhealthy and unhappy disaster. We attempt to improve ourselves by trying to fix the outside. This approach doesn't change a thing; it's like putting lipstick on a pig.

We buy creams, lotions, potions, and pills in the hopes of improving our appearance. These products only benefit those who manufacture and sell them. The only way to get healthy, have the clear glowing skin and improve the quality of your life is by addressing it from the inside first. We accomplish this by changing our lifestyle, psychology, and the food we eat. It's an inside job. If our biological supercar isn't calibrated and running at its peak, we could be left stranded on the side of the road.

How many are living their life with deteriorating health? Which of those are suffering with low energy, pain, mental fog, insomnia, digestion problems and bloating? The list could go on. We've come to the point of accepting that all this is normal. That it's part of life and the aging process. We conclude that some people are just unlucky with their health. More pills are ingested so we can continue abusing our body. We take no responsibility for the state we put ourselves in. There are no guarantees that we won't get sick with disease, or encounter acute health issues—however, it isn't normal that an increasing number of people are suffering with chronic disease.

WHY AM I ALWAYS TIRED?

I could easily say you don't get enough sleep, but that's not even close to being the full story. We're up against an evil so subtle that it can't be seen, but it's there. There is a hormone that is responsible for destroying your peace of mind, and physical health. Let's look at a typical day of the modern person.

Often, you get up earlier than your body wants to. You force yourself out of bed and get ready for work. This hormone gets pumped throughout your body to wake it up from its catatonic slumber. You quickly shower and get ready to face the world. If you have time, you make breakfast. I'm guessing not, but you've made your coffee, no doubt. Hopefully you've remembered to make your lunch the night before. You rush through breakfast, make lunches and get the kids ready for school. You're a good parent so you drop them off, take them to the bus stop, or make other arrangements. At this point you've dramatically raised this hormone through the roof.

Do you even have time to eat breakfast? If so, what did you eat? Did you eat it in your car, on the train, or as you walked? Do you know that most breakfast food jacks up this hormone? By now your hormone levels are already at insane levels. Are you late for work, the bus, or stuck in traffic? The more stress there is, the higher levels of this hormone. You may already be starting to crash and craving for another coffee to re-energize you, and you haven't even started work yet.

How is your job, anyway? Is it stressful? Do you have to deal with annoying customers and co-workers? Is your boss busting on you? You pray for lunchtime, and it finally comes. Well, that's if you don't work through it. What did you pack in your lunch bag? Oh damn, you forgot. Quickly, you rush out to grab some food, but you only have ten minutes left to eat. If you're a slow eater you're out of luck—don't eat, or train for the fastest-eater contest. I guess I don't have to tell you how much more you're overloading on this hormone. Back to work with undigested food rummaging through your stomach. You plow through your workload somewhat refreshed but still kind of tired. The stack of assignments mount, yet you're hardly keeping up. You grab another hormone boosting coffee for another pick-me-up.

Bam, the dreaded three o'clock crash hits you like a dank pillow right in the face. You struggle to stay awake, let alone be productive. You do your best to finish the rest of your work. Finally, your day is done and you get back into the traffic for home. The news reports that a tractor trailer has flipped over on the road you're on—your bus or train is delayed, even cancelled. The kids need to be picked up and brought to dance class, piano, hockey, or karate. Who is cooking dinner? Is it Drive-Thru or frozen dinner again tonight? Clean up, do the dishes, help your kids with their homework. You suddenly realize the dishwasher is still full, or worse, stopped working. A load of laundry needs to be done if you want clean clothes for tomorrow, but you have to finish a report that was due yesterday instead. You also have an early meeting with the boss before you start work.

How are you coping? Do you have more coffee, or knock off a few glasses of wine? Maybe you manage with indulging in other ways. You try to put the kids to bed but they resist, robbing minutes from your alone time. You turn on the television, the news declares another murder, child abduction and natural disaster. You lose yourself in binge watching your favourite show. It's late and you have to get up early. You're tired as hell, but you can't get to sleep because your mind is racing. Before you know it the alarm clock goes off. But you're too tired to use the bat under your bed to smash the shit out of it. Did you even sleep? This cycle continues, again and again. Maybe your marriage is on the rocks, you're having an affair, or your kid is being bullied at school. Is there a way off of this crazy train?

ONCE UPON A TIME

Once upon a time, we lived a more simple life. We spent a longer time doing and making things. Many indigenous people have lost their ancestors' abilities to read the clouds and observe how the leaves turn in the wind that predicts impending weather patterns. Our instincts were once more aligned with nature, like that of the animals. We've since disconnected, needing to get back to our innate nature and follow our Soul's inspirations and insights. We've been cut off from this inner wisdom. In the past, our main concerns were acquiring water, food, and shelter. Occasionally, our angst was due to a passing predator. Today things are moving so fast, we've lost touch with nature, and with ourselves. We've become severely stressed out.

Convenience has encouraged us to cram in too many things in one day. We are inundated with more information that we can process. We've lost our connection with nature's cycles and patterns. Technology was supposed to make life easier and give us more time. Instead, it has complicated things. I'm all for technological advancements and can't wait to see what's next, but at what cost does it come with? We are going nowhere fast. This is creating unnecessary stress in our lives, compounded with the mental anxiety many of us are plagued with. Everyone handles pressure differently. Some can have what appears to be the most stressful life, yet act as cool as a cucumber. Others can be on a tropical island without any care in the world, but be nervous wrecks.

Incidentally, with so many of our needs now being met with technology, we have the opportunity to explore who we are. We can slow down and become more mindful, understand how our body works and harness its full potential. Like a car, we need to take care of our human spacesuit. We need to learn which fuel is best for it, and carry out the proper maintenance and alignment that will afford optimal performance.

POSTURE

Our body's posture is a reflection of our inner emotional states. I've noticed that confident people stand erect with their chin up and level to the ground.

One may act confident, yet be very insecure. The body doesn't lie. Shoulders that are slouched with the head held slightly downward denotes a lack of confidence. In order for blood to flow easily through our arteries and veins, there needs to be no obstruction in the pathways. Heart and stroke sufferers can attest to this. The same occurs with our nervous system. If a nerve is severed or damaged, information can't properly be sent to and from the brain. Metaphysically, this also applies to our meridians, chakras and the nadis that run throughout our body.

Energy, or Life Force runs mainly up and down the spine, which gets distributed throughout the body via the aforementioned pathways. Damage to the spine, and all bets are off.

Did you know that a bad posture can affect your digestion, reduce circulation, interrupt sleeping patterns, impact your mood, promote pain in your joints, reduce motivation, give you headaches and create fatigue, to name a few? Our brain is a transmitter and receiver, the less obstruction the better the signal. The healthier the body, the more energy it has. We impinge on the quality of Life Force that is available to us by how we carry ourselves. When we slouch, entertain restless thoughts and fearful emotions, we drastically restrict the flow of energy. When we are aligned and open, we can receive and utilize more energy. You can immediately change how you feel by changing your posture. A smile is not always the result of feeling happiness. Sometimes a smile can make you feel happy. Try it now, make a big smile and hold it… "Ok, hurry up and take the picture already." We can hack our body, thoughts, and emotions by manipulating our physiology. We can change our posture and align ourselves by stretching, exercise, yoga and having a chiropractor adjust our spine. Try doing Tai Chi, Qi Gong or any other modality that aligns your mind and body.

Let's try an exercise:
I want you to stand up, drop your chin to your chest, slouch your shoulders forward, lower your chest, and form a sad face by puckering your bottom lip. Look sadly at your feet and let your arms hang lifeless by your sides. How do you feel? Now, take a

deep breath, raise your hands over your head like you're ready to catch something, put a big smile on your face, open your mouth and show your teeth. Look upward and anticipate catching a colourful beach ball. Open your hands and spread your fingers. Raise your shoulders and chest as you lift your hands to catch the ball. How do you feel?

I strongly suggest being mindful of how you carry your body. Doing so promotes strength, flexibility and increased energy flow. Pay attention to your posture when you are sitting, walking or standing. How are you holding yourself? This will be hard to remember at first, but after a while it will become second nature. Use your body to get yourself into a good mood whenever you're feeling down. Paying attention to your breath is just as important.

THE BREATH

Breathing is one of the most neglected and undervalued functions of our body. Many of us take it for granted. Do you know our brain can only survive six minutes without oxygen, and before our heart stops? Did you know that just after one minute without air the cells in our brain start to die? And after three minutes it experiences severe brain damage? How do you breathe? Is it quick and shallow, or slow and deep? A human breathes on average twenty-five thousand times a day. Deep breathing naturally releases the tensions in our body. Conversely, breathing shallow causes restrictions which holds the stress and anxieties of the day. Babies are supple who breathe effortlessly. As adults we stiffen, experience tension, pain, restriction and fear. Consider slow, deep breathing a drug-free way to cure stress, depression, tight muscles, insomnia, lower blood pressure, and trauma-induced behaviours and emotions.

For many of us, our cells are starved for oxygen. The deeper you breathe the more Life Force is drawn in. Did you know that the longest living creatures on Earth breathes the slowest and the least amount of times per minute? We can conclude that the opposite is true. The shorter-lived animals tend to breathe the fastest in that same timeframe. Breathing slower releases less stress hormones, resulting in lower anxiety levels. Did you know that every emotional state has a corresponding breathing pattern and structure? You can instantly gain control of your mind, body and emotions by becoming aware of your breath. Doing so brings your awareness into the present moment. This helps you focus and connect to your Soul. Deep breathing also helps you bring in positive thoughts and emotions. In addition, it draws in creative Life Force energy. Breathing should be natural and never forced. The next time you walk by a lake, ocean or a forest, try inhaling its healing aspects.

Lets try another exercise:
Take in short and shallow breaths quickly. Eventually, you will start feeling lightheaded. Now inhale slowly and deeply. Do you notice the difference? The quickest way to relax your mind and body is to take in a deep breath through the nose to a count of three, hold for three, and exhale for three out through the mouth. Do this three to five times or more until you feel

completely relaxed. Practice this in the morning and during the day and especially if you have trouble falling asleep.

Mantra: "I breathe in love and exhale gratitude."

Can breathing burn fat?

There is new research claiming that we can burn fat simply by deep breathing. Our fat cells store triglyceride which is a type of fat found in our blood—it's composed of carbon, hydrogen, and oxygen. Through oxidation, these atoms are released and fat is burned off as CO_2 and water. So every time you urinate and exhale you're technically releasing fat.

Miki Ryosuke, a Japanese actor, recently discovered a natural method that helped him lose weight. After experiencing back pain, Miki's doctor recommended he perform a certain exercise each day to help relieve his pain. After performing the exercise for a few weeks, Miki noticed that he had lost 28.7 pounds and 4.7 inches from his waist in just two months. He refers to this technique as the long-breath diet. How it's done: Stand in a position with your hips aligned to your shoulders. Place your kicking foot in front of your other foot. Place your weight on your back foot. Take in a deep fast three-second breath, while raising your arms above your head. Clench your butt cheeks while doing so. Hold for a second or two. Then exhale strongly for seven seconds, lowering your arms in an arching motion down to your sides. Contract your body and core as you quickly exhale—empty all the air and hold for a second or two. This exercise should take two to five minutes.

WATER

Water was going to be covered in the next chapter on food, however it's better addressed here. Water is life; it sustains us. Our body is made up by a majority of it similar to the percentage that covers the Earth. Without it, we will die after three to six days. There is no use talking about food if we are dead, right? We need to drink plenty of water; however I don't believe that we should be drinking gallons as some suggest. Drinking too much can be dangerous. You can kill plants by over-watering. Likewise, we can over-hydrate our body which can lead to water intoxication. An excessive amount of water in the blood dilutes essential electrolytes such as sodium and potassium. This causes the water residing outside the cell to go inside of it, causing swelling. There was a report of a military soldier dying from drinking ten litres of water within a three hour timespan. That equals to just 2.5 gallons.

Drink only when you're thirsty, not because you think you have to. Some believe that when you are thirsty, it's too late and you're already dehydrated. Not to panic, our body is a medical marvel and can adapt to many challenging conditions. It's suggested that we drink six to thirteen eight ounce glasses a day, more if necessary. Urine which is pale yellow that looks like lemonade is a good indicator of sufficient hydration. Colourless urine signals over-hydration, and darker signals dehydration. Water not only hydrates us, it helps our digestion, transports nutrients through our blood, aids in circulation, helps in the production of saliva, assists in maintaining body temperature, flushes out cells, helps bowel movement, and aids in keeping our joints lubricated, to name a few.

Symptoms of mild to moderate dehydration include thirst, reduced sweating, decreased urine production, dry mouth, dizziness, and reduced skin elasticity. An obvious sign is fatigue, and severe brain fog. When our body gets dehydrated, electrolytes become deficient and water is restricted from moving easily from inside the cells out into the blood. Reduced water levels can cause low blood pressure which can lead to lightheadedness, particularly when standing up suddenly. If water and electrolyte loss continues, blood pressure can fall dangerously low and result in shock and severe damage to the internal organs. These include the kidneys, liver, and brain.

The requirement for water increases and decreases depending on the circumstance. We would need more walking through the desert than if we were standing at the bus stop during the dead of winter. The more we sweat the more water we need to replenish what is lost. If you are naturally a profuse sweater or perform intense exercise, you'll most likely need to drink more. Those living at higher elevations also need to replenish more. The need for water increases when we are sick. During this time we lose vital fluid via mucous discharge, urine, and diarrhoea. Lactating mothers also require more than normal. In simple math: water out equals water in.

Try drinking clean, natural spring water if you can. Avoid the fluorinated stuff that comes out of the tap. Steer clear of flavoured water that claims to have been enhanced—they usually contain sugar and chemicals. Tea and coffee don't count as they are diuretics which have a dehydrating effect on the body.

There is a debate on whether chemicals leak out of plastic bottles. Nonetheless, they cause incredible damage to our oceans and sea life.

Consider investing in a Reverse Osmosis water filtration system. If you decide on drinking distilled, be sure to replenish the lost minerals by adding a pinch of natural sea salt to it.

CLOCKS AND RHYTHMS

Everything in nature is governed by rhythms and cycles. Seasons are the Earth's natural clock. The Solstices make the two main divisions of the seasons, which further divide into four by the Equinoxes. The same seasonal phenomenon can be found within the body of each living thing.

Hibernation occurs in the winter, thriving in the spring, and so on. A plant buds, flowers, produces seeds, and eventually drops its leaves so that it can regenerate again. The cycle of the seasons is seen reflected in the behaviour of all living things. There is birth, growth, aging, and finally death. The leaves of a tree complete their maturing process and die, this takes place in autumn. The tree's energy retracts and concentrates in its roots during the winter. (Similarly, during this time, more energy settles into our bones making them stronger.) As spring dawns, the energy awakens and rises up into the stem and into the leaves. In the warmer months, they flower, then blossom into fruit. The seeds are ready for the next cycle.

Humans are governed by biorhythms, lunar and seasonal cycles. Women are more in-tune physically than men are. This may be due in part by their higher emotional intelligence, and monthly menses. I believe that both genders are affected by lunar cycles. There is a cycle or clock that affects our mental, emotional, physical, and biological aspects.

THE CIRCADIAN RHYTHM

There is a 24-hour cycle that governs all humans, plants, animals and fungi.
This biological process is called the circadian rhythm. A disruption to this in humans can lead to insomnia, obesity, diabetes, depression, bipolar disorder, SAD (Seasonal Affective Disorder) and impair bodily functions. Environmental cues affect this cycle, light being the highest contributor. One such trigger is the blue wavelength that's found within the natural light spectrum of the sun. When the molecule melanopsin in our retina stops sensing light, it tells the pineal gland to produce *melatonin*. This hormone is responsible for making us sleep.

Our technology, (cellphones, computers, etc.) also emits a blue light. This may be fine in the daylight hours, yet it causes major problems at night. Using tech when it's naturally dark tells our brain that it is still daytime. This totally interferes with our sleep cycle.

Did you know that your melatonin levels can be reduced by a whopping twenty-two percent after two hours of screen time? Watching television, surfing on your computer and checking messages on your smartphone right before bed will prevent you from having a good night's sleep. If you have to use your technology later in the evening, use blue blocking sunglasses. They are great at filtering out this portion of the light spectrum. Some devices now have an automatic filter as part of their operating system. Way back, we had no choice but to follow Mother Nature's clocks. We ascended and descended with the sun and were in concert with her seasons. Lighting candles or fires weren't bright enough to throw our melatonin out of balance, unlike our modern tech and artificial lighting does.

HOW THE CIRCADIAN CLOCK WORKS

Just before you wake up, your blood pressure starts to rise. This happens around 6:30am to 6:45am. By 7:30am your melatonin secretion stops and cortisol secretion begins. Our need for a bowel movement is stimulated at around 8:30am. Testosterone is at its highest level by 9:00am, which may explain the crankiness of non-morning people. Incidentally, most men have a higher sex drive in the morning than do at night when testosterone levels decrease. By 10:00am we are most alert. In the afternoon at about 2:30pm a person's coordination is at its best. By 3:30pm reaction time is at its fastest. Cardiovascular and muscle strength are at their peak in the late afternoon at around 5:00pm. Blood pressure is at its highest at 6:30pm, and by 7:00pm so is our body temperature. Melatonin secretion begins at 9:00pm. The signal for fecal excretion is suppressed at 10:30pm. By 2:00am we reach the deepest state of sleep. Our body temperature is at its lowest at 4:30am. Cortisol levels are at their lowest during sleep, and HGH (Human Growth Hormone) is at its highest. Cortisol is the hormone that wakes us up, and melatonin is what puts us to sleep. Ghrelin, the hunger hormone, rises and falls within a twelve hour interval. At around 8am, it's typically at its lowest. By 8:00pm, it's at its peak as hunger increases.

These rhythms are inherent in our genetic makeup and are biologically precise in normal conditions. However, they are often disrupted and interfered with by our poor lifestyle choices. Conversely, we can take advantage of this knowledge and benefit from it. Next are a few hacks to optimize our circadian clock.

For example, the best time to exercise and workout is between 2:30pm and 8:30pm. This is when the testosterone and cortisol ratio is at its best. At 5:00pm the body is in its strongest state, and this is a good time to take advantage of it; additionally, it is a good way to avoid using a chemical pre-workout or stimulant. Since hunger is at its lowest in the morning—7:50am to be exact—we shouldn't force a feeding at this time. Insulin is also at its highest. This hormone is responsible for creating many of our health problems. The Europeans have figured this out long ago and typically eat their biggest meal between 12:00pm and 3:00pm. They keep breakfast very light, and some don't eat at all.

7

CHEMISTRY, SLEEP AND EXERCISE: PART 2

Our bodies are incredible biological machines. They are al-chemical marvels composed of DNA, microbiome, proteins, fats, cells, chemicals and water. An imbalance can cause havoc to the intellectual, emotional and physical aspects of our well-being. These chemicals consist of hormones and neurotransmitters, which regulate our body's processes. Neurotransmitters are the body's chemical messengers used by the nervous system to transmit signals between nerve cells (neurons) to the muscles.

The brain uses neurotransmitters to tell your heart to beat, your lungs to breathe, and your stomach to digest. Neurotransmitters belong to the nervous system, whereas hormones belong to the endocrine system. Hormones are released by the endocrine glands such as the ovaries, testicles, pituitary and pineal glads, thyroid, and so on. This isn't a medical journal so I am going to keep this as simple as I can. It's important to learn how this alchemical system works and how it affects us, so we can utilize it to our advantage.

INSULIN

Insulin is a hormone made by the pancreas that allows our body to use sugar from carbohydrates in the food we eat for energy, it also stores glucose for future use. Insulin helps keep our blood sugar level from getting too high (hyperglycaemia), or too low (hypoglycaemia). Cells in our body use sugar for energy, however, sugar cannot go directly into them without help. Typically, after we eat, our blood sugar levels rise, cells in our pancreas known as beta cells signal the release of insulin into our bloodstream. Insulin attaches to the sugar and signals the cell to absorb it from the bloodstream. This hormone is also important as it allows protein to enter our muscles to be rebuilt. Insulin is often described as the storage hormone. Consider it the *doorman with the key* who unlocks the cell. Unfortunately, if he knocks on the door too often, the cell is going to get pissed off, change the lock and will eventually stop answering.

INSULIN RESISTANCE

As with any drug, tolerance increases with excessive exposure, and it takes more of it to have an effect. Our cells will stop responding to insulin if we ingest too much sugar; they will become resistant. When this happens, the cell has nothing to eat because it has triple bolted the front door. The delivery guy is there knocking profusely; he's trying to deliver the double pepperoni pizza. The cell is going crazy, it's starving and yelling at the landlord (your brain) to bring in more food. There is a line up of delivery boys with pizza, chips, pasta and bread sent in by the brain. Since all the doors are closed where does all the food go? Unfortunately, these simple nutrients get quickly stored as fat. The body gets fatter and is starving at the same time. In an experiment, rats were made to be resistant to insulin, then they were starved. They died without accessing any of their fat stores. Did you also know that fat burning isn't possible when there is a high level of insulin in the blood? Insulin means insulation.

Excess sugar is transported to the liver and muscles to be stored as glycogen. Unfortunately, storage space is limited so the rest gets fatted away into the cells. High levels of sugar turned fat can lead toward many types of diseases and health problems such as a nonalcoholic fatty liver and insulin resistance. Tolerance depends on age and other factors. Children seem to be able to ingest copious amounts of sugar all day without gaining one ounce of fat. Granted, we may have to peel them off the ceiling, or deal with their erratic mood swings. Eventually, their body will become resistant due to the constant release of insulin. They may gain weight, or worst case, develop diabetes. The older we get, the greater the risk. When there is too much insulin due to high blood sugar, hypoglycaemia can result. To compensate for the body's low energy, cortisol, epinephrine, and norepinephrine are released. This creates the jitters, nervousness, and unhealthy behaviour. When the brain gets hypoglycaemic it releases the neurotransmitter glutamate. This causes excitability and hyper behaviour which has been linked to stimulate criminal-type activity. Could less crime, antisocial behaviour and suicide be reduced by eating less sugar and keeping insulin levels down?

What is too much sugar? The body can only handle five grams of glucose in its bloodstream at a time. Any more, or less can be dangerous. To put it into perspective, five grams is only one teaspoon. One cup of plain cooked pasta, unsalted with no sauce has around forty grams of carbohydrates. A plain bagel has fifty to sixty grams of carbohydrates. That's well over ten times the normal level of healthy blood sugar.

Having more than two teaspoons of sugar dissolved in our blood is considered toxic. It's no wonder why obesity and Type 2 diabetes is becoming an epidemic. Many of us are pre-Type 2 diabetics and don't even know it.

LEPTIN AND GHRELIN

These two hormones are responsible for our sensations of hunger and feeling full. Ghrelin is what makes us hungry. These hormones decrease and increase our appetite. Ghrelin is mainly produced and released by the stomach, but low amounts can be released by the small intestine, pancreas and brain. Leptin is produced by the body's fat cells. Interestingly, obese people are often affected by leptin resistance. Overeating releases high levels of this hormone, and eventually the brain's receptors become resistant, much like a cell becomes insulin resistant. Your brain loses its ability to tell you to stop eating. Conversely, dieting raises ghrelin, and may lead to more fat storage. Yo-yo dieting plays havoc with our body and these two hormones. As mentioned in the circadian rhythm section, hunger is naturally lowest at 7:50am and highest at 7:50pm. Avoid having a big breakfast as you are basically breaking a fast.

Did you know that during an extended fast, ghrelin peaks only during the first two days and then steadily falls? Most people report that after a couple of days without eating their hunger actually disappears. It appears obvious that heavier people have more ghrelin than thinner people, and that thinner people have more leptin. In the summer ghrelin is higher as there is more food available. In winter there is less of it, and coincidently, leptin is higher. This may be why animals in the wild don't get obese.

CORTISOL

Cortisol is known as the *stress* hormone. It's a steroid-hormone that's produced from cholesterol in the two adrenal glands located on top of each kidney. It is responsible for our immune responses, metabolism, and assists with lowering inflammation in our body. However, when persistently elevated, it has a negative effect on our weight and overall health. Cortisol provides our body with a quick release of glucose when needed. If there isn't enough available, it taps into our protein stores via gluconeogenesis in the liver. At this time, insulin production is inhibited to prevent the glucose from being stored as fat, so that it can be used by the muscles instead. Short-term stress like a sudden fall, a run-in with a bear, or any intense experiences spikes cortisol triggering our fight-or-flight response. When this occurs, less oxygen is available in our brain—the less we think—the more we run on pure instinct. Normally, after the threat is over, cortisol, insulin, and sugar levels normalize.

Unfortunately, our modern life causes us to experience long-term stress. Many have stressful jobs and a pressure filled life. This leads to prolonged higher levels of cortisol which keeps our body in an insulin resistant state. Nutrients and precursors required to sustain these abnormally high levels begin to deplete. Chronic stress can lead to a decline in important hormones and neurotransmitters such as testosterone, HGH (Human Growth Hormone), aldosterone, epinephrine (adrenaline) serotonin and dopamine. This can lead to Adrenal Fatigue, better known as burnout. Over time, the high sugar levels puts undue pressure on the pancreas and it fails to keep up with insulin production. This brings us back to our body's starving and paranoid cells who've barricaded their doors yelling for more food. We not only crave more sugar, but we often reach for stimulants like coffee and other substances to stimulate cortisol and adrenaline release. This just further exhausts our adrenals making us more sick, fat, and tired.

High levels of cortisol can lead to rapid weight gain, high blood pressure, irritability, collagen depletion, muscle loss and weakness, osteoporosis, mood swings, a short attention span, mental illness (including anxiety and depression), heart disease, hardened arteries, weakened immune system, irregular menses, menopause, and diabetes. Another danger of consistently raised cortisol levels may lead to a disease called Cushing's Syndrome. Symptoms may mimic the aforementioned with the addition of a fat pad behind the neck, kidney stones, extra hair on the face, a lowered sex drive, and lack of sleep. Medications can also cause Cushing's Syndrome such as steroids and prednisone. Conversely, having too low levels of cortisol may cause dizziness, fatigue and weight loss. Have you ever noticed how kids get cranky if they are over tired? Sleepovers pose challenges to parents who try calming down giggling children jacked up on adrenaline and cortisol.

Cortisol is at its highest first thing in the morning, but levels can raise up to fifty percent within the first thirty minutes of waking. During the course of the day this hormone normally drops off gradually, and is at its lowest in the late evening. We can't fall asleep with high levels. Conversely, as we sleep our stores are replenished. For those who work nights or experience jet lag, these levels adjust to compensate. This can result in the cycle becoming inverted which may lead to anxiety and sleepless nights.

How to lower cortisol

One of the first and most important things we need to do to lower cortisol and repair adrenal fatigue is sleep. Unfortunately, this is something many of us have a hard time doing. Next, we have to remove all of our stressors and triggers. Then we need to rebuild our body's adrenals and give it a chance to heal itself. To begin, I highly suggest removing all stressful people and environments, coffee, (caffeine, all stimulants), strenuous exercise, simple carbohydrates such as sugar, starchy vegetables, grains, rice, legumes, and low-fat dairy. Since cortisol is elevated in the morning, avoid anything that will spike it even higher. This includes coffee and simple carbohydrates. Doing so only increases inflammation, anxiety and fat storage.

Ironically, observing a strict no-carb diet can stress the body even more. Drastically reducing carbohydrate intake may cause low blood sugar which can lead to hypoglycemia and increased adrenal release. We can avoid this by upping fat intake and consuming electrolytes. This will be covered further in a later chapter. Many people wanting to lose weight simply can't if they have high levels of stress and anxiety, no matter how much they exercise. Cortisol makes you fat much faster than food can. Did you know that belly fat is a result of high levels of cortisol? The truth is, dieting only reduces calories, not the stress hormone.

In order to reduce our stress and the biological chemicals responsible for playing havoc on our health, I suggest doing the following: drink adequate water (add a pinch of Himalayan sea salt to help with hydration), go to sleep early, consume food containing B vitamins (B5 and B6 and B12 in particular) and vitamins A, C, D, K2, selenium, magnesium, potassium, and zinc, eat organic grass-fed organ meats (especially liver, oysters), leafy greens, asparagus, saturated animal and vegetable fats—butter, ghee, coconut oil, monounsaturated fats like avocados, nutrient dense proteins, lower inflammation by omega fatty acids, and curcumin, drink non-caffeinated herbal tea (chamomile tea and rooibos), go on relaxing walks, meditation, yoga, massage and other body work, take a nap, spend times outdoors (in the sun, water, lake, rivers), realign to your circadian rhythms, and finally, learn to say no and don't stress out by being a people pleaser. High stress equals high cortisol, creates high insulin and causes inflammation—which creates disease.

HUMAN GROWTH HORMONE

There is another way to combat high cortisol. HGH (Human Growth Hormone) is a peptide hormone that stimulates growth, cell reproduction and regeneration. It keeps us strong and lean. As we age, our body's HGH production decreases. Some say that by the age of fifty it bottoms out. Once we hit the age of thirty, we enter in what's called Somatopause. This is a point at which our levels of HGH begin to drop off quite dramatically. This decline of HGH is part of what drives our aging process. Maintaining HGH levels becomes increasingly important with age. HGH is the Yin to cortisol's Yang; they balance each other out. If there is too much of one, there is an imbalance of the other. During sleep our pituitary gland activates HGH which lowers cortisol. Levels increase during the time of puberty, by sleep, exercise, fasting, and consuming saturated fats (mainly animal). Levels are decreased by stress and high sugar levels in the blood.

IGF (Insulin-like Growth Factor) is a hormone that is similar to HGH which is produced by the liver that regulates fat burning. Insulin regulates sugar when you are eating, and IGF regulates blood sugars when you're not eating, and while sleeping. Every time we eat, insulin is released. If we don't eat solid meals but graze throughout the day, we don't give our body a chance to produce HGH. This is why it's better to have two to three meals a day, without snacking.

SEROTONIN AND DOPAMINE

If you've ever experienced addictive behaviour, a lack of motivation or depression, you can thank these two neurotransmitters. Too much or too little amounts can throw us out of balance. Serotonin makes you feel good, relaxed and self-confident, and dopamine helps us get things done. Serotonin impacts every part of our body, from our emotions to our motor skills. Not only is it considered a natural mood stabilizer, but it also helps with sleeping, eating, and digestion. Serotonin converts to melatonin (the sleep hormone) so we need it available for a good sleep. Both a hormone and neurotransmitter serotonin is found in our brain, but mostly in our gut. There is a strong connection between low serotonin and IBS (Irritable Bowel Syndrome). Gut health and mental health go hand-in-hand. The more serotonin we have in our body, the less cortisol. Conversely, chronic stress decreases serotonin and dopamine. This results in feelings of anxiety, depression, insomnia and as some believe, OCD (obsessive compulsive disorder). Could this explain why depression and the use of antidepressants are at an all-time high? When our serotonin levels are normal we feel good, happy, calm, relaxed, more focused, less anxious, self-confident and more emotionally stable.

Men make serotonin faster than women do, but lose their dopamine faster.

Women have higher dopamine, but lower serotonin, and are twice as likely to experience depression, anxiety, and other mood disorders than men. Sugar cravings is the brain's way of trying to increase serotonin. Unfortunately, although carbohydrates raise tryptophan (a precursor to serotonin), cortisol and insulin are released. This lowers blood sugar causing us to crash and experience mood swings. Could this be why women generally seem to crave sugar more than men? They are also more likely to exhibit carb cravings, emotional swings, and binge eating. Men on the other hand generally have less of a sweet tooth and are more prone to alcoholism, ADHD, and impulse control disorders. Alcohol and drug use affect dopamine and serotonin levels. Withdrawal symptoms are a result of a sudden drop in serotonin. Continued stress, quitting smoking, PMS, and SAD (winter depression) can also lower serotonin. The nicotine in cigarettes raises serotonin and may be a major reason why quitting is so difficult. It's a vicious cycle: we eat, drink and take stimulants to make us feel better, but those same substances will make us feel like crap. One step forward, three steps back.

Do you have any symptoms of low serotonin? If you don't know, here are some things to look for. Do you quickly anger, are sensitive to pain, binge eat, or have intense carbohydrate cravings? Do you suffer from SAD (Seasonal Affective Disorder), migraines, are easily overwhelmed, or feel deep sadness? Lowering our cortisol and curbing sugar addiction can remedy many of these symptoms. So can aligning with our circadian rhythm. Gut health is also very important—this will be covered in the next chapter. Some foods to consider for raising serotonin are eggs, cheese, pineapple, salmon, nuts, seeds and turkey (tryptophan). Research from the Larner College of Medicine at the University of Vermont has found that a daily 248mg dose of magnesium has been found to help reverse depression.

Serotonin synthesis can be a two-way street. It can affect your thoughts, and your thoughts can affect it. Try exerting yourself to feel happy when you are feeling down. Also, when you are craving those carbs, try eating some healthy fat and protein instead. The next time you do eat or drink unhealthy, or watch negative media, notice your mood during the next day or two. Is there any correlation?

DOPAMINE

Catecholamines are hormones produced by the adrenal glands. These hormones are released in response to physical or emotional stress. Dopamine, epinephrine (adrenaline), and norepinephrine are the main catecholamines. These hormones are released as part of the fight-or-flight response. Both adrenaline and cortisol are involved in this stress response. Dopamine is associated with the reward and pleasure centre of the brain. High levels can encourage us to take risky behaviours. This molecule is behind most of our sinful and irrational behaviours such as: gambling, thrill seeking; *sex, drugs, and rock n' roll.* There are pros and cons to everything. Dopamine can be great to get you excited about doing something. Or, it can lead to addiction and depression that can exhaust the adrenals, create anxiety, or cause mood swings and paranoia. Too much of anything eventually overstimulates and desensitizes corresponding receptors which leads to resistance. Symptoms of dopamine resistance are chronic boredom, feeling tired, chronic fatigue, a decrease in physical energy, no desire for exercise, over-sleeping, a low sex drive, sudden weight gain, and increased cravings for sugar and alcohol.

Did you know that low dopamine levels has been known to lead to Parkinson's disease? Do you know that an adrenaline rush usually happens in seconds, while cortisol can take minutes to kick in? The takeaway is choosing healthy behaviours that raise dopamine levels naturally. Artificial substances and extreme behaviour release higher than normal levels of dopamine. This gets us too high, which results in the subsequent crash. The higher up you go, the harder you'll fall.

TESTOSTERONE AND ESTROGEN

Both genders produce these hormones, but each are dominant in one. They often become imbalanced due to our diet, stress and lifestyle. They can dramatically influence our thoughts, emotions, and overall health. In addition, they can greatly affect the shape of our body and sexual functions. Women produce estrogen in their ovaries and other reproductive tissues; they can also synthesize testosterone. Men can only produce estrogen by transforming testosterone with an enzyme called aromatase.

Oxytocin is a hormone that's more dominant in women. It is produced by the hypothalamus and secreted by the pituitary gland. Oxytocin tends to make people more social and generous.

Testosterone—which is typically more dominant in men—can have the opposite effect. This is better suited for success in defending and hunting. Oxytocin is known as the love and cuddle hormone, and is produced by sexual activity. Studies show that it's responsible for keeping men monogamous. When men and women get stressed, their cortisol levels rise which can invert these hormones. Women experience higher levels of testosterone, and men experience higher levels of oxytocin. These have to be reverted back and replenished. Testosterone reduces stress in men, and oxytocin reduces stress in women. This is why men want to retreat into their man-cave to recharge, and why women want to talk their feelings out after a stressful day. Also, to the differing age-related sex drives: this seems to be another cosmic joke responsible for challenging relationships.

Did you know high and sustained cortisol levels can lead to adrenal exhaustion which can result in estrogen dominance in men? Males lose testosterone with high levels of estrogen and cortisol. For women, fat on the body affects estrogen levels which may influence moods and increase the negative effects of menopause.

SLEEP

In addition to proper breathing, posture, drinking adequate water, following circadian rhythms and understanding chemicals, we cannot neglect the importance of sleep, meditation and exercise. If one instrument is out of tune, the orchestra cannot play in perfect harmony. The entire performance will suffer dissonance. The body needs movement for circulation, and it has to develop strength and endurance to move through life. Most importantly, it needs to rest and repair. Many in the Western world follow the eight hour model of work, sleep and recreation. Consider yourself lucky if your slumber is close to eight hours; many can't even get six. How many hours of sleep is enough? Your body will tell you. When we don't get enough, it's obvious. Either way, too much or too little isn't good.

A correlation has been observed between obesity and hours of sleep. Presently, Americans have a seventy percent obesity rate, and thirty percent claim to sleep well. The connection between weight and sleep patterns can be observed all over the world. During sleep our body produces HGH which builds and repairs our cells and immune system. It also lowers cortisol. This is when protein synthesis occurs. Sleep helps our food cravings; the less we sleep the hungrier we become. Darkness and longer sleep reduce ghrelin.

Sleeping also helps purge our thoughts and emotions, it clears and regulates our memories from the days events. We would go crazy otherwise. For some, it's lights out as soon as they hit the bed, others are more like a dimmer switch. The brain produces two types of sleeping patterns: One is REM (Rapid Eye Movement) and the other is SWS (Slow Wave Sleep). As we fade into sleep we align with the SWS cycle. Most of our night's sleep is in this state. When we reach REM, our body and muscles become paralyzed, but our brain activity is very active. Some experts believe that we need to have at least five quality REM cycles each night to reap the full benefits of sleep. If our body has stimulants coursing through it, our melatonin production is impeded. Many suffer from racing thoughts inundating their mind. There is no way one can sleep in this state.

If you can't get a good night's sleep, try the following suggestions. Reduce stress, stop ingesting coffee or stimulants at least six hours before bed, drink chamomile tea (no caffeine), take 500mg of magnesium citrate, and unplug from all technology emitting light (Television, WiFi, tablets, smartphones). If you must, wear blue blocking glasses. Avoid watching the news or engaging in any negative thoughts (media, gossip, horror shows, books) and focus on positive thoughts. If negative ones creep in, put each in a balloon and send them off. Avoid sleeping pills, have sex to relax the mind and body (which produces oxytocin). If you're alone, take matters in your own hands.

A powerful way to fall asleep quickly is by this simple meditation: bring your awareness down to the spot located two finger widths below your belly button and begin breathing deep into it. Breathe in three counts, hold for three, and exhale for three. Do this as many times as you need. This helps us to connect with our body and aids in bypassing our thought and emotional processes.

BRAIN WAVES AND MEDITATION

There are Spiritual Masters in India who can quickly get into deep mental states by meditating. They can literally slow their heart beat to a snail's pace. Doing so gives the body a chance to heal and regenerate. In most cases, it's better than the deepest states of sleep. Meditation helps reduce stress and anxiety, and it improves concentration. It also helps one to become more aware of the self, increases mindfulness, acceptance of all conditions, and increases happiness. Meditation is great for strengthening the immune system and a plethora of other health benefits. These claims are being proven by ongoing scientific studies. Praying is how we speak to Source, and meditation quiets the mind so we can listen for the response. This introspection helps us get in touch with our intuition and knowing the true nature of who we are.

Meditation alters our brain waves. Eventually, we can learn how to better control them. There are different types of brain waves we experience daily. Slower wavelengths equate to more time between thoughts. Quicker waves relate to less time between them. The faster the wavelength, the more we experience anxiety and stress—more cortisol and adrenal levels in our bloodstream. The deeper we breathe the calmer we become. The different types of waves from slowest to fastest are: Infra-low (0.5 Hz), Delta (0.5 to 3 Hz), Theta (3 to 8 Hz), Alpha (8 to 12 Hz) Beta (8 to 12 Hz), and Gamma (38 to 42/100 Hz). Tibetan monks can reach Delta, which occur in the deepest meditative states, and dreamless sleep. Theta takes place when the body's senses withdraw from the external world; when the mind enters into the inner landscape. Alpha is a calm state and a detached awareness. This occurs when there's a strong link between the conscious and subconscious wavelengths. Most of the time we are resonating in the Beta cycle. This is the dominant waking state where we perform cognitive tasks, problem solving, and are attentive and alert. The Gamma cycle is the fastest of all the others and pulsates beyond the typical neural firing spectrum. Here is where spiritual awakening occurs, were we feel bliss and higher states of compassion and awareness.

On a side note: Taoist Master Mantak Chia says that if we stay in total darkness for seven days and nights we can dramatically raise DMT (Dimethyltryptamine) levels naturally. High levels of melatonin convert to serotonin, which can convert to this psychedelic chemical. DMT is naturally occurring in the body. This chemical can be found in sacred plants used by Shamans to give us spiritual experiences and awakenings.

MEDITATION

If you've never meditated, try this simple one to get you started.
Make sure you won't be disturbed for at least fifteen minutes. Turn off your cell phone and other electronic devices so you're not interrupted.

Sit in a comfortable chair with your back straight and feet flat on the floor. Keeping your head level, place your hands on your lap with your palms facing up. Make sure your shoulders are not slouching forward. Close your eyes and take in three slow deep breaths. Hold the breath slightly at each end of inhalation and exhalation. If you can, breathe in through the nose and out through the mouth. Otherwise, breathe in and out through the nose. If you have any nasal obstruction, then breathe entirely from your mouth. Breathe as naturally as you can without forcing your breath. Just observe it. Listen to the sound of the air naturally flowing in and out until you feel at one with its cycle. Let the breath breathe you.

Thoughts will come and attempt to engage you. One cannot stop them from surfacing. The secret is not to entertain them, just watch them pass without judgment. Some find it helpful to imagine a flowing river and watch each leaf, as a thought, drifting by. If it helps, you can imagine those thoughts being placed into bubbles or balloons, watch them float away. The mind loves to be engaged, and it won't stop looking for things to get caught up in. By witnessing the sound of our breath, we are giving it a task. This will be enough to distract the mind from attaching to too many thoughts. It will take time to train your mind, yet don't fret if you feel that you're unsuccessful the first time you meditate. Keep practicing. The more you do, the easier it will become.

EXERCISE

When you think of exercise, what comes to mind? Is it walking, running, cycling, or lifting weights? We each have different fitness goals and expectations. Some become excited at the thought of exercising, while others cringe at the notion. Exercise can be classified by being either cardiovascular or resistance training—or a combination of both. Each have varying intensity levels and affect the body in different ways. They can be performed separately or incorporated with varied intervals. Levels can be low, moderate or high, and are reflected by a person's maximum heart rate. This rate is based on an estimated calculation by subtracting a person's age from 220. For example, if one is fifty years of age, their maximum target heart rate should be no more than 170 BPM (beats per minute). To find an accurate percentage, we simply multiply it by 170. To calculate 50%, multiply 0.50 by 170 to get 85 bpm. To determine 70% of one's maximum—170 x 0.70 = 119.

HIGH INTENSITY

One's heart rate is raised as close to their maximum age related as possible. This intensity type is usually performed in quick bursts, alternating between high and low, or followed by a rest period. Interval periods vary but usually exertion time equals the rest time. They can be anywhere between thirty to sixty second intervals. This type of exercise is typically called HIIT (High Intensity Interval Training).

PROS:
High Intensity exercise does release adrenaline and cortisol, however, levels decrease quickly as do glycogen stores. Testosterone is released which builds our muscles. Human growth hormone is also produced which helps our body burn excess fat. In primitive times this meant developing greater strength and agility for further predatory attacks.

CONS:
It can cause potential injury and stress on the heart; and shouldn't be sustained for long periods of time; especially as one ages.

MODERATE INTENSITY

This intensity level can be achieved by running, riding a stationary bike, brisk walking, the elliptical, and so on. The target heart rate should be sustained between fifty and seventy percent of your maximum heart rate.

PROS:
Runners high—great for mental health (exercise increases the amount of endorphins released in the body), excellent circulation and lymphatic drainage.

CONS:
Endured for long periods can raise cortisol which leads to increased glucose and insulin spikes in the blood. These fluctuations can result in sugar cravings which can cause one to consume more calories than what were burned off by the exercise. To burn off a hundred and twenty calories, you'd have to run fourteen minutes. That's only a five ounce glass of white wine. Many fall into the trap that they've earned a reward. Furthermore, the high cortisol released from excessive cardio restricts the production of T4 which is produced from a properly functioning thyroid. T4 is converted to T3 which is responsible for your metabolism. Low T4, or low T3 (hypothyroidism) results in a slower metabolism resulting in easier weight gain. The body's self-preservation instinct kicks in and lowers T3 to conserve energy. This means you become more efficient, burning less calories during moderate cardio. It can take as little time as one month for the body to adapt and go into hypothyroidism.

LOW INTENSITY

Low intensity exercise doesn't challenge the heart. This intensity type is low impact and doesn't increase one's breathing or heart rate. In most cases, it actually lowers it. Activities include restorative yoga, walking, stretching and so forth.

PROS:
Low intensity doesn't spike cortisol. In fact, it lowers it while reducing stress.

CONS:
Not the best for weight loss.

FINAL THOUGHTS ON EXERCISE

It has been said that losing weight is eighty percent diet and fifteen percent exercise, while genetics accounts for the rest. Increasing exercise increases hunger and the need to eat more, which means having to workout more. This cycle leads to another sequence by producing more cortisol and inflammation. This causes an increase of sugar cravings. Moreover, many of us are overtraining, which doesn't give our body a chance to properly heal.

The solution is simple: eat and workout less to get better results. Muscle recovery is important and often neglected by many weightlifters. I suggest at least three days of rest for the muscles to properly heal. To regulate cortisol spikes during lifting, perform slow movements in each direction while breathing deeply. Weight training is important for tone and function as it reshapes the body. Cardio as mentioned before has circulation and drainage benefits. I believe both should be incorporated.

There is strong evidence suggesting that as we age (especially aging males), resistance training and high intensity interval training is more beneficial than performing longer cardio sessions. It's better to do HIIT (sixty-second intervals) for fifteen to twenty minutes versus thirty or more minutes of moderate sustained cardio. Yoga, stretching and mindful breathing is just as important as is weight and cardiovascular training. Holding a pose allows tension to arise that we aren't consciously aware of. Breathing into these blocks helps dissolve and release them. Combining all modalities of exercise helps us become aware of our body and mind connection. Stretch every day, especially when we age to keep our muscles flexible.

FORGING THE PLAN

This and the previous chapter together combine to create a powerful blueprint that we can follow to achieve balance and harmony with the totality of our body. We can better manage our energy, thoughts and emotions. By amalgamating correct posture, breathing, hydration, and understanding our circadian rhythm together with understanding our chemistry, we are closer to personal triumph. There are many additional factors to be conquered before we can achieve Self-Mastery and the ability to create consciously. These will be addressed in the following chapters.

Here are a few more things you can do to prevent disruptions to your natural state of being. Eat your last meal (keep it light) three hours before you go to sleep. Lower artificial lighting when the sun sets. Meditate fifteen minutes a day (preferably twice—before and after sleep). Unplug your WiFi router at night, or locate it away from your bedroom. *Experiments were conducted where seedlings were placed near WiFi routers. Many of them died, those that did not showed impaired growth.* Refrain from placing your cell phone by your bed. Try leaving it in another room, or set it to airplane mode. Better still, turn it off altogether. To keep in alignment with melatonin production (9:00pm), go to bed early—10:30pm at the latest. Get at least eight hours of beauty sleep. Exercising and consuming caffeine late in the evening will keep you awake and interfere with HGH production. Avoid eating sugary food when cortisol is high. Wear blue light blocking glasses. Get outside into the fresh air and sunshine as much as possible.

Whenever you are stressed, take in deep breaths, relax your body and muscles, and release all tension you're holding on to. Imagine all tensions flowing out of you like a waterfall.

8

GUTS AND BOLTS: THE ALIENS AMONG US

Knowing how our body works is one thing—understanding how food affects it is another. My intent with this chapter is to present a whole new perspective on how our environment and what we eat interplay with one another. Some believe that what we eat is all that keeps us alive. Stuffing food into a corpse will not bring it life, thus proving that without Life Force, the body cannot live. Beyond this notion, there is more needed to be understood beyond food, and can be the difference between a thriving and a deteriorating body.

IT TAKES GUTS TO BE HEALTHY

Have you heard the joke between the brain, blood, lungs, stomach, and rectum? They were all discussing who should be in charge, and who was the most important to the body. The brain said, "I run all of the body's systems." The lungs retorted, "I oxygenate everything." The blood responded, "I carry everything; no blood, no life." The stomach snapped, "I process all the food to give you all the energy!" The rectum confidently said, "I am the most important and should be in charge because I deal with all of your shit." All the other body parts laughed at him. So to prove a point, the rectum shut down. Within a few days the brain started hurting, the stomach was in pain and bloated, and the blood became toxic. Only then they all agreed that the asshole was the boss.

One of the most overlooked, yet most important aspect of our health is having a healthy gut. We can discuss which food is the healthiest until we are literally sick and tired. But until we address the real cause of ill health, we will be forever chasing the answer, forever elusive.

What is the gut?

Most think our gut is the intestines. Some believe it's a place where we feel our intuition, or warnings of danger. In truth, the gut is much more than that. It starts at the nasal passages, into the sinuses and the mouth, down the esophagus, into the stomach, along both large and small intestines, and all the way to the rectum. The gut is the largest macro membrane in our body. Did you know that it's only half the width of a human hair? This cellophane-like layer is what separates our immune system from the outside world. Some call the gut the second brain and believe that it contains more neural connections than the actual brain does. Imagine if our brain was simply a processing unit that responded to the commands sent to it from the other parts of the body. What if our entire body is collectively our total brain? This would radically change our concept regarding our body and health.

The gut lining is composed of protein structures called tight-junctions. They are looped together to create a watertight barrier. These junctions let the good bacteria through, and keep the bad ones out. Did you know that over sixty-five percent of our body's immune system is right behind the gut lining? Sadly for many of us, these junctions have been damaged. This allows everything to pass through and enter our bloodstream. In addition to pathogens and other invaders, food particles also flow through the severed barrier. This is called Leaky Gut Syndrome. Not knowing who the good and bad guys are, our immune system starts attacking everything that crosses the lining. This is the cause of our food allergies, inflammation, autoimmune disease and a plethora of other ailments. The greatest factor that causes disease is inflammation, via poor gut health. Could the increase of autism, cancer and other maladies have anything to do with this? Remember, serotonin is mainly produced in the gut and low levels can lead to mental health issues and depression. Did you know that the Vagus nerve which is the longest nerve in the human body is a communication superhighway of connectivity between your gut and brain? It connects from the brainstem to the lowest viscera of the intestines. Science is barely scratching the surface of the importance of our gut and Vagus nerve.

ALIEN ABDUCTION

Depending on who to believe, there are between thirty-seven to seventy-trillion cells in the human body. Seems like a lot, doesn't it? There's a strong belief that our body is one hundred percent human in origin. I hate to break it to you, but we are hardly human at all. We'd like to believe that the bacteria living in our body is in the minority. Outnumbering our cells ten to one, are the microbiome living inside our guts. Did you know that there are over thirty to forty-thousand known species of bacteria, three hundred thousand species of parasites, five million species of fungi and an unknown amount of viruses living on the planet? We also have a multitude of parasites living on our body. They can be found on our eyelids, in our sweat pores and places where you'd never think. No, they can't be washed off. In fact, we need them for our survival. They help us regulate and normalize healthy cellular functions.

One would surmise that out of all the bacteria, parasites, fungi and viruses living around and inside us, that they would have killed us off by now. If they didn't want us to be here, we wouldn't be. Maybe they aren't out to get us. Perhaps there is no such thing as bad bacteria, parasites or fungus. Evolutionary maps show our connection as humans to our primate ancestors who share similar genes. New research suggests we include all the aforementioned bugs as part of our evolutionary family tree. Many of our human genes which make up our biology have been acquired from non-human microbes. This is called horizontal gene transfer. Did you know that the water flea has more genes than we do? They have thirty-one thousand genomes to our twenty-three thousand. Could the difference between our pattern of evolution simply be from the types of microbial aliens we've exchanged information with?

A STORY ABOUT GERMS

I'm assuming that we've all heard the term pasteurization? This is where a liquid or substance such as milk, cheese, yogurt or wine is heated up enough to kill off microorganisms without changing the taste of food. This process was named after the French biologist Louis Pasteur. By his discovery, he concluded that germs, or microorganisms cause disease. As a result of this statement we were led to believe to fear germs. The theory implies that we catch bugs which cause disease. This created a mindset that we have to kill them before they kill us. Currently, we do so by disinfecting and killing everything by using soaps and drugs. These we believe, are safeguards and preventive measures against getting sick.

Like usual, history doesn't always reveal the true story, and is most often written by the victor. Louis Pasteur was accused of plagiarizing his ideas from several earlier scientists. Antoine Béchamp, another French researcher and biologist, was one who did. Béchamp opposed Pasteur's theory by proposing that living entities called microzymes created bacteria in response to host and environmental factors—he coined this, Host Theory. This hypothesis suggests that people don't catch germs which cause disease, but rather a disease is caused by an imbalance or weakness of an internal environment. Meaning, pathogenic germs are the byproduct of the disease, not the cause of them. Unfortunately, the better salesman won.

WEEDS

In a healthy ecology everything works in concert. Each organism is part of the whole, they all support and communicate with one another. When there is an imbalance, things tend to go awry. Did you know that when soil is denuded, the first thing that crops up are weeds? Do you know why? The weeds arise to help restore the soil. Weeds grow faster than plants, they also produce carbon and other compounds quickly. Each species of weed draws certain nutrients up from the deeper levels of soil and brings them to the top.

As they compost, they release further nourishment to the plant and soil. In addition to supplying essential minerals, they also help loosen the earth assisting the plant's roots to penetrate deeper into it. An abundance of these plants indicate which nutrients are lacking in the soil. A wise farmer can tell what the soil is depleted of solely by the type of weed that's growing in it. Weeds not only protect, fertilize and condition soil, they give shade and help prop up some plants. They also attract beneficial insects which help balance the ecological system. So before you reach for the weed killer, think again. If this is true with the bacteria in the soil, can it not also be for those in our gut?

Did you know that penicillin is a secretion from bread mould? Imagine, a mould making an antibacterial? It does so because it's trying to be in a cooperative relationship with the bacteria. Can you guess what bacteria make? They make anti-fungals, anti-yeasts, antivirals and anti-parasites. So, if you suffer from any intestinal bacterial overgrowth such as SIBO (small intestinal bacterial overgrowth), chronic bacterial, yeast, or parasitic infections, your internal gut flora is most likely out of balance. These conditions are present because the body wants to heal the disproportionate ratio of pathogens to beneficial microbiome. This is true with any disease. We need to pay attention, and investigate what is really going on.

Are you starting to see the bigger picture? What if we take into account all the microscopic life living everywhere in and outside of our body, and realize how everything in our Universe is interdependent? How would you live knowing this? How would you treat all life with the understanding that its entirety communicates with itself the way it does?

DOES CANCER HAVE AN EGO PROBLEM?

Cancer is a cell that has become damaged by an imbalance of our inner microbial environment. This may be caused by an overgrowth of uncooperative bacteria, fungi, parasites or viruses. Other causes of injury may include toxins, heavy metals and the accumulation of harmful environmental substances. Some believe that emotional stress is what causes this disease. Self-hatred and regret are what literally *eats one up inside*. Whichever the case, the cell has become impaired. In a healthy or balanced microbiological environment, the cell's mitochondria could call out for help. A multitude of healthy bacteria are able to communicate with each other. Unfortunately, the cancer has lost contact with the body's communication network. With the system down and depleted microbiome, the damaged cell can't repair itself, nor self-terminate. As with all life, the basic instinct is to survive, at all costs. In desperation, that's exactly what the cancerous cell attempts to do. It's starts dividing, until eventually it becomes a tumour.

There is no difference between our Soul and our ego. The ego—like the cancer cell—feels alone, afraid and angry. It has become unaware of its connection to Source energy, or the collective Oneness of all things. From the ego/cancer's perspective, everything that threatens its existence is considered an enemy.

This activates the survival instinct, and the response to kill, or be killed. This not only applies to these paradigms, but to the current state of our world affairs: politics, religion, cultural differences, and every type of relationship. We go to war, build bombs, use drugs, chemotherapy, and to a lesser extent, use antibacterial soaps to kill the enemy. Ego is the cancer of the Soul that's living in fear.

What if the healing of all these elements can be accomplished by re-establishing love, support and communication? Did you know that our thoughts and emotions affect our bacteria, which also affect us and our emotions? Macrocosmically, whatever crops up that's considered an enemy is simply a result of an imbalance. Instead of fear and fighting, pay attention to what is being mirrored, and nourish it.

GUT KILLERS

There are many substances that destroy the gut. Ironically, one major culprit is weed killer. Glyphosate is the active ingredient in weed destroyers. The weed killers we use today is an evolution of an invention discovered by the military. Do you remember Agent Orange, the spray that was used in the Vietnam war? This chemical was used to defoliate the enemy's terrain to literally weed them out. Did you know that glyphosate is actually an antibiotic, antifungal and an anti-parasite? This salt compound has a toxic effect on the tight junctions of our gut lining, and on our blood-brain barrier.

Glyphosate kills single-celled life on contact. It kills the plant and the soil's bacteria through the same mechanism. It works by preventing plants from synthesizing amino acids necessary for their growth. Basically, it stops them from eating, so they die. It blocks an important enzyme pathway called The Shikimate Pathway. This enzyme pathway produces the ringed aromatic amino acids. As humans, we don't possess this pathway and is the reason why glyphosate is deemed safe for humans. The shikimate pathway is a seven step metabolic route used by bacteria, fungi, algae, parasites and plants for the biosynthesis of the aromatic amino acids (phenylalanine, tyrosine, and tryptophan).

Since we don't have this pathway we need to get these essential amino acids from bacteria, plants, or the animals that eat them. Glyphosate not only destroys phenylalanine, tyrosine, and tryptophan, but also glycine. How can we properly build and heal our body with these four essential amino acids missing from our body and food sources? We can see the results of this by the increased cases of medical and behavioural diseases and conditions. If the plants are blocked from making these amino acids, animals won't be able to obtain them, either. So where can we get them? We have a big problem as glyphosate seems to be everywhere. The stuff is in the air, soil, and in the water tables. This means that it's most likely in all of our vegetation. I don't trust that organic farms can claim their one hundred percent status because of this spillage and cross-contamination.

There are other contributors that destroy the gut and should be avoided even if you're not experiencing gut issues: autoimmune disease, or any type of inflammation. The following substances kill our precious microbiome: aspartame, pesticides, herbicides, GMOs (all corn is modified), alcohol, antibiotics, carrageenan (a food thickener which causes inflammation), wheat, NSAID's (Non-Steroidal Anti-inflammatory Drugs: Aspirin, Advil, etc.), steroids, birth control pills, infectious diseases, bottle feeding, pollution, radiation, toxic chemicals, vaccinations, dental work, lack of sleep, intense exercise, smoking, antibacterial soaps, and constant washing and disinfecting. Some factors such as age and to a lesser extent stress are impossible to avoid, we can only do our best and control what we can.

RAW AND UNCUT

Many believe that eating raw, organic, and vegan is the correct way for achieving optimal health. Perhaps for some it may be, but for many it can be the cause of their deteriorating health. Uncooked vegetables can be the root of one's gastric woes, and may even be slowly killing them. Raw and fibrous food often irritates the gut lining which increases inflammation. One such food, and considered to be the king of superfood, is garlic. Did you know it's an antibacterial with an acid pH of 3.3? Some research claims that if any amount gets into the bloodstream, it may kill you. This is bad news if you're a practicing vampire. If you must eat it, cooking may reduce its toxic effect.

If your intestines are indeed raw and cut, the best way to heal them is to simply stop consuming substances that damage them. This means avoiding all food that triggers inflammation. You want to give your gut a chance to heal itself. The next step is to consume food that will proliferate the colony of microbiome and help repair the tight junctions. Since most of the food we eat is missing the essential aromatic amino acids, we need to find food sources that contain them. Having all the essential amino acids helps to repair cell to cell communication. Some suggest supplementing with spirulina and chlorella as they contain the absent aromatic amino acids. Others warn that these types of algae are toxic and stored unused in the liver.

NUTRIENTS AND ANTI-NUTRIENTS

Nutrients provide nourishment to our body, anti-nutrients reduce its ability to absorb them. Anti-nutrients contribute to inflammation. Some of these substances are found in many of the so-called healthy food. Saponin exists in grains, quinoa and white potato, and can weaken the gut lining. Glucosinolates can be found in broccoli, cabbage and cauliflower (they have been known to affect the thyroid). Oxalates are found in many foods, especially raw spinach and rhubarb, as they reduce the solubility of calcium iron and zinc. High oxalate levels can lead to kidney stones. Flavonoids in tea, coffee and wine can reduce mineral absorption. This is not to say that all of these are toxic; many have been shown to be beneficial to our health.

LECTINS

Not everyone is susceptible to this sticky protein, but they affect us all in some way. About thirty percent of food contains significant amounts of this anti-nutrient. Lectins can be the source of one's inflammation, leaky gut, heart disease, arthritis, and autoimmune response. They are usually behind one's food allergies and sensitivities. Lectins are a type of protein that bind to cell membranes. Small amounts may help stimulate one's immune system, but high amounts can pose serious problems. Lectins can rip holes in our intestines. In plants they are its defence system against other microorganisms, pests, and insects. Like humans, animals and most all life, plants don't want to be eaten. They want to live and procreate. Some have evolved to the point of being able to ward off predators by producing these toxic proteins. Lectins are resistant to human and animal digestion. They pass through the digestive tracts untouched—a good strategy for unsuspecting animals to replant their seeds and keep its lineage alive. These fruits and vegetables are usually colourful and send off enticing aromas that entice predators to eat them. They can fool an animal once or twice, but not always. Unfortunately, they have been fooling us forever. There is wisdom in nature.

You may have heard of gluten. Many are unable to tolerate this endosperm. Although it is a lectin, it's a minor one and isn't generally the problem.

Agglutinin, which is found in the hull of wheat grains, is to blame. Yes, whole wheat is worse than is refined. Lectins are found in all grains, rice, legumes, potatoes, and nightshades (tomato, eggplant, peppers, goji berry). Other popular foods that contain lectins are lentils, chia seeds, squash, and cashews.

Peanuts are not nuts, they are legumes. If they don't instantly kill you with their proteins, they have been known to cause heart disease and colon cancer. Peanuts contain a toxic fungus called aflatoxin (aspergillus flavus). Some say that cooking reduces lectins, but if this were totally true, peanuts would be rendered safe after roasting—they are not. Removing the skin and seeds in tomatoes and peppers greatly reduces their lectins. Italians and Mexicans must have known this as they char, peel and deseed their tomatoes and peppers.

Have you ever noticed your nose running, or eyes watering after eating hot peppers? Our body produces mucus so their lectins stick to it and can be flushed out. Did you know that raw kidney beans contain between twenty to seventy-thousand lectin units? Eating as little as four of these beans raw can kill you. Cooking them brings their countdown between two to four-hundred units. Did you know that a few salt-sized grains of the lectin ricin, which is derived from the castor bean, can kill a human adult? *Breaking Bad* fans know how Walter killed Lydia using this powder. If you are experiencing any type of disease caused by inflammation, consider omitting the foods mentioned from your diet. If you must eat them, cook, soak, sprout or ferment them to reduce their toxic effects.

OTHER POTENTIALLY HARMFUL FOODS

Soybeans are not only high in lectins, they are also GMO (genetically modified organism) unless specified. Soy (tofu) contains phytoestrogens which are endocrine disruptors and confuse normal hormonal function.

When they enter the body, estrogen receptors treat them as if they were estrogen. In males, estrogen adds to weight gain and a lowered sex drive. Phytoestrogen interferes with the adrenal and thyroid glands and is responsible for adding weight. Soy also contains goitrogens which affect the thyroid gland and cause lower energy levels. They also contain other substances like phytates, oligosaccharides, oxalates, and protease inhibitors. These are linked to cognitive problems like Alzheimer's and dementia.

Protease breaks down protein and peptides. Phytates bind to minerals and lower their absorption. High levels of oligosaccharides can cause intestinal gas, bloating, stomach cramps, and diarrhea. Soy has been shown to lower vitamins D and B12, and disrupt digestion. Some believe that soy causes cancer.

There is a debate on whether dairy is healthy or not. Casein A1, the protein found in milk, converts to a protein called beta-casomorphin which can cause inflammation. This is also an opium type peptide which is responsible for dairy addiction—cheese is crack. Some believe that the casein A2 found in heritage cows is much healthier than the genetic mutation of the casein A1 breed. Incidentally, unpasteurized milk and fermented dairy products tend not to cause inflammation due to their living enzymes and pre digestive bacteria.

EAT OR BE EATEN

You may be asking, "What the hell can I eat, then?" You may be one of the fortunate who's able to eat everything. Not everyone reacts the same to a certain food, nor does one size fit all. Food restriction may be a choice, or it can be forced on us. Many times what we can't eat, is what we love. Conversely, food that agrees with our body doesn't always resonate with our taste preference. It's unfortunate when our favourite food becomes the enemy. Either way, we have to learn how to eat differently.

In the cycle of life, all living things need to eat other living things for their survival. This applies not only to humans, but to bacteria, cells, plants and animals. Together we all have a symbiotic relationship, and are dependent on one another. We are malleable with our environment, we adapt and evolve by exchanging energy and information. Would you be surprised if I told you that when we eat, it isn't for our body? Instead, it's to nourish the non-human microbiome living within us. Bacteria take the food and turn it into a form of energy our cells can use, namely Adenosine Triphosphate (ATP). We feed them, they feed us. The alien invasion has already occurred. They are not here to kill us, but to keep us alive.

When our microbiome is properly colonized, it's able to communicate with one another and provide us with everything we need for optimum health. They know exactly what toxins need to be released, which cells need care, and which vitamins and minerals are lacking. They can manufacture anything we need, create hormones and even metabolize our fat. Bacteria and parasites also consume the dead cells released by our body. This network is self-sufficient, but we interfere with this process. We kill them off by unhealthy living and eating, by antibacterials, and by consuming isolated vitamins and supplements. Unknowingly, we've become micromanagers doing more harm than good. Whole food is complete and contains the correct proportion of nutrients, and is in resonance with nature. This is the perfect relationship. Unfortunately, if our gut doesn't have a healthy ecosystem, none of this is possible.

PREBIOTICS, PROBIOTICS AND ANTIBIOTICS

You've no doubt heard of the term antibiotics, and have most likely taken them. These are prescribed by a doctor in order to kill off harmful bacteria when we get sick. Did you know that taking a single course of antibiotics can wipe out most of our microbiome and damage our gut? If the chlorine in our tap water acts as an antibiotic that kills microbes, can it not also kill the ones thriving in our body? Not all is lost, because bacteria can double every twenty minutes.

What are prebiotics? They are non-digestible carbohydrate plant fibres which act as food for our microbiome. Our gut bacteria consume these glycans, which are the bonds that hold polyphenols together. Polyphenols are a great source of prebiotics; they are a large class of chemical compounds (phenol units) that are found in plants. Polyphenols are powerful antioxidants and can neutralize free radicals, reduce inflammation, and slow the growth of tumours. The best sources include: raw chicory root, dandelion greens, leaks, asparagus, onions, Jerusalem artichokes, all berries, pomegranate, curcumin, green tea (matcha) and dark chocolate (raw cocoa). The heat caused by cooking destroys these chemical compounds. Polyphenols are the Yin to the lectins' Yang.

Probiotics are the living bacteria in food that become part of the living colony inside our gut. Sadly, many of us have very low levels of microbiome. We can trace this back to our parents and grandparents and the quality of their gut health. Bacteria are passed down from parent to child. C-section babies suffer greatly by not receiving the natural and beneficial antibodies from their mother. Instead, they are inoculated with the harsh bacteria from the hospital. Vaginally birthed babies collect all they need during the constricted passage through their mother's birth canal. Breastfeeding is another way the child receives the essential microorganisms needed to build their immune system. Furthermore, the newborn's umbilical cord should not be cut until after it stops throbbing. Doing so will prevent additional antibodies from being transferred.

It wasn't long ago when a mother would invite their children's friends over who were afflicted with chicken pox, or measles. They wanted to expose their children to these viruses quickly just to get it over with. Old wisdom has been lost to fear mongering and biased science. When viruses and bacteria come in naturally, our body starts to build permanent immunity to them—unlike when pathogens enter direct to blood, the immune system can weaken. Colds and flu viruses are constantly mutating so we can't be immune from every one. Don't be in fear of getting sick. Instead, build a healthy immune system. Stop washing and disinfecting everything to the extreme. Start getting soiled, play in the dirt, and in between the sheets. Antibacterials and antibiotics kill the beings that give us life. Colonize good bacteria and feed them, not the bad ones with garbage food and unhealthy living. Being sick means that you have an unhealthy overgrowth of uncooperative bacteria; these microbiome are in fact attempting to right the ship.

A COMMON MISTAKE

We not only kill beneficial microorganisms and prevent their opportunity to recolonize, we make the mistake of consuming the wrong ones. The microorganisms claimed to be in commercially produced supplements, dairy products and fermented foods are typically sterile. Did you know that probiotics bought off the shelf are not the best choice? This also includes those kept in the fridge. Store bought probiotics have a low species count, and most are killed off by the acid in our stomach. The billion plus count you see on the bottle are only copies of a few strains—a narrow spectrum containing billions of clones only creates a monoculture. This only makes things worse. We need much more than the typical seven to sixteen strains typically found in these pills. How many? One or two hundred? If you guess thousands you're getting close. We need an army of them that are able to communicate, work together, and defend us through a solid network. What we have instead is a weak and declining village with sick and dying inhabitants. They've lost contact and have become unable to interact with each other. The sheriff is gone, and the town is overrun with outlaws and gunfighters. So what can be done?

I highly suggest making your powerful army by fermenting your food. There are many books available on this topic. Almost any vegetable can be brewed. A typical favourite is fermenting cabbage. All that's necessary is to chop some up and place it into a bowl. Add natural salt and massage it to release the juices, and to break down the fibre. Place it in a mason jar and top up with non-fluoridated water. Spring water is the best. Weigh it down with a plate and screen it over with a cheesecloth. The natural bacteria in the air will inoculate and ferment the cabbage. In as little as two weeks you'll be well on your way to recruit your bio-infantry. To harvest even more species take your cabbage out for a walk. Expose it to other environments with different species. You can save the juice left over from a previous batch and use it to start another.

There are different types of microbiome responsible for the breaking down of each food type. When we abstain from one variety altogether, we may lose the corresponding bacteria. If gluten isn't a problem for you and you stop eating it, the bacteria responsible for its digestion will die off as they have nothing left to eat. If and when the food is re-introduced, there could be serious digestion problems as a result. Since that specialized bacteria aren't available to properly assimilate it, the pathogens oblige and instead create toxins.

INFLAMMATION AND OXIDATIVE STRESS

Oxidative stress is when the balance of free radicals to antioxidants is uneven. Free radicals are unstable molecules with a missing electron. They steal that electron from healthy cells that have balanced electrons.

This action ends up destroying the balanced cell. Oxidative stress is also what causes metal to rust. Antioxidants are molecules that reduce free radicals before they can do damage. These cells donate an electron to spare the healthy cells. Oxidation is both beneficial and harmful as this process is important to help the digestion of food, and metabolizing fat and vitamins. Free radicals are also important as they can help fight off pathogens which can lead to infections. The cause of free radicals are stress, inflammation, intense exercise, smoking, and radiation. Oxidative stress also contributes to aging.

If you experience inflammation, eliminate food known to cause it. Then, slowly reintroduce them and see how they affect you. Disease has a formula: stress + toxins + unhealthy gut environment + bad diet = inflammation.

9

FOOD MYTHS AND TOXINS THAT CAN KILL

Whatever we enjoy indulging in that's considered unhealthy, we try to justify their benefits. This can be with food, drugs or any behaviour. We can always find facts and studies which will support the positive side of anything. This type of rationalization gives us permission to ignore the negative aspects. In most cases, the good doesn't always outweigh the bad. Our lust for something prevents us from seeing the bigger picture.

In many cases, we convince ourselves that it doesn't apply to us. Deep down we may know that something may be unhealthy, but because of our addiction to it, we remain numb and purposely ignorant. Just because something is socially accepted doesn't mean that it isn't harmful. "Everyone is doing it, so why shouldn't I? What about everything in moderation?"

Have you considered that maybe what you believe to be moderate is actually an extremity? Those who try to lead a healthy lifestyle by reducing their sugar intake are often accused of being extreme. When in fact they are only getting back to what is normal. This is how far off centre we have become. One trip through the Drive-Thru of a famous fast food chain can contain up to two hundred grams of carbohydrates. If you remember, more than five grams in the blood at one time is considered toxic. This is only one meal which includes a hamburger, fries, drink and an ice cream sundae. What about the other meals eaten throughout the day?

Coffee and alcohol are considered staples in our lives. They are integral parts of our social interactions. No one questions their toxicity and affect on our psyche. These substances are socially accepted coping mechanisms similar to other drugs. They can be debilitating to our mind, body and emotional well-being. Yet, they are not seen as such. Coffee in the morning to start the day, and wine at night to end it. Why give up something that gives you the energy to grind through the day, and another that sedates and help you unwind? Even Elvis Presley loved his uppers and downers. "Wine is good for you!" you may say. "It has antioxidants, so does coffee!" Evidently, resveratrol, catechin, epicatechin and proanthocyanidins are also found in fresh red grapes. Unfortunately, you can't get drunk on grapes. Ironically, one can heal your liver, the other can destroy it. Coffee is said to be great for increasing energy and burning fat. Java also contains beneficial nutrients that helps ward off Alzheimer's, Parkinson's and dementia, and increases one's lifespan. "What about its harmful effects?"

Canada has a ridiculous Low-Risk Alcohol Drinking Guideline to help adults moderate their intake. The recommendation is that men and women drink no more than two drinks and three drinks a day respectfully. That's ten drinks a week for a woman, and fifteen for a man. A recent report later confirmed that having just one drink is dangerous. We've been lied to so often, it's hard to know who to believe. My intent is to shed some light on all this. You are free to reject what I say, and anything else in this book. In fact, I encourage you to challenge everything written here. You may even get upset, but before you do ask yourself these questions: "Have I researched both sides of the argument? Am I secretly committing acts of self-sabotage so that I don't have to face my pain? Do I want to be the best version I can be?"

Life is meant to be enjoyed, but if life is enjoying you, then it may be time to consider reassessing your lifestyle. This choice is yours, read on and decide if this is true for you.

ALCOHOL

Alcohol is considered a social lubricant. It's referred to as liquid courage. Drinking has been ingrained into the fabric of our culture and society. We see this in almost every movie, television show, and advertisement. They depict people having fun, or show the badass cop having a whiskey and a smoke for breakfast. There seems to be little focus on the damaging long-term effects of drinking, both physically and mentally. In the Catholic church wine is used to symbolize the spiritual blood of Jesus. If the priest drinks it, then it must be good, right? How often have you heard, "Let's grab a drink?" God forbid you say you don't drink. You'll be looked at as if you had two heads. "What do you mean you don't drink?" The assumption is that you must be a recovering alcoholic, or a prude for not indulging. Drinking is so hard-wired into our psyche that not indulging seems unusual. Why is there a stigma attached to the teetotallers of the world? Many cringe at the thought of not being able to have a drink, socially or recreationally. Maybe they'd miss out on fun if they didn't? Any graduate who's earned their Bachelor's, Master's and Doctoral Degrees in drinking can reassure you that you're not missing out on anything. Actually, that's not entirely true; you'll pass over the wretched hangovers, fatigue, and mental fog that typically follows a swig fest.

Did you know that heavy drinking can spike insulin that can lead to hypoglycemia? If you recall, low blood sugar can elicit unhealthy and criminal behaviour. Irritability often results when craving a sugar fix.

The appetite for alcohol can be reversed by treating hypoglycemia through a change in diet. Have you ever heard anyone say, "What's your poison?" when asking you what you drink? Being drunk is referred to as being inTOXICated. If you recall, alcohol destroys the mucus lining in our gut, loosens its cells and kills off our precious microbiome. It destroys our health emotionally and physically, our relationships, social status, and keeps us from realizing our dreams. Highly successful people aren't usually substance abusers, and if they are, it won't be long until they crash and burn.

Do you know where the word "alcohol" comes from? Astrologers say that Algol is considered to be one of the most unfortunate and violent stars. Algol is also associated with death by decapitation—the name of the slain snake head belonging to Medusa. In Islamic folklore it is believed that there are three divisions of sentient beings. Angels, Jinn and Humans, created in that order. Angels are considered neither male nor female and have no free will. Jinn, like humans, are gendered, and have free will. The Jinn are usually considered evil, or tricksters who often lead us astray. There are five types of Jinn, one of which is called The Marid. He is considered the most powerful of them all and is associated with the Genie in the bottle. Jinn in the bottle? How about a Gin and Tonic? Another type of Jinn is called a Ghoul. In Arabic, Al Ghoul means demon, an evil spirit, or devil. Al-Khul, Algol, or alcohol may be spelled differently, but all carry the same phonetic energy. Ghouls are thought to be zombie-like Jinn who haunt graveyards and prey on human flesh—body eating spirit. The English word for alcohol is derived from the word Al-Khul. A ghoul is also considered to be a ghost, and what do ghosts say? "Boo!" or "BOOze" to be exact. Do you think this is just a good attempt at word play?

Is it a coincidence that alcohol is also referred to as "spirit"? In terms of alchemy, alcohol is used to extract the essence of a substance. It could be an essential oil, tincture, or the very essence of a Soul. When one drinks in excess they may experience no recollection of what happened to them while they were drunk. This is called blacking out. When this occurs our Spirit checks out and allows a lower energy to take a joyride with our body. During this time, we are temporarily possessed by these malicious spirits. Our Soul is extracted for a while. These spirits are usually more hedonistic than how we normally are. Have you ever felt different, more sexual, less inhibited, or more violent after drinking excessive amounts of alcohol? Sometimes people change so dramatically that their words and actions are not even close to when in their normal states. Alcohol numbs our senses, lowers our spiritual vibration and awareness. The only Spirit you should be consuming is the one you distil from within. If you want to be at the top of your game, consider abstaining.

COFFEE

This is a very delicate subject, as many are protective of their coffee. Most of the world wakes up to this warm and sometimes cold beverage. The majority of those who do drink coffee are dependent on it, and need it to wake up. I believe that java is actually a legalized and socially accepted drug. Don't believe me? Try going without it for a few days and see what happens. For some, the withdrawal symptoms can be overwhelming to say the least. Whenever something is deemed socially accepted, we assume that it's safe. How many of you smoked in the 60s and never thought twice about its health ramifications? I often hear, "I'm not addicted to coffee. I can stop at any time. I only have one or two a day in the morning and that's it."

Overuse of coffee masks our chronic fatigue. We've stopped noticing how tired we really are. As our body acclimatizes by increasing its tolerance to caffeine, we need more of it to get the same kick. We can become so desensitized that it doesn't stop us from falling asleep; even though our cortisol levels are through the roof. When I say coffee I am also referring to caffeine in all its forms. The worst possible combination is sugar and caffeine. Hello energy drinks and cheap chocolate. Did you know that caffeine, although milder, is a psychoactive drug very similar to cocaine and methamphetamine? Do you know that methylphenidate is better known as Ritalin? Caffeine triggers the same neural pathways as when a snake hisses at you. Too much coffee can tap out adrenaline stores by raising cortisol and sugar levels, which produce epinephrine and norepinephrine. It can cause heart palpitations, raise blood pressure, and overstimulate the nervous system. Brain scans have shown that less than one cup of coffee can decrease blood flow to the brain up to fifty-two percent. Like alcohol, coffee is a toxin to the body, and is also acid forming.

Do you know that drinking lots of coffee can make you fat? It can raise cortisol levels for up to eighteen hours and increase sugar in your bloodstream. This is bad news for Type Two Diabetics. Caffeine also interferes with REM sleep which is when you burn the highest amount of fat, and produce HGH. If you recall, cortisol and low HGH are the biggest causes of weight gain. You may agree that coffee is a drug only after you kick the habit, and are free from its effects. You'll feel so good and liberated without it that you'll wonder why you didn't give it up sooner. This is also true with alcohol.

There is a mould that grows on coffee, it's a fungi called Ochratoxin A.

It has been shown to cause cell degeneration in humans. Roasting cannot destroy it. In fact, the longer coffee beans are roasted (darker blends), the more carcinogens like acrylamide are produced. Did you know that caffeine consumed on an empty stomach can raise hydrochloric acid? This will eventually reduce your body's ability to produce it. Moreover, caffeine is known to relax the esophageal sphincter allowing stomach acid to rise and cause heartburn. It is an irritant to the stomach and small intestines that can lead to IBS (Irritable Bowel Syndrome) and Crohn's disease. Caffeine acts as a laxative and a diuretic which can impede the absorption of essential minerals and nutrients. Caffeine is responsible for much more damage to our body than I have listed.

Medicinally, caffeine has its place. It is a great way to help alleviate headaches, fatigue and jet lag. Like alcohol, we are abusing it.

SUGAR

Sugar (sucrose) is made mostly from sugarcane, or sugar-beet. All green plants produce simple sugars called glucose. An excess of this fuel is stored in their roots, much like how we reserve ours as fat. Root vegetables have more carbohydrates than do other vegetables. Unlike plants, consistently high levels of sucrose can lead to many diseases in humans. Many of us are unknowingly suffering from pre-diabetes and damaged metabolisms. Did you know that sugar is eight times more addictive than cocaine? Both release high levels of dopamine in the brain, but sugar lights up more of its pleasures areas. The withdrawal symptoms can sometimes be worse than that of other drugs—it's that addictive. No one looks twice when someone eats a doughnut, or a bag of chips—it's a different story if they snort a line of coke. There isn't much difference, one is socially accepted and the other is not. Keep this in mind when you are trying to give up sugar. Withdrawal is not easy, so don't be too hard on yourself.

We don't realize how much sugar we're consuming, it's hidden everywhere. I once saw a television commercial that promoted a breakfast cereal. "Make Spesh-X part of your daily healthy breakfast." The scene had a bowl of their cereal on a table with a glass of orange juice, milk, and toast with jam. They could have shown yogurt with fruit, pancakes with maple syrup, waffles, croissants, or oatmeal with berries; it wouldn't have made a difference. Each of these foods contain large amounts of sugar in the form of *carbohydrates*, *fructose* and *lactose*. Don't be fooled—processed whole grains are just as bad, if not worse. Remember, coffee spikes cortisol which is already high in the morning. High insulin with all that sugar is a recipe for disaster. There is a false belief that you'll be able to burn off all those calories during the day. As you already know, more than a teaspoon gets packed away as inaccessible fat. The brain will then tell you to eat more carbs as your blood sugar starts to drop.

There are obvious and not-so-obvious culprits that raise your blood sugar and insulin, which leads to the accumulation of fat and disease. These include: all grains, rice, legumes, root vegetables, baked goods with grain flour, soda pop, all-commercial juice (pasteurized and devoid of enzymes), beer, alcohol, wine, and all low-fat dairy (skim milk and yogurt) which still contains lactose (milk sugar). You're better off with the higher fat varieties. Sugar is also hidden in salad dressing, ketchup, some bacon, breakfast sausages and Beef Jerky. You may be under the impression that because you're vegan or eat healthy, you're not consuming lots of sugar. Did you know that it's hidden in so-called health foods? Anytime you see "*-ose*" in an ingredient, it's really sugar by a different name. So is corn, oat or brown rice syrup, agave and any fruit juice made from concentrate. They are finding new ways to make it sound healthy. The best is organic evaporated cane juice. Who cares if it's organic—it's still sugar and your insulin doesn't give a damn.

Do you eat whole grain bread, pasta, cereals, jams, and naturally sweetened baked goods? Fruit is packed with sugar and should be eaten in lower quantities. Did you know that even natural sweeteners alleged to be safe still spike insulin? Products such as Stevia, Erythritol, Xylitol, monk fruit, and any other natural sugars trick the brain via the tongue to release it. Even chewing gum will deceive the mind that we're eating. These artificial sweeteners also damage our gut lining and should be avoided.

Another cause of spiked blood glucose is due to food devoid of its fibre. The less roughage, the quicker the absorption—fibre slows the absorption rate. You can find the carbohydrate to fibre ratio on the nutritional facts label on food you buy. If it's listed as having four grams of carbohydrates, and two grams of fibre, it really means that there is only two net grams of absorbable carbohydrates. We arrive at this by subtracting the fibre from the total carbohydrates. There is a term called the *glycemic index* which is the value assigned to a food based on how fast or slow it enters and raises our blood glucose levels. Eating a solid tomato is less glycemic than eating tomato sauce. Cooking vegetables breaks down the fibre, carrots are sweeter cooked. Conversely, avocados have a lot of carbs but because of its high fibre, it cancels them out. One avocado has around nine grams of carbohydrates, but contains seven grams of fibre. That's equal to only two grams of glycemic sugar. As a result, all fruits and vegetables should be eaten whole. Let your body do the blending and juicing naturally.

FRUIT ISN'T ALWAYS HEALTHY

Although fruit is a great source of antioxidants, vitamins and minerals, eating large amounts can put undue stress on the pancreas. Fruit is still sugar which will raise insulin. One can put themselves at risk for developing diabetes or worse, pancreatic problems. Many Fruitarians experience nutritional deficiencies such as: zero good fats, vitamin D, A, B12 and protein. They also face increased tooth decay and cavities. Nonetheless, Mother Nature designed us to gorge on whatever fruit was in season long ago, when there wasn't much food around and we had to load up when we could. Days could pass before we'd eat again. Unfortunately, modernization has made fruit in season all year long. Eating fruit tells our brain to fatten up because for all you *Game of Thrones* fans, winter is coming. Think of what a bear does to survive the winter. Our ancestors feasted on nature's candy to endure the colder months when food was scarce. Did you know that any produce containing seeds is considered fruit? This means cucumbers, tomatoes and zucchini technically aren't vegetables.

SUGAR AND CANCER

The Mitochondria is a cell's nuclear power plant which produces most of its energy as ATP (Adenosine Triphosphate). They can divide using their own strand of DNA—there can be more than one found in each cell. They can also trigger cell death by releasing a chemical called Cytochrome C. Nearly every Mitochondria use glucose, fatty acids and amino acids as their source of fuel.

There is one type, however, that can only use glucose. Can you guess which one it is?

In 1931, Otto Heinrich Warburg won the Nobel prize in physiology. Otto discovered a phenomena that was later called The Warburg Effect. He noticed that cancer cells have a different energy metabolism than all the others. Cancer has a design flaw much like the thermal exhaust port of the *Star Wars* Death Star. Cancer's main source of fuel is *glucose*. There is strong evidence that supports cancer can be starved out by not feeding it. Can this be a cure for the disease?

SUGAR AND DISEASE

Isn't it strange that no one questioned the harmful effects of sugar after it ate away our children's teeth? Or, that it made them incredibly hyper? How many clues do we need? Besides destroying teeth and creating little monsters, sugar leads to premature aging. Yes, it gives you wrinkles. High sugar consumption leads to anxiety, hyperactivity and a lowered immune system. This sweet evil acidifies the body and is responsible for feeding harmful pathogens and microbes. Sugar has been associated to be the primary cause of insulin resistance diabetes, obesity, heart disease, chromium deficiency, accelerated aging, tooth decay, gum disease (associated with heart disease), behavioural cognition in children, increased stress, fatty liver, brain fog, Alzheimer's, Parkinson's disease, and dementia.

Most diseases thrive in a sugary environment. As you can see, sugar is worse than you probably thought. Why is it loaded in almost every food? Why do we let our kids devour it? Unknowingly, we are addicts raising addicts. No one should be consuming it. Did you know that sugar acts like sandpaper against our arteries? Do you know that's what causes them to inflame?

The rabbit hole gets deeper…

A PRESIDENT AT HEART

We've been told for years that fat and cholesterol cause heart attacks and strokes. To combat this lie, we're advised to eat low-fat (usually high sugar) and avoid cholesterol. In 1955 President David Dwight Eisenhower of The United States of America suffered his first heart attack. Over the next thirteen years he suffered six more. On March, 28, 1969 at the age of 78 he passed from his final one. American physiologist Ancel Benjamin Keys, who was very popular at the time, had studied the influence of diet on health. As a consequence of the president's death, he hypothesized that dietary saturated fat causes cardiovascular heart disease and should be avoided. Ancel convinced the world of this unproven conclusion by cherry picking data that supported his biased claim.

British physiologist and founding Professor of the Department of Nutrition at Queen Elizabeth College of London, John Yudkin warned that sugar is dangerous to one's health. He wrote several books on the importance of eating a low carbohydrate diet. Yudkin cautioned that sugar is the factor in the development of dental cavities, obesity, diabetes, and heart disease, to name a few. He also noticed an obvious correlation between the sudden rise in heart attacks and the rise in sugar intake. As with the Béchamp-Pasteur battle, the bully won. In fact, Yudkin was ridiculed and even criticized by Ancel and his cronies who were behind the pro-sugar industry. Since then, we've been told the same lie again and again without ever questioning it. Fear is a powerful emotion.

In the summer of 2017, the AHA (American Heart Association) declared that eating saturated fats such as butter and coconut oil should be avoided to cut one's risk of heart disease. Instead, they advised us to replace them with alternatives. For years we have been told by the AMA to eat grains, and avoid saturated fats. They endorsed the consumption of harmful fats such as canola, corn, soybean/sunflower oil and processed omega-6 vegetable oils and margarines. You have to love Poetic Justice because just months later, on November 17 another president, fifty-two-year-old cardiologist John Warner of the same AHA suffered a heart attack in the middle of a speech at a heart health conference. How can people keep buying this bullshit? Even after the president of the Heart Association almost died following his own advice. Lucky for him the conference house was full of cardiologists to save him.

FAT AND CHOLESTEROL ARE NOT THE ENEMY

Who remembers our parents and grandparents cooking and eating beef tallow, lard, fat and butter? Do you want to know the truth? Fat and cholesterol does not cause heart attacks! Science has proven that excess sugar (in all its forms) causes clogged arteries and heart disease. How can something be so bad when every organ in our body is dependent on it for its survival? Our brain is composed mainly of fat and cholesterol. Our body will eat every other part of itself first to spare its brain and heart. Do you know that our cells are composed mainly of fat and protein? In fact, our whole body minus the water is constructed by both of these (amino acids and lipids to be exact). Fat is basically stored energy for when we need it. It helps our body produce collagen in our skin, and build muscle. It's essential for our reproductive health, for better brain function (mood stabilizer—less depression), for stronger bones (combats osteoporosis) and immune system. Fat is beneficial for our skin and eyes, it strengthens our lungs, help absorb toxins, and is hydrating. If our body is dependent on fat and cholesterol, why are we told to reduce it?

We have been told that LDL cholesterol (low-density lipoprotein) is bad, and that HDL cholesterol (high-density lipoprotein) is good. Did you know that LDL is an antioxidant made by the liver to reduce inflammation in the blood vessels? Did you also know that HDL is simply the carrier of LDL? This means that HDL cleans up the LDL and brings it back to the liver. As usual we have it backwards. If you have high levels of LDL, all it means is that there is lots of inflammation in your body. Do you know that cholesterol is essential in the formation of vitamin D and important *hormones*? Did you know that the liver uses it to make bile? Cholesterol insulates our nerve cells, helps create cell membranes and protects them from sudden temperature change. The insanity is that we're told to lower nature's perfect healing solution against this inflammation by taking statins. Anti-cholesterol medicine has been proven to damage muscles, cause pain, damage the liver, increase blood sugar, Type 2 diabetes, memory loss and confusion, and has even been linked to cancer with long-term use. Cholesterol production decreases as inflammation does. Studies show that high levels of cholesterol is indicative of a long and healthy life.

Why is cholesterol so vilified? This may be due to how LDL oxidizes, or becomes damaged as it penetrates the walls of inflamed arteries. Over time this builds up as hardened plaque. Arteries are further damaged and lose their elasticity by low levels of nitric oxide. Sugar is what really irritates the arteries, as does smoking, stress, and consuming omega-6 vegetable oils. Cholesterol is blamed the same way weeds, cancer, and bacteria are for creating the problem. Again, we fail to understand that they are there because of the condition, not the cause of it. We keep killing the Cavalry that's trying to save the day.

BAD FOR BUSINESS

Have you ever asked why fat and cholesterol is defamed by so many corporate and government associations? Why are heart health stickers plastered all over cereal boxes and on low-fat food packages that are loaded with sugar? We have been brainwashed to believe that these proven toxins are the path to our health. Imagine what would happen if we stopped listening to them. Eating healthy fats, and avoiding excess sugar (in all its hidden forms) will reduce and in most cases eliminate the need for statins, insulin and possibly even chemotherapy. Eating foods rich in pre- and probiotics would reduce if not eliminate the need for supplements, and vitamins. These are the most beneficial. Our skin would glow, our teeth would be strong and shine. We could then even say goodbye to beauty products. You mean food can help lower or eliminate diabetes, heart disease, stroke, and even cancer? This doesn't sound good for business, does it?

Have you noticed that every time a new variation of a high fat, low carb diet resurfaces, it explodes in popularity? The reason is because it works, and people experience results. There are lots of cunning people in the big corporate syndicates. They've been to more than one rodeo. It doesn't take long for them to sink anything that poses a threat to their trillion dollar monopolies. Diets like South Beach, Dukan, Atkins, Paleo, and the Keto diets all share one thing in common: the reduction of simple carbohydrates.

How many industries would perish if we radically changed our diet and lifestyle? Unfortunately, this would cause a chain reaction and affect the honest farmers and producers that have been built on grain and sugar production. Slowly, however, we can transition and build better business models based on transparent and authentic practices which benefits everyone. The problem is we can't help ourselves—we are addicted to these poisons, and they know it. Until we take control of ourselves, nothing will change.

10

FOOD

I trust that you now understand the backbone of what true health is really all about. Without it, food cannot be the cure. In fact, it can become the opposite. Good health is not just a result of what we put in our mouths, but just as important is the environment of our mental and emotional states. It's about our attitude and lifestyle—one in which should be enjoyed, and is sustainable.

Food has been integrated into our cultural identity. What we eat is often influenced by our social and geographical environment. Eating is a slippery slope because it's a necessary indulgence for our survival. Food can act as a nutrient, or as a drug which can be very addictive. Many cultures use food as a form of nurturing and/or a display of love. Growing up with this model may result in establishing an unhealthy relationship with food. Instead of regarding it as nourishment, we associate it with receiving pleasure and reward. When we celebrate a birthday or graduation we get cake, if we behave it's candy, and so on.

The relationship we have with ourselves greatly affects how we eat. When we are sad or bored we tend to make poorer food choices in the hopes of raising our spirit. We reach for edibles that quickly raise our serotonin and blood sugar levels. Many times we eat in haste or absentmindedly, failing even to relish it. We forget to be mindful and grateful for what's on our plate. Reestablishing a healthy relationship with our food is imperative.

We have to navigate through our past conditioning and see how it affects our dietary choices. Everything in moderation works for those who possess self-discipline. Without it, is like telling a recovering alcoholic that just one drink is fine. Our aim is to find the balance between nourishment and enjoyment—want verses necessity.

Ask yourself what your relationship is with food. Do you consider food more than just fuel? Are you an emotional eater? Do you seek it for comfort? Do you eat out of boredom, fear or guilt? Do you worry about fat, calories, cholesterol, and so forth? Do you enjoy each morsel fully? I'm not a fan of counting calories, weighing food or tracking macronutrients. This seems a bit obsessive and contrived. Did you know that emotionally sensitive people tend to gain weight under stress? Can the opposite be true for those who lack empathy? At times, it may seem like we're on an extreme roller coaster ride as we try to figure it all out. We try different approaches until we find out what works, at least for a short time.

New studies reveal the new perfect diet, then another, and on it goes. Contradictions appear to be the only sure thing. One week something is supposed to be good for you, and the next it causes cancer. This can be so frustrating, and over time we stop believing everything altogether. We surmise that everything is going to kill us anyway, so why not eat whatever you want. Or, we become orthorexic (the obsession with eating a pure diet) and allow it to govern our entire life—even avoiding social interactions and catered functions. There has to be a sensible answer, a balance in between. It is my intent that you will find that balance with the information that I'm sharing with you.

NEW ATTITUDE

The solution doesn't exist in the empty promises pledged by the next miracle pill, supplement or gadget. We are sucked in by quick fixes, and preyed on by our desire for simple and easy. Most of us will try everything except for what works—slow and steady. But it's not a race; rather, it's a process toward health and vitality. Hunger is a condition that's not permanently cured by eating, it always comes back. Like all things, health and eating is not a destination, but a journey. Wait for the weight to go, fat loss is simply a bonus of being healthy. Our sickness didn't happen overnight; neither will our healing. To some of us, sadly, it only matters how we look on the outside. Many don't care what's going on inside the body. Have you ever heard of the saying, "You are what you eat?" In truth, we become what we eat—the choices we make today affect who and what we become tomorrow. I believe we should be eating food closest to its natural state. There is a saying, "Living food living body, dead food, dead body." Cooking food denatures, and kills it.

Being healthy is not about buying more time on this planet, it's about the quality of what we have left on it. Mother Nature provides everything we need in terms of shelter, food, water and herbal medicines. When we deviate from this we experience disease. A common misconception is that there exists one or more superfoods that can cure all diseases, reduce weight and regain health. There is no one panacea food, list, or nutritional category that addresses everyone's dietary needs—we are each different. Being a vegetarian doesn't guarantee one perfect health. In fact, there are vegetarians who suffer more health problems than do meat eaters. A fraction of a peanut can be suitable for one person, or a death sentence for another. We are going to need more than one brush to paint this picture. There aren't any hard and fast rules.

Inflammation and insulin resistance isn't exclusive. Like gravity, there is a common ground that applies to everyone.

Sometimes we need to eat just to nourish the Soul. This means eating the food from our parents' Mother country. These are the building blocks that helped build our DNA. Life is not always about regimes and sacrifice, it's about having fun. Our Spirit innately knows what it needs—sometimes it's pierogies and pasta. At times it may be eating nothing at all (fasting). The secret is not continuing to eat what made you ill in the first place. I invite you to experiment and see what works for you. Observe which food affects you, and how it leaves you feeling. Maybe you can't ever indulge in gnocchi without feeling like the Vesuvius is erupting inside your bowels. Start a journal and log everything you eat. Notice what bloats you, gives you gas, loosens your stools, gives bowel discomfort, muscle or joint pain, skin conditions, energy levels, sleeplessness and so on.

Start your journey to greater health by eating what is right for you. Have fun, and enjoy the process.

THE ANATOMY OF FOOD

Food is not only calories, it's information which affects our DNA. When you boil it all down, food is composed of macronutrients, micronutrients, and microminerals and enzymes. Who knows what science will further discover? Macronutrients are composed of proteins, carbohydrates and fat. Carbohydrates are made up of small chains of sugar which the body breaks down into glucose. Protein is essential for repairing and regenerating the body's cells and tissues. It builds a healthily functioning immune system, and manufactures hormones. Proteins are composed of twenty known amino acids: nine of which are the essential ones, which the body cannot produce on its own. There are four different types of fat. *Saturated* fat solidifies at room temperature and can be found in animal products. *Monounsaturated* are in avocados, nuts, olives and seeds. *Polyunsaturated* are found mainly in vegetable oils. Then there are *trans fats* which are changed by the process of hydrogenation. Healthy fat such as saturated and monounsaturated help improve brain development, overall cell functioning, protect the body's organs and absorb vitamins found in foods. Micronutrients consist of vitamins and minerals. Macrominerals are calcium, magnesium, phosphorus, sodium and potassium, etc. Microminerals are iron, copper, iodine, zinc and fluoride. These are needed only in trace amounts. Plants produce substances called phytonutrients. These chemicals act as antioxidants and anti-inflammatory compounds.

TO EAT OR NOT TO EAT MEAT

Like it or not, to eat is to kill another life form so we can sustain our own. Did you know that plants can feel pain? Cows and pigs can express fear better than chickens and fish. This is why they resist more when their life is threatened. The more highly evolved an animal is, the more it can express its reluctance to die. Conversely, the more evolved we are the greater awareness we have about killing beings who have a higher consciousness. A plant can't yell, "Don't eat me!" They can only produce toxins such as lectins to deter predators like us from eating them. One school of thought suggests that if you can kill it, you can eat it—many can't. Would you be able to slaughter an animal if it cried out, "No?" It's much easier to buy on the shelf already prepared. Could you eat an animal that was loved and raised with respect, fed the best food, and euthanized properly?

Some believe that animals with lower consciousness have incarnated simply to sacrifice themselves to sustain humans. Doing so would elevate their Soul to a higher state for their next incarnation. Many Hindus believe that an elephant is in its last animal embodiment before taking on a human form in its next life. A number of alternative doctors believe that varying blood types and body constitutions dictate the need for meat. Some do not thrive on flesh. In addition, many women find that eating red meat once a month replenishes depleted iron during their menses. It is believed that eating meat provides strength and increases aggression.

There are those who are convinced that because India's majority population is vegetarian, they've become passive—which has allowed others in the past to invade their country countless times.

Ironically, vegetation not only thrives on other dead plant matter but also on meat-based fertilizers. The root systems of trees are known to take on the form of carcasses which have been buried near them. Who knew Mother Nature was a carnivore? Each fig fruit contains hatched eggs and dead remains of wasps. When the males mature they mate with the female inside the fruit. The males tunnel out a path for the female, then die. After the female collects enough pollen from the mature fig she escapes, finds another fig, lays its eggs and dies. The line between vegetarian and meat eating is blurred. One day we will also become the fleshy food that nourishes Mother Earth.

VEGAN ~ VEGETARIAN ~ CARNIVORE

This is a battle that is waged daily, with all sides fighting 'till the cows come home. One will milk it, another will kill it, and the third will object to both. Which way is right? Meat eaters swear on this way of eating, claiming that it's the only way God made it. Alternatively, one can thrive on a vegetarian diet as long as it's done correctly. This can be achieved by eating high fat dairy and eggs, and reducing the intake of excessive carbohydrates. I would question a diet that required the need of additional supplements to fill in the missing nutritional spectrum. We weren't designed to ingest synthetic pills and powders as our food. If your health deteriorates because you don't get enough concentrated nutrition from vegetables, then for heaven's sake, eat some animal fat and protein. Human life takes precedence over a chicken or fish. If you'd rather jeopardize your body and get sick for spiritual reasons, or to save an animal, then that's a personal choice which I respect. Good health isn't reserved for ethical ways of eating. There are healthy and unhealthy people in each dietary category.

Isn't it ironic that Hitler was a vegetarian, and Jesus ate meat? Many believe gorillas which are the closest to us biologically are vegan—this isn't true. They may eat up to sixteen pounds of leaves a day, but they also eat many insects and the flesh of other small animals. Wildlife identified as herbivores have been filmed eating other animals. This may not be the case all the time, but it happens. If you want to pursue a spiritual life, then eating little to no meat is preferable. This is based simply on observing non-violence, consciousness, empathy and energetic vibration. If your lifestyle is one that demands heavy labour, or if you pursue goals that require strength, nature has designed itself to thrive on a carnivorous diet. Harassment in any form should not be used to belittle anyone for their dietary choices. Nor should violence, nudity or damage to personal property be a means to enlighten others with different points of view. Wouldn't a loving and cooperative approach work so much better?

Life is a contradiction, it is duality. Either way, what's important is that we practice conscious eating. Listen to your body. What works for another may not work for you. This means questioning your food choices. We are not the script we were taught, we are what we choose to create. Be cool, bless your food.

CAN YOU STOMACH IT?

Did you know that cows have four large stomachs called rumens? They contain parasites, bacteria, flukes, fungi and other microorganisms that help break down grass and plant matter. Do you know that only microbiome can digest a plant's fibre? A cow chews grass over two hundred times swallowing and regurgitating it until the bacteria breaks it down enough to pass through its intestines to be absorbed and pooped out. Omnivores have single and smaller stomachs with high levels of hydrochloric acid. These can only digest meat, fish, dairy and eggs—with the help of pepsin, bile and pancreatic juices. Healthy human stomachs do not contain microbiome and therefore cannot digest fibrous plant matter. Pre-digestion starts in the mouth by chewing which releases the enzyme amylase. An omnivore's bowels resemble the rumen of ruminants. Protein and fat are not absorbed in the intestines; they are broken down in the stomach to be absorbed in the intestinal path.

Our body, cells and organs are constantly rejuvenating. We need building blocks to allow this process to occur. Animal products are the perfect resource. Veggies are not building materials, they are powerful cleansers and detoxifiers that contain polyphenols, antioxidants, and vitamins. Meat, dairy and eggs have similar amino acid structures to the human body. A plant's amino acid structure isn't in the correct proportion. This means that the protein found in broccoli can't be utilized as efficiently by the body. Plants also contain unhealthy fats such as polyunsaturated. Vegetables should be cooked, sprouted and fermented (pre-digested) to make them better digestible.

Eating vegan is basically a form of fasting. This is why people feel fantastic at first. When the cleansing is over the body will tell you to eat animal products again. Many override this signal and over time crash and experience deteriorating health. Plants clean us, they don't feed us—we need both.

GRAZING IS FOR COWS

Cows need to graze because their food (grass) is very low in calories but is high in nutrient density. We eat higher caloric food with a lower nutrient density. Eating a balanced nutrient to calorie food satiates us and gives our gut bacteria what it needs to feed our cells. This involves eating whole food which includes some fibre and compact micro and macronutrients. Eating simple refined food never fills us up, in fact it makes us even hungrier. This is why we can eat a whole bag of chips and still crave more.

When we graze or eat frequently, we keep insulin constantly elevated. This turns everything to fat, and may even convert the healthy cucumber. Remember, every time we eat, insulin is released. The goal is to eat less frequently. This doesn't mean to eat less food. Eat all of your daily calories in one or two meals instead of five to six—no snacking. Many body builders believe that dividing calories into more meals is good to build muscle. This may be true short-term as insulin helps cells absorb protein. But over time this causes damage to the metabolism, depletes the adrenals, and creates inflammation. In addition, the more one exercises the more cortisol and free radicals are produced. One can never work off a bad diet. So eat less and workout less. A relaxed body has time to repair and build, giving you better results.

WILL YOU CAVE, MAN?

Have you ever wondered how our ancestors—AKA cavemen—could go days without eating food? How could they still maintain their strength and mental clarity to hunt? Nowadays, many of us can't even go three hours without wanting to eat our hands off. We hit the proverbial wall and become hypoglycemic. When our blood glucose drops, so does our energy and mental clarity. We become lightheaded, irritable, sluggish and forgetful. We get hangry! We want something sweet, a coffee, or anything that will give us energy and raise our serotonin levels. This results in a yo-yo effect of energetic ups and downs, mood swings and weight gain. How long have you been playing this exhausting drama—a seesaw of spiking and declining cortisol, adrenaline, and insulin? Eventually, this plays havoc with our health and leads to metabolic damage, and adrenal burnout.

There is a solution, a way to restore balance and sustained energy. We need to get back to our natural way of being, of primal eating. Presently, the typical Western diet consists mainly of refined carbohydrates. The common belief is that the body and brain require glucose for its fuel and cell function. Unfortunately, we have gotten to the point of overloading our bodies with too many refined carbohydrates. If we looked back in time to our early ancestors, we'd realize that they didn't eat how we do today. They didn't eat pasta, or bake cookies. They didn't have access to a fast food joint on every street corner. Agriculture and milling grains are relatively new practices in the historical timeline of our species. The truth is, the body doesn't need carbohydrates or sugar to function. There is a better and more efficient fuel source.

CLEAN AND DIRTY FUEL

Natural gas is the cleanest burning of all fossil fuels. $CO2$ emissions are about fifty percent cleaner than coal and about thirty percent cleaner than oil is. Did you know that too much oil in a two-stroke gas engine will cause it to smoke? There are different types of gasoline for your car. Higher grades burn cleaner and leave less residue behind. Some claim to actually clean the engine. Have you ever placed a bunch of newspaper on a fire? You get a huge flame, then nothing. A fire needs fuel to sustain—the more fuel it has, the hotter it gets. Paper burns quickly without creating much heat. However, when a log of wood is used, the fire will burn hotter and for much longer.

Imagine fire being our energy, body fat is the log, and simple carbs is the kindling, or paper. Eating carbs is like throwing paper continuously on a fire. All the while, there is a pile of wooden logs waiting to be burned. The irony is that the more we replenish the fire, the hungrier it gets—while the stack of logs keeps piling up. Nature has our back, but also our tummy, thighs and hips. Fat is stored on our body for a reason—it's our fuel reserve. There is one problem: fat is like money deposited into our bank account; it's hard to access. Carbs are like having quick cash in your pocket and is readily available. Here is the second problem: we cannot access our fat stores if we are dependent on sugar for our fuel—insulin closes the bank.

Our body is like a high performance car. Top of the line vehicles need premium gasoline to perform the way they were designed to. Sugar is considered the dirty fuel, and fat is a cleaner one. We are the jealous lover who puts sugar in their cheating partner's gas tank—our body.

WE NEED CARBOHYDRATES, DON'T WE?

"Isn't it dangerous if we stopped eating carbs? Doesn't our body need them? I can't give up bread. Grains are a part of life. Won't you get fatter when you start eating carbs again? What about everything in moderation?" Let me ask you, "Who told you it's dangerous to stop eating simple refined carbs?" Cells can and do use glucose to function. Our body is an incredible biological machine and can adapt to whatever shit we feed it. The liver can convert stored glycogen back into glucose and release it in our bloodstream if needed.

Wheat is cheap and filling, and many lower income people greatly rely on it. What an amazing business model, a food that's cheap and keeps people hungrier for more. Carbs make you feel good, but they also make you feel bad. When you cut them out, you will feel so much better. Why would you want to start consuming something that made you feel sick in the first place? This is about a lifestyle change, not a quick fix temporary solution. Simple refined carbs such as sugar are what leads to yeast, fungus and uncooperative bacterial overgrowth. When the good guys have nothing left to eat, they die off and let the bad guys take over.

Did you know that a cow's microbiome digests seventy percent of what it eats (grass) to create fat and protein? Who knew that cows were on a low carb, high fat diet? If saturated fat was bad, why does our body convert excess glucose into it for storage to be used later?

Changing Fuel

The goal is to start using wooden logs as our primary fuel instead of highly flammable paper. How do we do this? First we need to change the macronutrient ratio of the typical Western diet. This is accomplished by eliminating or drastically reducing refined carbohydrates. Eat more whole foods and stop being afraid of good fat. This isn't easy, as the majority of us are addicted to sugar and carbs. Second, we have to burn up the remaining glycogen in our body before we can get to the stored fat. The quickest way is to do a total fast.

What happens when we stop eating carbohydrates? Initially, we will experience low blood sugar. Symptoms include fatigue, weakness, sugar cravings, dizziness, brain fog, irritability, and difficulty focusing, to name a few. We'll also experience significant water loss as carbohydrates hold on to fluid. For every gram of existing carb in the body, about three grams of water is retained. Imagine putting a piece of bread in a glass of water—notice how it acts like a sponge. Fat, on the other hand, doesn't hold fluid like carbohydrates and salt do. When we dramatically reduce carbohydrate intake, glycogen stores start to tap out. When there is no more sugar to burn, our body finds an alternative fuel to use instead. Your pancreas not only creates insulin, it also creates the enzyme lipase which breaks down stored triglycerides into fatty acids. When these travel to the liver, ketones are produced. Ketones are considered to be a cleaner and a more efficient fuel than sugar. Actually, our brain prefers them and performs much more coherently. This process is called Ketogenesis.

To achieve this state, the following foods must be avoided at all costs: all sugars, grains, rice, tubers, legumes, beans, lentils, low dairy, or low-fat anything. This is difficult for those who's diet depends on them. This is still possible if one sticks to green leafy vegetables, avocados, nuts, seeds, eggs and high fat dairy. Foods must be eaten whole. If you eat meat, consume wild organic, and grass-fed—do not remove the fat. Drink adequate amounts of water. I do not suggest attempting this without first educating yourself.

TRANSITIONING

When our glycogen stores tap out, the body will transition. This isn't always fun and can feel like a junkie who goes through withdrawal. For the majority of our lives we've relied heavily on sugars (a drug) to fuel us. Insulin not only carries glucose to the cells, it also signals the kidneys to hold on to salt. Low sugar means low insulin, which means sodium is released from the body, taking with it lots of water. Fluid loss also means electrolytes are lost, as well.

This is why we lose tons of weight at first, but it's only water. One way to remedy this is by adding a pinch of unprocessed sea salt to your water. In addition, you can add potassium and magnesium. Hydration is imperative, or you'll feel terrible if you don't. During the first day or so, your body will be using the stored glycogen within your liver and muscles—the cells in your pancreas release glucagon which the liver turns into glucose. This process restores sugar levels. Lowered insulin also activates the fat burning enzyme HSL (Hormone-Sensitive Lipase). Eating higher amounts of fat as you transition will help your body during its adaption to burning its own stored fat. Don't over do it. Some people swear by using MCT oil to help through the changeover as it quickly turns into ketones which keeps the brain happy.

THE MOST COMMON MISTAKE

When glycogen (your body's sugar storage) is low, and protein intake is high, amino acids from your meals and your muscles are used as fuel. This also happens when you're stressed and cortisol levels are elevated.

Your liver will perform a trick called gluconeogenesis. This literally translates to the making of (genesis) new (neo) sugar (gluco). During gluconeogenesis, the liver (and occasionally the kidneys) turn these non-sugar compounds into sugar. If your body continues to convert amino acids into fuel, it can keep you from getting into ketosis. Eating too much protein is one of the biggest mistakes committed by low carb newbies. This is also a great strain on your kidneys. More protein is not better. In fact, it's the same as eating sugar. This is why initially, some may experience an increase in body fat, and a decrease in muscle mass during the first couple weeks. Protein cannot be stored, it is a muscle and tissue builder, and shouldn't be used as fuel.

Low carb, and high fat doesn't mean high protein. The formula to fat burning is consuming macros in the ratio of 80% fat, 17% protein and 3% carbohydrates. Don't be afraid of fatty meats. Lean meat and fish quickly turn into sugar and spike insulin. Ditch the skinless chicken breast and white fish, and bring on the marbled beef and fatty salmon.

It takes about two weeks to curb cravings, and this is when our ghrelin levels reduce. Calories in and calories out still applies. If you are eating too much fat, your body won't use its own stores.

ARE YOU FAT ADAPTED?

Being able to eat like our primal ancestors who could easily go hours and days without eating can take months to achieve. Depending on the severity of one's metabolic syndrome, it can take as little as a few weeks. Metabolic syndrome is a combination of many conditions that increase your risk of heart disease, stroke and diabetes. These include high blood pressure, high blood sugar, and high levels of triglycerides (fats from the food we eat). The best evidence of being fat adapted is having increased energy without feeling hungry. Energy will be steady and even, and will not fluctuate. Unfortunately, we may be tricked into thinking we've transitioned. When in fact, we may be on the road to adrenal fatigue and burnout. Consistent high cortisol levels will deplete adrenals and destroy our muscles to compensate. This happens when we are in a hypoglycemic state. Many criticize the ketogenic approach: they say it's dangerous and that the body is actually starving. This fight-or-flight response happens for only a short time until our body adjusts. Like with any drug, withdrawal symptoms will be experienced.

Don't confuse reducing carbs with starvation. There is a big difference and many get themselves in trouble by not understanding this. If we keep our body on a low caloric intake without being adapted, we run the risk of gluconeogenesis. Restricting calories while still being dependent on glucose will indeed keep your body in starvation mode. Your body will not go into ketosis—instead it will start eating itself to survive. Only when you have healed your metabolism and are fully adapted, you can switch between carbohydrates and fat burning. This is called metabolic flexibility. So many people have injured metabolisms and cannot switch between both. Those relying on sugar need to replenish constantly, or they won't have the energy to sustain themselves. Sugar burners don't have access to their fat stores. This is the reason why many athletes need to carb load before, and replenish after a workout or long run. The stored glycogen in their liver and muscles burns off quickly. Using ketones for fuel, one has access to all the fat they'll ever need—it's stored all over our body. Once accessible, fat is a highly concentrated energy that's ready to use at any time. Protein and carbohydrates both contain four calories per gram, while fat provides nine—the perfect fuel.

There are many reported benefits to being a fat burner over a sugar one. Low carb diets have been known to prevent and reverse cognitive diseases such as autism, bi-polar, Parkinson's, Alzheimer's, dementia, and epilepsy. Further benefits include repairing metabolic syndrome, easier menses, stabilized mood and hormones, Poly Ovary Syndrome (PCOS), diabetes, cancer, headaches, obesity (weight loss), MS, aging (more collagen due to fat) better brain function, greater focus, memory and clarity, IBS, better mitochondrial function, less inflammation, acne, and heartburn.

Being fat adapted also means that you can observe fasting without the discomfort typically associated with it.

FASTING

Fasting is instinctively practised by animals when they are sick. This behaviour is also observed by many of the world's diverse religious faiths. Have you noticed that when you get sick your natural instinct is not to eat? This gives a chance for our body to heal. Fasting is also the quickest way to detox from addictions and cravings. This allows time for the corresponding and over-sensitized receptors to reset. There is a misconception that fasting will result in muscle loss. This is true, and also false. As was mentioned, reduced calories can lead to gluconeogenesis. Fasting means no food, so glycogen can deplete and not keep the body in starvation mode. The fact is, HGH (Human Growth Hormone) will preserve your muscle for up to five days before muscle cannibalism begins.

When our cells have nothing to eat they enter into a process called autophagy. This is a natural process that literally means self-eating. Think of this as our body's innate way of regenerating itself, like recycling. The faulty parts are purged to create new ones. These include pre-cancerous growths and old dying cells. This carnage is used to fuel the process and provide energy for our body. Autophagy makes us more efficient biological machines. It stops metabolic dysfunctions like obesity and diabetes. In addition, it helps control inflammation and strengthens the immune system. Autophagy can be the key to slowing the aging process by inhibiting the accumulation of sugar molecules bonding to protein or fat molecules. This process is called glycation, and occurs when insulin doesn't metabolize sugars properly. Glycation destroys the collagen in blood vessels and in the skin, causing them to form plaque and become brittle.

Do not attempt fasting without first understanding how it's properly done.

INTERMITTENT FASTING

The beneficial effects of autophagy kicks into full force after eighteen hours of fasting. You can take advantage of this daily by observing intermittent fasting. This is when you eat only in a specified eating window. An example is eating between the hours of 10:00am-4:00pm. This gives you the required timeframe. Start slow and increase the fasting time by gradually decreasing your eating time. You can work up to eating only two meals a day, at 12:00pm, then at 4:00pm. This gives you twenty fasting hours, and a couple of full-on autophagy. Some people have adapted to eating only one big meal a day. Eating less frequent doesn't tax your metabolism, it maximizes fat loss due to less insulin production.

If you prefer, you can do a total fast one day a week, or three full days a month. I do not recommend more than three consecutive days. Twenty-four to forty-eight hours is ideal. Ease into normal eating when observing and breaking a longer fast. The riddle of starving a cold or a feeding fever is solved either way.

Pump You Up

Whether you are fasting or dramatically reducing carbohydrate intake, you need to pay attention to water and electrolytes. Our body's cells are like batteries and run on electrolytes. The sodium-potassium pump moves sodium ions for potassium ions through the cell's membrane. One molecule of sodium attracts twenty-five molecules of water. If there is no sodium around the cell, say goodbye to the water, potassium and other electrolytes in your body. This leads to increased urination which may cause dehydration. As a result, you'll experience headaches, flu like symptoms, low energy, cramping and other adverse side effects. To replenish those lost minerals, especially potassium (K), eat at least seven to ten cups of leafy greens every day. Our body's daily K requirements are between 4700-6000mg. Did you know that potassium helps create stomach acid for digestion and also helps with insulin resistance?

You can make an electrolyte infused drink to help you. Add 1 tsp of potassium chloride (salt substitute), 1 tsp of sodium chloride (Himalayan pink salt), and 1/2 tsp of magnesium (food grade Epsom salt) to two litres of pure water. Consume this daily during your full fast or fat burning transition to help nourish your cells and sustain your energy.

11

BACK TO NATURE

We can't be great human beings if we don't honour and respect our planet. Mother Earth is (ME) and spells Heart when we move the H (symbolizing Home) in front of it. We need her more than she needs us. We have lost our relationship with Her by our material pursuits, selfishness, technology and misinformation. These have led us away from intimately interacting with our Earth Mother. We stay indoors under artificial lighting, and in stagnant air infused with unnatural electro-magnetic fields. We are eating processed food, use toxic hygiene products and cleaners. More children are being born with diseases that normally afflict the old. It has been said that for the first time in history, in this generation, parents will outlive their kids.

Our current lifestyle is severely affecting our health. We are developing more allergies and suffering from more diseases like cancer and heart attacks. There is an increase of depression and suicide. We've cleared vegetation to make room for concrete cities. We tread on Earth like packed sardines in trains and buses, congested in traffic. Let's not disrespect the rats, this human-race cannot be won. We are not meant to live this way. This abuse is happening at an alarming rate, never seen or known before. I'm not trying to be a doomsday preacher, but the alarm bells are blaring and we aren't listening. We are in denial as we find more ways to numb out and distract ourselves. We have no time or energy to be the superheroes we've been born to be. It's time to wake up!

SOILED BY IGNORANCE

We have lost our sacred connection to the soil, the life-giving substrate that supplies our food. Gone is our respect for the delicate balance between the microbiome and the ecosystem. Modern agriculture has destroyed the soil, it has denuded it and is contributing to the demise of our planet. Our land is stripped of all life such as insects and bacteria, the water tables are poisoned. We have stopped growing our own food in the name of convenience. Instead, we source this out to corporations that value the all mighty dollar over our health and well-being. We are forced to trust The System to keep us in their best interest, knowing that they are more interested in filling their pockets.

Today, many of our seeds are genetically modified to withstand the very chemicals that were created to help them grow unnaturally. These Frankenstein seeds create monstrous food that our body doesn't recognize. Genetic Use Restriction Technology (GURT) is a method that restricts GMO plants from creating second generational seeds. This terminator technology creates sterile suicidal seeds. Why? To hold farmers hostage and dependent on buying only from them, the agricultural mafia. Sure, these seeds create visually stunning produce. So what? Who wants tasteless and nutritionally devoid produce that's harmful to our body? Given the choice, many of us do.

We are doing the same to our own bodies by adorning and altering them with labels, products and surgeries. How can we trust anything called organic when neighbouring farms and water tables are saturated with glyphosate and other harmful compounds? Livestock is taken off the natural land, separated and raised on cement floors. The animals are fed grains and dead animal remnants, and who knows what else they shouldn't be eating. Are we so far removed that we can't see all this? Have we gone insane?

The whole system is rigged to keep us sick. We need more drugs to treat more ailments which leads to more drugs, which never ends up healing anything. It's a great business model, one we are blind to.

NOW YOU KNOW

In nature, monocultures don't exist, vegetation is scattered. Mother Earth favours a polyculture and abhors how man grows fruits and vegetables together in rows. In response, she creates disease, pests and predators to cull these unnatural crop formations. In the wild, yield is normally low and exposed to hungry wildlife. Perhaps we weren't meant to eat an abundance of vegetation. Do you know that backyard gardeners find it difficult to grow a high enough yield to feed even one person for the year? The only way to manipulate this is by diligent effort, and with chemical fertilizers. This may explain why organic produce isn't cheap.

The same concept applies to raising animals. Sustainable farming involves honouring both the animal and the land. Together, they create a brilliant ecosystem. The animals are pasture raised on natural grasses. They eat, digest, defecate, and urinate their waste onto the soil. This reintroduces microbiome and compost which fertilizes the earth. It takes about four months for the soil to regenerate back into optimal quality food for the livestock. If left in one area for too long or tightly fenced in, animals will eventually destroy the grass and its roots system. The farmer has to move them to greener pastures. In the fields, sheep need a herdsman to relocate them. In the wild, Mother Nature provides predators to act as her shepherd. This forces the herds to stick together and move as one to fresher grazing lands. Sometimes an animal is killed in the process, but that's the cost of doing business.

Raising pasture fed livestock isn't very profitable and is very challenging for large scale production. The only model that's lucrative is the inhumane way. Where animals are caged, crammed together, beaten, tortured, and pumped up with antibiotics because many become sick as a result. Alternatively, growing grains with chemicals and machines is very profitable, and easy.

Big Agra isn't stupid, they have some of the best minds on the planet. They devised a scheme so clever that no one would have ever considered. Religion and politics have been pulling the same trick on us for years, even the church has to make a Prophet. The coin has two sides, yet they are one of the same.

Those that hold it give us a false choice, heads or tails. The most sinister scheme of them all is the illusion of good and evil. Angels and demons play for the same team, both have a job to do. After their shift is over, together they go for a drink at the local pub. This is true for both defending and prosecuting lawyers who shake hands after the trial is over. We are all kept distracted and powerless fighting amongst ourselves. Unfortunately, many can't wrap their heads around this insidious model.

The corporate elite know that there will always be people eating meat regardless of how it's produced. They also know that many will be opposed to their inhumane practices. Similarly, there are those who believe in global warming, and those who do not. How would you devise a plan that could hedge your investment and capitalize on all sides? This scheme would have to be so cunning that it could play both sides against each other. Could there be such a sinister plot in place?

GLOBAL WARMING IS NOT ABOUT BULL SHIT

What if greenhouse emissions where actually caused by the destruction of soil and not from farting cows? Do you know that humus is the organic component of dirt created through the decomposing of plant and animal waste? It is mainly composed of carbon. Agricultural chemicals and plowing destroys the soil's humus and releases the carbon into the atmosphere. This turns into carbon dioxide, or greenhouse emissions. Humus in soil is like a spongy gelatine that attracts and can hold up to ninety percent of its weight in water. This means that healthy soil needs less watering and can contain vital nutrients. Since damaged soil cannot retain water, runoff occurs which creates flash flooding and swelling rivers.

What if we are the victims of misinformation who are being told lies by the corporations that own the agricultural industry? What if those animal torture videos were purposely designed to stop us from eating meat altogether? Showing the unethical treatment of animals would turn most people off eating flesh, especially young children. The message is, "Eating animals is heartless and wrong, and the only solution is to be Vegan." Tell this to the tribes and cultures who depend on meat for their survival—where their climate affords little vegetation. In truth, the way in which animals are being raised and slaughtered is disgusting and beyond cruel. This must stop!

Interestingly, a pure plant-based diet relies exclusively on the Industrial Agriculture Complex. Have you ever considered that eating vegan plays right into the hands of Big Agra and Big Pharma? This model is the cheapest and most profitable way of producing food. Less meat, more grain, more disease, more chemicals, more drugs and more supplements that fill their coffers. Isn't it interesting that people like Bill Gates who is known to support human depopulation has invested in pharmaceuticals and artificial meat products? What if there wasn't really a food shortage in the world? Do you know that the agricultural industry overproduces around fifty percent of the grain it grows? This can feed the poor! Why are all these surplus grains either thrown away, or fed to animals that shouldn't be eating them? Animals require grass, not toxic cereal crops. Grains make livestock fat to fetch a higher yield on the markets—they also fatten us up, too. What if those starving countries actually have embargoes set on them by their own governments and global political agendas? Why are natural farmers discouraged from growing and raising grass-fed livestock and organic produce? Why are they not subsidized like the commercial puppet farmers are? In fact, they can be fined and even jailed for selling raw natural dairy.

FIXING GLOBAL WARMING ~ MORE COWS

The way out of this mess is not simply to stop eating meat. Animals should never be raised by the agricultural model—nor should we be supporting it. The solution is sustainable farming. This means healing the soil by raising more livestock on the pasture, and planting more trees. This way, more carbon is absorbed from the air and redirected back into the soil. Saving the planet means supporting natural farming, not shunning it.

We used to grow vegetable gardens, rotate the crops and practice companion planting to keep soil lush, pests and disease away.

The community shared its yields, and traded resources. Instead, we turned to killing both the soil and plants with chemical pesticides. When weeds come to replenish the soil, we kill them, too. Then we try to reclaim the denuded soil by adding even more chemicals and fertilizers.

We have the opportunity to change all this and get back to a sacred way of living. Collectively, we can reclaim the soil by composting and recycling, and by raising a few pasture animals. Many of us are unable due to our urban lifestyle. The answer is to buy local, organic, and support natural farming and cooperatives. Consider getting back to small communities, make your own hygiene products such as soap and toothpaste. Heal your gut and avoid products that harm you. Rekindle a healthy relationship with food. Let food be thy medicine. Stick it to the Man. They need us, we don't need them. We have the power to reclaim what is ours.

A REGION, A SEASON, AND A RIGHT TIME

For every food there is a region, a season, and the right time to eat it. Maybe not the best play on that saying… nevertheless, mother nature provides the proper food according to the geographical area. This means eating indigenously and whatever is available in season. We forget that at one time, refrigeration, freezing and transportable food wasn't available. The Chinese believe that food has either a cooling (Yin), warming (Yang) or a neutral effect on the body. Not surprisingly, most tropical and summer growing food tends to have a cooling effect. Examples are fruit such as pineapples, grapefruits, oranges, cucumber, and watermelon. Conversely, food like ginger, garlic, onion, pumpkin, squash, chestnuts, and walnuts tend to warm the body. These can be preserved and easily stored for longer periods over the course of the winter. We never used to be able to drive five minutes to the grocery store and buy pineapples in the winter. Just because we can, it doesn't mean we should. Eating cooling food when it's cold out upsets our body's thermal and energetic balance. Nature knows best, but when we don't follow her wisdom, we get sick.

Here in North America—Canada, to be exact—the native cantaloupe offers us the nutritional profile needed for our body and its climate. Likewise, the tropics provide the papaya for the same needs. Two highly dense nutritional fruits for two different climates and geographical regions. In the name of convenience, we jeopardize our health. Be mindful and follow these principles as we do our circadian rhythms and natural clocks. Those who live in tropical climates year round fair better when eating more fruit and vegetation, and less of animal flesh. In contrast, the Inuit and polar bear rely mainly on seal meat and seaweed for their sustenance. Climate has a strong bearing on our food choices and availability.

I invite you to start eating only fruit and vegetables that are in season. In Canada, cherries are in season in June and July, peaches in August, and apples in September and October. Research other produce that grow in your area. Produce is offered by nature to warm, cool and fatten us up for the changing seasons. It also gives us the correct nutritional profile to thrive in changing conditions. Natives hunt, kill and use all of the indigenous animal's resources, wasting nothing. They even pray for the safe passage of their Spirit into the Afterlife. Did you know that honey from local bees can treat one's allergies? It all relates to the floral source in question. Some claim that this is only effective within a twenty to thirty kilometre range. Get back to nature, honour it. Be an artist with your food, and eat the rainbow. The darker the food's colour, the more nutrients it has. Rotate your food options and be diverse. Try, and see what happens.

UNPLUG

Have you ever heard of Earthing, or grounding as some people refer to it? Earthing is similar to grounding your energy after a meditation or healing session. Before we started wearing rubber soled shoes, we naturally connected to the Earth. The Earth is abundant with negatively charged free-electrons. They're available to us when we connect with her directly. Free radicals are created in our system when we eat poorly, smoke, ingest pollutants, and exercise excessively. Negative ions are known for being a great antioxidant to remove these toxins. We are bombarded with electromagnetic radiation from computers, mobile phones, tablets, radio, the television, WiFi, and most anything that's plugged in. These fields disrupt the subtle energetic communications in our body.

The easiest way to ground yourself is to walk barefoot on grass or soil, anything in nature will conduct. If you are hardcore, get naked and bury yourself in a hole for twenty minutes. Swimming in a lake or ocean is a great way to absorb the healing properties of negative ions. More skin—more surface—more contact. This decreases inflammation and stress, you'll sleep a lot better too. Grounding offers an array of other benefits. More and more people are swearing by this method of pain management and overall well-being. Take off your shoes and socks, and give it a shot. Try hugging a tree.

Living unplugged is the best way to restore our health and vitality. In modern society this is difficult to do, unless we live far away from the city. Spend as much time as you can in nature. Go camping, or rent a cottage (preferably by water) as often as you can. Shut off your cell phone, clock radio, computer and all technology. This includes television and radio. Try going completely powerless. Did you know that you can regulate your serotonin and melatonin levels simply by going without artificial light for a month? You may love the city and all its amenities, but what you don't know is that it's slowly destroying your health and creating disease. It will do you good to get away from the rat race, the noise, and the sea of electro and physical pollution. Even if it's only for a few days or a week, you'll feel the difference. Start connecting with real interactions, not with web connections.

Our physical health is a result of our inner mental and emotional health. However, we have to be mindful of what we physically expose our body with. Challenge the safety of fluoride in tap water, wheat, coffee, alcohol, aluminum and mercury in vaccines, cell phones held close to the brain, microwaves, MSG and other chemicals in processed foods, chemotherapy and other pharmaceutical drugs, Tylenol and other painkillers, antidepressants, pesticides, GMO food, chemical fragrances, air fresheners (plug in), cleaning products, and the chem-trails that can be seen in the sky. It's not about being paranoid—research with an open mind. Look at both sides and decide for yourself.

THE SUN

Without the Sun of God there would be no life. Yet, over the last few decades we have been conditioned to fear it. The invention of sunglasses and sun blocking lotion have given us a false sense of safety. We should be afraid, not of the sun but of these fear-based innovations. They are a detriment to our health. Ever since sunblock became available many types of cancer have skyrocketed. Do you know that sunglasses block and filter essential light from entering our eyes? Our health is dependent on these solar rays. There is information, or light codes contained in this light. These solar codes enter through our skin and eyes. Typically, the lens in our eyes fracture the white light into the seven colours of the light spectrum. These hues enter the pineal gland and get passed on to the cells in the body. According to Andreas Moritz a medical intuitive and author, each beam of colour corresponds to different structures in the body. Red fortifies the blood, green assists in bile production, and so on. He believes the replacement of plastic lenses due to eye surgery may impede this process.

Ultra violet rays are required for the pineal gland to produce the stimulating hormone called melanocyte. When sunglasses block the light from entering our eyes, our brain thinks it's nighttime. The hormone melanin which is what protects us is not produced. To further jeopardize our risk of getting a skin disease such as cancer, we apply a toxic sunscreen. This lotion not only blocks essential vitamin D, but unnaturally prolongs the time we're exposed to the sun. There is a reason why our skin burns—it's telling us we've had enough! We are not supposed to be in the sun all day long. If you have fair skin then wear a hat, or expose yourself only at sunset and at sundown. Our skin is the largest organ of the body. Whatever you apply on it, you're basically eating. Would you eat sun tan lotion? Take a look at the ingredients. If a plant can die without light, what happens to us? What's the effect of constantly being under artificial light? Get outdoors as much as possible.

The sun's electromagnetic radiation is what charges our energetic field, our body, and its cells.

12

ENERGY LIFE FORCE

"If you want to find the secrets of the Universe, think in terms of energy, frequency and vibration."
—*Nikola Tesla*

THE ELECTROMAGNETIC SPECTRUM

Did you know that we can only see 0.0035% of the known electromagnetic scale? This is what we call visible light. Just because we can't see what's beyond this range doesn't mean it doesn't exist. Our physical senses aren't calibrated to these subtle energies. Yet, dogs and cats have a much greater perception. The electromagnetic spectrum is the range of the different types of waves which are positioned according to their frequency and wavelength. Electromagnetic radiation is the stream of photons that is emitted from electronic and natural sources. These travel in wave-like patterns, and the photons of each type contain either high or low amounts of energy. The lowest are the radio waves which have the longest wavelengths. Conversely, the Gamma rays have the highest amount of energy and the shortest wavelength. Imagine waving your hand in front of you with your palm positioned vertically, thumb up. Sway your hand slowly side to side to mimic the radio wave, like a dolphin's tail swimming. Now move it faster and tighten the distance and movement. This imitates the wavelengths of the gamma rays. The only difference between sound, heat, and light are the rates of vibration.

This can be proven if somehow we could hook up a device to a steel rod which can receive different rates of vibration. A slow vibration would first cause the rod to vibrate. As the vibration increases the rod would create sound. Initially, the tone would be low, then it would become loud and piercing as the pulsation increased. Eventually the sound would recede, and for a short time no physical evidence would be noticed. After some time, heat could be felt, getting hotter as the vibration increased. Eventually light would emanate from the heat, the rod would glow as it became red hot. The next stage thereafter would produce ultraviolet light, and other non-visible radiation would be emitted.

The following are the known electromagnetic waves starting from their longest to shortest frequencies: short and long radio waves, television, FM, microwave, infrared, visible light, ultraviolet light, X-ray and gamma-ray. Just because we can't see them doesn't mean they don't affect us. X-ray and ultraviolet radiation can have harmful effects on us physically. I believe that Life Force and Cosmic Rays resonate beyond the gamma-ray range. Scientists say that all matter is in a constant state of vibration.

BEYOND THE SPECTRUM

What if one day a device is created that can measure all the energy that is emanating from the Universe? Perhaps that day is upon us now. One frequency I haven't mentioned yet is the one that resides between the radio and microwave portion of the electromagnetic spectrum. I find it alarming that a signal that's so close to one that can cook food is being broadcast into the air. Although we can't see WiFi (We-Fry), it carries an unlimited amount of information. Without a device to decode it, proving its existence would be difficult. As we evolve, we can become the mechanism that distils the unseen, and limitless wisdom of the Universe.

We exist in a sea of energy much like fish do in water. Like the fish, we are unaware of this permeating Life Force which is sustaining us. There are many names for it: *Prana, Ki, Chi* and so forth. Our physical world appears real from our third-dimensional perspective. However, science tells us that everything is made up of empty space. Things feel solid because of an electric force. This force is dense, much like our physical body.

It contains similar amounts of negatively charged electrons and positively charged protons.

THE CHICKEN OR THE EGG?

There is a great debate on whether the chicken or the egg came first. Some may argue that the egg did, since dinosaurs laid them well before chickens.

This same question applies to all physical matter in physical creation. Which came first, the seed or the plant, the mother or the child?

Every physical form on this Earth plane has an energetic skeletal frame on which it's built on. Physical matter is held together vibrationally by an energetic blueprint. This electro-skeleton is constructed of sacred geometric shapes that are formed by the will of Source Energy. Before the chicken or its egg can be physically assembled, it has to be constructed non-physically in energetic form first. This applies to all things existing in our three-dimensional world. It's much like how CGI (Computer-Generated Imagery) is used to create realistic images in movies and in video games. The process uses a carefully constructed wireframe in which texture is built onto it to create a three-dimensional form. Have you ever built a papier-mâché craft in art class?

Whether you are an atheist or deeply religious, you must agree there is something beyond our scope of awareness that is accountable for initiating life. Some type of intelligence has to be at play here. There is an algorithm, a patterned sequence responsible for creating and sustaining our three-dimensional world. Humans do not create anything, we can only alter what is. We can transform wood, steel and the earth by means of heat, cooling, burning, and applying blunt force—all things are malleable. Chemistry shows us that we can add, remove or change any element or molecules of the known chemical and periodic tables. Could we not also alter these energetic structures and waveforms? First, we need to understand how matter is derived from pre-matter.

SACRED GEOMETRY

The study of Sacred Geometry explains how creation works on an energetic level. Briefly, sacred geometry is patterns and grids that are created by pure consciousness.

In the beginning there was nothing—no time or fixed distance. Source had to establish a point of reference by projecting its consciousness forward, from a single point into six directions. These trajectories consisted of equal distances: front, back, left, right, up and down. This process created lines which, when connected together, at their end points creates a sphere. Thus the hidden and true meaning of Adam's rib to create Eve. Lines are considered male, and circles (curves) female. After this motion is complete, Source's consciousness moves to the edge of the sphere and repeats this pattern again. After six spheres have been established or realized, one vortex motion is completed. The result is six spheres within one sphere. This formation is called the Seed of Life, which is the foundation of the creation of all physical matter. This process is the true meaning of God creating Life in six days, then resting on the seventh. When a second vortex motion is created, an additional six spheres are conceived. After the third vortex motion occurs, it gives rise to the Flower of Life. This pattern can be found etched in stone at sacred sites all around the Ancient World. Additional vortex patterns create the Fruit of Life.

The Egg of Life is derived from the seven circles from the Flower of Life. The shape of the Egg of Life is said to be the shape of a multicellular embryo in its first hours of creation. Nature uses this embryonic process to create life's living organisms. The Fruit of Life is an extension of the Egg of Life which gives birth to all the platonic solids and their corresponding elements. These solids are the energetic templates behind the creation of matter and the elements: Tetrahedron (fire), Octahedron (air), Hexahedron (Earth), Icosahedron (water), and dodecahedron (ether). When pure Life Force is modified it becomes ether, which, when condensed, becomes the four physical elements of Earth, Air, Water and Fire.

A HINDU PERSPECTIVE

Life Force (Prana) is the great sea of cosmic energy of life itself, it is omnipresent and permeates all space. When it is transformed it becomes a substance called Akasha. When this is modified, it becomes ether. As the ether vibrates it creates different vibrations called the Tattwas. When these condense or crystallize they form the four physical elements of Air, Fire, Water and Earth—in that order. First appeared the space, from which appeared the sequence of the four physical elements. Hindu philosophy states that Akasha (ether) is the fifth substance. Maya is the Sanskrit word for illusion. It suggests that everything we see in the physical world is not actually real. This concept is retold again in modern day science fiction by movies such as *The Matrix*. We are living in a projected virtual reality; a hologram. The goal of our journey is to realize this ultimate truth and transcend its Maya.

KEYLONTIC SCIENCE

There exists units of consciousness of potential which are called Partiki. Science hasn't discovered these minute units of matter… yet. These units are both electronic and magnetic in nature. They pulsate between unity and fission, alternating between positive and negative states. Partiki form Partiki-grids, which in turn form Keylons. These are sequences of complex structures, or units of consciousness that group and move together to create crystalline structures. These are the base of the form-holding templates that create the Morphogenic Field. Keylons compose the frequency fields of sound and light upon which the entire Cosmic Matrix is structured. They are also what create the Morphogenetic template upon which Chakras, DNA, genetic coding, and the physical body is built on. Keylons are electro-tonal and electromagnetic energy; they are the initial step in the transition from pure consciousness to pre-matter substance.

Imagine if you could influence the Keylon codes. You would be able to activate and alter DNA, genetics, cellular memory, and even change physical formations.

IN ENGLISH

Are you confused? If so, here it is simply: thoughts, emotions and sound are vibrational waveforms that program the morphogenic field/templates/matrix/grid/hologram or whatever you want to call it. When an intention is held vibrationally, the template is created energetically and is ready to manifest in the physical. This is similar to the papier-mâché and CGI analogy mentioned before. You are the programmer of what you experience. Be mindful of the thoughts and words you use to program your reality. All the more, be mindful of what it is that's programming you. Change the energy structure—change the physical mass. Simply put, thought precedes matter.

DIMENSIONS

The physical world is built within the construct of time and space, it is formed in the third dimension. The nature of the physical world is one that is dual. The sun goes up, and it goes down, there is light and darkness, hot and cold, and so forth. Duality and dimensions are covered in greater detail in my book *The Ultimate Journey*. Here is a brief overview of how energy is and can be directed within each dimension.

There are many levels, or dimensions which are superimposed upon each other. Due to the density of physical matter in the Third Dimension, altering it takes massive amounts of focused energy. We need to harness and direct Life Force electromagnetically by combining and willing both our thoughts and emotions. Physical action is required to get things moving. We don't yet have the capability of Master Yoda to be able to lift an X-wing fighter out of the water. Manifesting in the fourth dimension can be accomplished solely with focused thought and emotion, without taking action. Manifesting in the fifth dimension only requires centralized thought. Manifesting begins beyond the fifth dimension, then descends downward through the denser realms until eventually, it solidifies in the physical. This only happens when all aspects are aligned and energetically sustained.

A snail was in a bar having a beer. Suddenly two turtles came in, roughed him up and stole his wallet. When the authorities asked what had happened, the snail said, "I don't know, it all happened so fast." Physical matter is denser than the non-physical, it resonates and responds at a slower rate. As a result, we feel like the snail. We become impatient when things don't happen right away. Manifesting wouldn't be so difficult if we weren't up against physical density, and our past conditioning.

RADIO AND BROADCAST TOWERS

We are transmitters and receivers of vibration, just like a broadcast tower and a radio. Our thoughts and emotions are what send and decode these waves. As previously mentioned, when we send out a signal non-physically, it is sent into the morphogenic field. This is where the energetic templates begin to form. When we hold on to and focus this vibration it expands and attracts similar resonating energy. The resonance of similar vibrations are what create the synchronicity, luck and opportunities that happen along the way. This is how the Law of Attraction works. What you send out also activates in others, inspired thoughts and impulses which create magnetic attraction. Only cooperating energies respond, we can't impose our will on another. Everyone has free will, forcing our intentions on someone who doesn't share them is manipulative and a violation. Heads up to all the practicing witches out there.

When a tuning fork is calibrated to 261.6 Hz which is the key of Middle C, and a tone generator or instrument is set off to oscillate at the same cycle, the tuning fork would vibrate in unison. I believe that increasing the volume or intensity of the oscillation would expand its range. If there were other tuning forks present with each calibrated to a different Hz (Hertz - the measurement of a waveform's cycle per second) none of them would resonate. Whatever our vibration is, is what we attract to us, and send to others. Each of us have a set point in our vibrational output, much like a baseball player's batting average. We can use the example of a heating and cooling system. When we set the thermostat to a desired temperature, the system responds accordingly. If the thermostat is set to 68F/20C and the surrounding air temperature is colder, the heater kicks in and gradually warms to that setting. Conversely, if the temperature is hotter than what the thermostat is set to, the cooling system kicks in.

Changing our vibration can take time. Our thoughts and beliefs have to be recalibrated and aligned. We attract what we are set to, not to what we want—our habits haven't yet been set to the desired vibration. The intent with this book is to reprogram our vibrational set point, to create a new blueprint. We are the sum total of what we vibrate.

CASTING SPELLS AND DRAWING SWORDS

It has been said that the pen is mightier than the sword, however there is something much greater than the blade. The Druids used to make their magic wands out of holly wood. Likewise, Hollywood casts their magic on us through the silver screen. We also have a magic wand that can cast spells, it is through our words—our *sword*. Words are not just elements of speech or writing, they make sounds which direct and move energy. Whenever you speak or spell words, you cast these vibrations out into the Universal sea of energy. You can heal another by raising their energy, or hurt them by stabbing them. Is your *sword* one of truth, or of deception?

Do you believe in magic? We may be led to believe that miracles only come from God, and that magic is evil, and from Satan. Countless miracles happen every day, from the marvel of a baby being born, to a tiny seed growing into a mighty tree. Long ago, those that understood science and chemistry could fool people into believing so. Magicians use deception and sleight of hand to create the illusion of it. *Is there such a thing as real magic?* Do you know that we cast spells every day? We are magicians and alchemists with the power to create, and also to destroy—the power to spell and dis-spell energy. We are unknowing wizards unconsciously directing unseen powers. The very Law of Attraction is the ability to attract into our lives whatever we focus on. We achieve this by drawing energy toward us like a magnet. Have you noticed that the word magic is derived from mag*net*ic. What are you magnetically drawing toward yourself?

When communicating with another, it's very important that what you say matches your intention. In terms of vibration, thoughts and feelings are the same as when speaking them. Since the Universe responds to vibration only, it can't be fooled. Furthermore, our subconscious can't decipher between what is real and what isn't. So there is no difference between conjuring up an experience via the senses, or by our focused imagination. We can use this to our advantage.

CHANGING MATTER

You may have read about the renowned Japanese researcher, Masaru Emoto. He discovered that water changes in relation to the information it is given. He gave the water data, froze it, then photographed how the crystals formed. Mr. Emoto would put water in vials and attach a label with written words on them, such as love and hate. After they froze, he took photos of each droplet. To his surprise, and after countless attempts, he noticed something miraculous. The water infused with love produced beautiful crystal formations. However, the water subjected to hate, fool, and other negative words produced incomplete and unpleasing formations. Water is an element that's more sensitive to our thoughts than are other solid forms. If mental energy can be directed to a substance, could we not also be affected and altered? We are made of mainly water. If this is true, then our self-talk and emotions will affect us, too. What about the words written on our shirts, tattoos on our skin, and environment? Be mindful of what clothes you wear and what symbols you engrave on your skin. Keep them positive.

I once blew out a car window with intense rage. There was no physical contact. It was all energetic, directed by intense emotion. I share this experience in *The Ultimate Journey*. A charged up emotion can be a very powerful force. Similarly, if you align sound to vibrate specifically, you can shatter almost anything.

SOUND

In the beginning was the word, the word was sound. Sound turns energy into matter by forming the sacred geometrical templates. When we think or feel thoughts and emotions we set off a sound wave, or vibration. This affects all matter, including our cells and organs of our body. There have been many experiments done by placing sand on a metal plate and vibrating it at different pitches using a tone generator. The result is amazing; varying shapes and formations form in accordance with each tone. The study of the effects that frequencies have on matter is called cymatics. In other words, the translation of sound vibrations into visible patterns. This makes one wonder how the quality of music and environment actually affects us. We know that every thought and emotion sends out a frequency into the ether. We also know how we are casting spells with the words we use. Energy itself is neither negative or positive, it's all in how it is directed. What kinds of words do you use when you think or speak?

Let's do an experiment. Feel the energy of the words, "I can't." Now feel the difference of, "It is possible, I am capable, and I am worth it." One feels empowering, the other doesn't. If you're feeling down and don't feel good enough to say, "I can!" with conviction, then you have to build up to it. Like changing the setting on the thermostat. Changing the energy behind a word or feeling sometimes requires doing so in baby steps. The best way to do this is to look for the next best feeling or word that is closest to your present state of being. "I can't" can be slightly raised energetically by asking, "I wonder how I can." Keep searching for the next best feeling and thought until you eventually can say with absolute feeling, "I can, and I will!"

Once again, consider the difference between, "Sorry I'm late" to "Thank you for waiting. I need to ~ I choose. I want ~ I intend. ~ I hate ~ I prefer. I hope ~ I trust. It's too hard ~ A challenge that I haven't overcome yet." Can you see how powerful changing the vibration (sound) of words can be?

CHANGING YOUR ENERGETIC VOCABULARY

Etymology is the study of the origin of words. Our English language is based on this structure, consider them to be energetic templates. Words and the sounds they create are energy patterns. Pay attention to those you use and which are said to you.

Words to start using:
I can, I am, I'm excited for, it feels good to know, It's coming and will be ready for me at the perfect moment, everything always works out great for me and happens in perfect time, I am always in the right place at the right time, everything works out better than I imagined, I trust and listen to my higher guidance, I love feeling excited because I know it's coming, this is so awesome, this is the greatest day ever, my Highest Self has already become what I desire, it's coming and will arrive at the perfect moment, I love refining my desire with every experience I create—I am grateful for each one, I am open and ready to receive, all is well.

Words to remove, and their alternatives:
I have to, need to, must, change to, "I choose." Stop saying, "Would have, should have, and could have." We need to own our choices, what's done is done. The words *always* and *never* are rigid and absolute. Be in the present moment, allow it to unfold as it will, this takes pressure off the future. Instead of saying, "But" use, "And"—as but discredits everything said before it. Remove all these words immediately: "I can't, I'll try, it's too hard, I have no time, maybe." Think twice before saying or texting things like FML (fuck my life) even as a joke.

We can tell what we are manifesting simply by what is showing up in our lives. Observe your life around money, your relationships, your health and career. Have you noticed that negative people draw to them other negative people and circumstances? There are those who are so happy and go-lucky that everything consistently goes good for them. You may consider yourself to be a great person and wonder why bad things keep happening to you. You may indeed be a good person, though probably have a crappy vibration. Sometimes the nicest people are the ones who are trying too hard. Their confidence may be low and is what's attracting bad shit to happen. Energy doesn't lie. We create our reality well before it happens. Some claim it takes two to five years for a disease to manifest in the body brought on by negative thoughts and emotions. Careful of how you are laying out the energetic template of an upcoming event, or vacation. The quality of your magnetism will draw on to you the appropriate experience. When you continue complaining about something, you keep that vibration active within you.

We want to create empowering patterns and pathways with proper programming. Start paying attention to the words you use in your thoughts and how you express them. Mantras and affirmations are the programs that create our reality. When you set intentions, they have to resonate with you. Too often we use an other's words or clichés, these become mechanical and irrelevant. Reciting words without believing them leads to disillusionment. This is dangerous and where many feel betrayed by the promises of the LOA (Law Of Attraction). When our Soul expresses itself with passion, then we see results quickly.

Break the spell and take control.

13

CONTROLLING AND DIRECTING ENERGY

Now that you know how energy works, you'll need to learn how to harness and direct it to create what you want. The only way to do this is in the present moment. The mind must be conquered before you can take control of anything. An undisciplined mind dwells in either a memory, or an expectation—it's in a constant mode of trying to escape the now. It can never accomplish this feat because it's always now. No matter how hard it tries to avoid or deny what is happening, it will always fail. The mind designates a timeline, it divides the now, thinking needs time and space. It measures time and events linearly, or sequentially. Moments are conceived and categorized as having happened, happening, or have yet to happen. The mind believes that whatever has happened in the past defines its identity. It also believes that something better is waiting for it beyond the present moment. Worry, fear, and anxiety are the result of projecting into the future. The fear of what may happen. Guilt, regret, and shame are the result of dwelling in the past. The undisciplined mind continuously relives what has happened, and in most cases keeps resisting it. This paradox is the cause of our inability to let things go.

Why does the mind desperately avoid the now moment? Because, like the ego, it cannot exist within it. The ego has no identity in the present moment, all of its stories are irrelevant. Since it's always now, the mind/ego will forever be searching, never finding what it's looking for. We are Divine Spirit, first and foremost—we are timeless and undefinable. Time and space don't apply. Our experiential awareness passes through an experience, but it is not that. Moving through an event is like placing your hand in flowing water, the water you feel passing is never the same. Yet, your hand is still and unchanged, it's in the present moment. The passing water represents the passage of time. This can also be related as the Light Source that passes through the lens of an old film projector. We are the light, the timeless, and the unaltered non-physical form. The film passing through represents time and the passing of life's events. You can't judge the quality of the present with anything that has happened in the past. Nor can you enhance it by anything that may or may not happen in the future. Stop being a slave who waits for a future event for their salvation, or happiness. This includes waiting for a condition, an authority, or a person. Embrace the now, cut the chains of memories past. The future hasn't happened yet, so how can you control what doesn't exist?

If tomorrow never comes, when will you do the things you want and love to do? Your future is dictated by how you feel, and what you do right now—no exceptions. Similarly, your present now is a result of how you thought and felt in the past. When you are attached to the mind everything matters, but ultimately nothing does. This puts a different twist on being out of your mind, for it has no bearing on the present moment. Now is all there is ~ embrace it fully.

A RADICAL SHIFT IN PERSPECTIVE

The now moment is the empty container. Time and space is the canvas which allows experiences to unfold. Nothing can exist without the void. The empty space in the cup is where the water is held.

"The music is not in the notes, but in the silence between them."
—French composer Achille-Claude Debussy

The space between these letters is what allows you to see the words. We get caught up in the identification of what we perceive to be real. If you remove your arm, are you still you? Of course, because you are still you without an arm. You can continue imagining this until only your torso remains. Yet *you* still remain. When you drive, are you the car? Or are you just the driver? Likewise, you are not the body. You are not your Halloween costume. When you say, "My car, my body," you are only perceiving them as yours. What you observe you cannot be, because the perceiver cannot be perceived. We are pure consciousness and pure awareness, everything else is observed. Who is watching the perceiver? When there is no one left who can discern…you are that. You are the space and the silence behind all things.

Our ego is a collection of thoughts and experiences fused together to create a character. *I think therefore I am*, becomes the mind, the car, the body, and the ego. How do we begin to live in the present moment without getting caught up in the ego mind? The way out, is the way in. First you have to be aware of the space or the emptiness that is behind everything. Then observe whatever is happening in, and occupying that space. Watch without analyzing, simply allow it to be. Events will arise, then subside, just like the waves of the ocean. There is a beginning, a middle, and an end. Start becoming aware of the silence and space behind everything you perceive. Observe the emptiness behind and between your thoughts. If you are currently sitting, pay attention to the space around your body. Feel the emptiness around the chair, and the space that it occupies. Feel how the chair is supporting you.

The mind uses thought to interpret what the eyes and ears perceive. This is a low frequency of perception. Consciousness, on the other hand, uses a higher level of perception which is beyond the conflict of duality. Pure awareness allows what it observes without resisting, judging or comparing. The mind is what desires to narrate the moment. It tries to enhance, remove and add to what it doesn't like. Pure consciousness is empty and silent, but is filled with all possibilities that exist simultaneously. When you are not in consciousness, you are in mind. The intellect invests in a narrative, which drives its desire to defend these stories it creates. In pure awareness, nothing is taken personally. How can anyone question or ridicule something that is not real?

THE RESTLESS MIND

Once there was a devotee who asked his Guru how to levitate like a Spiritual Master. The Guru told his student that he had to meditate for one hour every night and chant a special mantra. "After one month you will come back to me and I will teach you the next step." "Wow," he thought, and thanked his Guru. Excited, the pupil headed for the door. "Wait," said the Guru, "I almost forgot to tell you something very important. When you chant the special mantra, whatever you do, do not think of a monkey!"

The student went home and immediately went to meditate. Before starting, he mentally affirmed to himself, "I must not think of a monkey." As much as he tried not to, all he could think of were monkeys. The more he resisted the greater they were dancing around in his mind. A month later he went back to his Guru. With anger he barked at him, "You told me that all I had to do was meditate and chant the mantra, but all I could do was think about monkeys!" The Guru smiled and replied, "I wanted to teach you that your mind is not ready yet, it's untrained and restless. Unless you have mastery over your thoughts, you cannot achieve any success."

The ego/mind believes it can control a situation by thinking around it. This is the trap. The Universe works vibrationally and only responds to the energy we are resonating. What we think about we bring about, this applies to our thoughts and emotions. Whether we complain about something or appreciate it, we are sending forth that energy pattern into the Morphogenetic Field. Energetically speaking, trying not to think of a monkey is thinking of a monkey. By bringing something into your attention, you are sending out its vibration—regardless if you want to think about it or not. If I told you not to think of a white dog on a skateboard, would you not think it? Similarly, don't focus on what you don't want, or fear. You will attract it. We've become slaves to our mind. Being thought-less is actually a good thing.

CONTROLLING THE MIND AND SENSES: THE CHARIOT

In The Bhagavad-Gita (Hindu Scripture) Krishna tells Arjuna about the Chariot. The *chariot* represents the *body*, the *charioteer* is the *intellect* and the *reins* represent the *mind*. The five *horses* that pull the chariot represent the *five senses*. The passenger that sits behind, is the Soul. In most people, the mind has been taken over and is controlled by the senses. The horses desire pleasurable things—the mind isn't exercising restraint on the senses. The intellect submits to the pull from the mind, and the Soul has no control of where the chariot is heading. It's like walking five large dogs who are out of control. Who's walking who?

Typically, the human mind has an average of fifty to eighty-thousand thoughts a day. Up to seventy percent of them are negative. This averages to about three thousand per hour, or fifty per minute. That's almost one each second. The intellect has to reclaim control over the mind, which has become of slave to the senses. Although this may be difficult, it's not impossible.

This is like taming a wild horse. Eventually with determination you will be able to mount it. We have to hold the reins firmly and control the mind. We must keep at it, it's like building a muscle.

A powerful way to do this is through Yoga (which literally means union). The purpose is to connect to our true nature (to Source). We don't have to do yoga poses (asanas) to overcome the mind, although it helps. Discipline (self-control) can accomplish this.

CONCENTRATION

As a child, did you ever play with a magnifying glass? If you have, then you've most likely used the sun to burn holes into things. You would hold the glass up and focus the sunlight into a localized point. The more it was centralized the hotter it got. Likewise, concentrating means taking your mind off of many things, and focusing it on one. We live in a world full of distractions and overstimulation, forcing us to multitask. This scatters our attention which disrupts our ability to focus. We have no discipline, or the chance to develop it. How can we when we're perpetually distracted?

Our nervous system is overstimulated by neurotic thinking, pleasure seeking, and media of each type. Boredom arises when there is nothing available to fill the void—we're afraid to be still and silent. Have you noticed that those who don't know what to say are the ones who talk the most? They jump from subject to subject, and can't stay still. They're consistently trying to make others happy and fit in by editing their speech and behaviour. These people are exhausting and difficult to be around. When thoughts and emotions become erratic they override one's discretion, and cause their body to become unsteady. If you've ever seen anyone in deep concentration you'd notice that they are still. Their eyes are focused, they don't blink, and their breath is slow. On the contrary, one may appear to be in a deep state of concentration, but are in fact distracted, and may actually be tuned out.

THE BOOB TUBE

Boob is a slang word that denotes a stupid person. This may be why a woman's breast is called that, as it renders some men dense. Similarly, television reduces our ability to concentrate. A better name would be tell-a-vision, or tell-lies-vision—it's not called a TV *program* by accident. In 1969 an experiment was conducted by Herbert Krugman. Through many trials he noticed that after one minute of watching the boob tube a person's brain waves shifted from Beta to Alpha. When the person stopped watching, their brain state gradually returned back to Beta (if you remember, this state is associated with active and logical thinking). This means that by watching television, our ability to think logically drops off.

We literally tune out as we tune in. You can see this when children watch their favourite shows—their eyes are fixated on the screen, mouths are open, and they appear to be in a zombified state. Not everyone is affected the same; nevertheless, it does influence everyone in some capacity. I'm sure advertisers know full well that when potential consumers are in a passive and suggestible state that it doesn't hurt their sales. During this mental state, they can anchor the benefits associated to their product and implant triggers that can easily be activated. How do you respond when you see the golden arches of a famous fast food restaurant?

MEDITATION FOR CONCENTRATION

In chapter seven, I shared a meditation to help calm the mind down. A quiet mind reduces the static caused by thoughts. This allows us to hear the whispers of our intuition. Chapter four discussed practicing mental toughness by consciously delaying pleasure. That alone isn't enough—we need to still the mind, and control the senses. This is achieved by concentrated focus.

Many people don't know how to meditate. Some find it too hard. If one's mind is like a monkey, then this will be the case. Nonetheless, it's impossible to stop all thoughts—we can't stop the mind from thinking. We can, however, learn to quiet it down and allow its chatter to recede into the background.

When our senses are withdrawn inward, thought can be focused, sustained and directed however it's desired. Whether you seek spiritual or material pursuits, mastery over your thoughts and senses is essential.

CONCENTRATION STRATEGIES

Before you begin, turn off all tech and limit any possible distractions. Begin by breathing deeply and slowly watching your breath enter and exit your mouth, or nose. Get into a relaxed state, refer to the meditation in chapter seven. Becoming aware of your breath, posture and the present moment will help you get into the zone quickly. I suggest practicing these exercises fifteen minutes or longer every day.

The Lake

The following is an effective technique for controlling the mind. You are the witness watching it. You are the observer of the thoughts that appear; they don't define you. Close your eyes and imagine that your mind is a vast lake in front of you. Each thought is a ripple, or wave. Watch them arise, ebb and flow. Make no effort to control your thoughts, they are like waves in the ocean. Simply witness them. Do not engage, offer no resistance or narrative.

Imagine that each thought is like a stone thrown into the calmest lake causing ripples to circle outward. Fix your attention on the entry point of the splash. Hold your focus on the mark, not on the expanding ripples. Mentally affirm, "I am not the mind,

I am the witness." Eventually, you will have less identification with your thoughts. You will become their master, no longer their slave. As you do so with emerging thoughts, allow bodily desires and sensations to arise and then subside. Awareness of the breath is very important during this process.

The Candle

Place a lit candle on a table one to two feet away from you, preferably at eye level, or slightly downward. Darken the room if possible. With your back straight, arms relaxed and hands placed on your lap, gaze at the flame steadily. I suggest gazing for no less than a few minutes. Do your best to keep from blinking. Take deep breaths while keeping your body as still as you can. Stay mindful of your breathing, let it happen naturally. When your eyes get tired, or when you feel the time is right, close them. You will see the image of the flame dancing in your mind's eye. Direct this light to the space between your eyebrows (third eye). Hold it there for as long as you can. If you can't see the flame, stare at the candle again. Repeat this as needed to sustain the image. If you feel inspired, guide the light downward to the heart centre and hold it there.

The Apple Of Your Eye

We don't have to use a candle, we can use any object. Try this with an apple. Look at it for a minute or so, longer if you want. Move it around in your hand, view it from every angle. Smell it, and notice all of its textures, colour, skin, and so on. Does it still have a stem? Notice the size of the sepal (that's the bottom part). When you are ready, close your eyes and recreate the experience.

Focus on the space between the eyebrows. Practice holding the vision of the apple, rotate it around. Bring back its fragrance, texture, and if you can, imagine how it tastes. Bite into it and hear the crunch, feel the juice squirting out and hitting your face. Be in the moment. If you need to, open your eyes, look at the apple again and repeat the process.

Mantras can help you keep your mind focused when you don't have a candle available. These are words which are repeated that pacify the mind so it doesn't wander. Mantras are magic spells that direct energy into the Morphogenic field—they also help reprogram the mind. Not everyone is lucky enough to be born with a photographic memory. Some may never have a perfect ability to crystallize an image in their mind's eye. Nonetheless, it can be developed. Like building any muscle, you need to keep exercising it.

During the course of the day, call to your mind's eye the images that you practiced with. This will help you build your ability to concentrate and dramatically improve your focus. After a while you'll be able to hold on to a picture, scene, and even sensations. As you progress, you can challenge yourself to take it further. Turn in into a movie, add a soundtrack, and even brighten the colour.

HEART AND MIND

There are countless references between what the heart wants and what the mind thinks. Ask any person going through a romantic hardship. The general perception is that the mind is responsible for our thoughts, and the heart our feelings. Most times they don't cooperate. Thoughts are *electrical* and emotions are *magnetic*. When they merge, emotion is created (thought in motion). E-motion becomes a magnet that attracts similar frequencies onto itself. The merging of thought and feeling creates and becomes a powerful *electromagnet* of attraction. This happens when belief and desire align, they become charged with passion.

When we are in heart awareness, we feel the emotion of love and a connectedness to all things. This is a sign that we're in alignment with our Higher Self. When we feel separated from it, we feel fear which signals a state of resistance. These emotions include anger, hate, jealousy, guilt, shame, and so on. When referring to Love, I'm not talking about the kind you feel when your heart flutters toward a lover. There is a difference between conditional and Unconditional Love. Conditional love is a polarized emotion that arises from the ego. It is dual in nature, and shares an opposing emotion called hate. This type of love has to be earned on certain conditions and expectations being met, whether they are unconscious or not. Conditional love is unstable, limited and fleeting, which leads to doubt and insecurities. If our partner complies we love them, if they don't we push them away.

Unconditional Love has no opposite polarity. It's inherent within us, there's no need to search for it. There aren't any requirements, no qualifications. Unconditional Love is free, it's our Divine Source—it's who we are. Unconditional Love is the most powerful force in existence. No amount of darkness can extinguish its light. Yet, the smallest amount of light can singe away the darkness. This means that all we have to do is align with our heart. No other action is needed.

The mind is dual, the brain has two hemispheres. The intellect quickly gets confused in the web of its own changing thoughts. The mind forgets things and is very restless, it can't be relied on. Our heart is singular, it is fixed and stable. It doesn't suffer from regret or worry from the past and future, it resides in the present moment. The heart bypasses the neurosis of the mind. Sometimes, there is no sense in *sense*. Many studies show that the brain actually receives signals from the heart.

The longest journey is for our awareness to travel from the mind, to the heart.

HEART AND MIND TECHNIQUE

Earlier we learned that Life Force condenses into the four physical elements of Air, Fire, Water and Earth. There are seven energy centres located along the spine of our body called chakras. The lower ones which are the root, sacral and solar, represent emotional energy. They're depicted with warm colours ascending in the order of red, orange and yellow. They also represent the elements of Earth, water and fire. The higher chakras are the throat, third eye, and crown, which represent thought energy. Their colours are cooler and consist of blue, indigo and violet. Ether is represented in the throat chakra, the seat of consciousness is the third eye centre, and our connection to cosmic energy is via the crown chakra. The heart chakra is the bridge between both, containing the warmth of emotion, and the coolness of thought. The yellow of the sacral that is blended with blue of the throat makes the green of the heart.

Focus on the point between the eyebrows, or as known as the third eye chakra. Hold the vision of what you desire here like a laser beam. Breathe inward and visualize energy being drawn downward from the top of your head. Imagine that this white light is coming from hundreds of feet above. As it passes through the third eye, envision the energy passing through the throat centre (ether). Then downward into the heart (air), then down to the lower chakras of (fire, water and Earth). As you exhale, visualize red energy being drawn up from deep within the Earth, up through the lower chakras and into your heart. This will animate the chakras which will send these codes out into your energetic field (aura). Your third eye and heart centres are what focus and charge your auric field into a powerful electromagnet.

A simpler approach would be to hold the image firmly of whatever you want in your mind's eye. Fill your heart an intense feeling of exhilaration. The only thing that gets in the way is a lack of focus, thoughts, and emotions.

We don't create solely by action, we do so by vibration. It is the loving vibration that inspires us to take the proper action. Mindless action and brute force get you nowhere fast. A sustained will and a charged heart can accomplish anything.

14

ENERGY FLOW

I trust that you now better understand how energy works, and are beginning to learn how to control it. In this section, you will understand how it flows.

The physical and the non-physical are intertwined. The outer is a representation of the inner. Energy, like water, needs to flow, or it will stagnate. When any current is obstructed, it stops circulating and resistance builds. This creates tension, which leads to all sorts of difficulties. Something is either in flow, or it is not. Don't confuse integration with stagnation. Sometimes, things need to dissolve or assimilate before they can begin regenerating and start moving again. In terms of energy flow, the stagnation that can accumulate has to be cleared so it doesn't block the pathway. The river may still run even if there are obstacles in its way. They may slow it down a little, but if there are too many obstructions, there will be considerable restriction. Energy works the same way. Sadly, we've become little beavers building physical, mental, and emotional dams that are blocking energy from flowing freely within and around us.

When you send an intention, you create an energy stream that connects you to it. This pathway leads you to your desired target which is waiting in the Mesomorphic field. It's up to you how fast you want to get there. Imagine that you're on a cosmic canoe in the river of life. Do you surrender to the current, or paddle against it? We have been taught to fight and resist the flow. There is a belief that only dead fish go with the flow. Have you ever walked in a room and felt the tension in the air? Or, that something felt off? An argument may have happened, a death, or a very erratic person may have just lost their shit. You may have sensed the imprints left behind as a result. Objects that sit for long periods can collect and hold energy which can become stagnant. I suggest getting rid of articles that are no longer congruent with your present energetic state. These may be carrying the vibration of old, limiting and negative people, or experiences. This includes old love letters, gifts, objects and clothes from former lovers, family and friends who no longer add value to your life. You can't move forward if you're stuck in the past.

I'm not suggesting you throw everything out, or shun everyone you know that isn't on your sailboat. Nor do you need to dump your favourite throw pillows because you've had negative house guests sitting on your couch.

According to ancient Inca Wisdom, there is no "bad energy". The concept suggests that energy is either dense, or it's light. This means it's good, or varying degrees of less good. We can remove and displace stagnant energy simply through banging or shaking an object, or opening a window and placing it out into the fresh air and sunshine. If you move into a new house, you can use sage to purify the space. Washing and painting also works well. This is why some who are sensitive to energy will not buy used clothing, jewellery, or antiques that belonged to other people. No one wants a possessed Annabelle doll in their home.

THE PITY PARTY

Do you like throwing parties? Some do, especially pity parties. This isn't a celebration at all; instead it's an observance of failure and sadness. Empathic people are sensitive to an other's energy, and often become prey to those seeking attention or sympathy. Don't tolerate this behaviour in yourself, or from others. There is no better way to lower and stagnate your vibration than to be ungrateful, negative and feeling sorry for yourself. Stay away from energy vampires and pity-partiers. If you get an invite, don't accept. You will get sucked dry, and become tired and sick. When afflicted with the "poor me" virus, you will feel like you're wearing an extremely heavy housecoat. The tapestry woven by negative emotions and limiting beliefs will leave you feeling weighed down and powerless. This heavy robe will rob you of all motivation. Take it off and stop moping—snap out of it. This is where anger would be a positive energy to channel. Say, "No! I am a powerful Spirit that isn't going to give in to this bullshit of a story!"

SHIFT, OR LOSE IT

Are you ready to break up the stagnation? Now is the time to stir up the shift, and plunge those clogged blocks. Let go of the old crap that's holding you back. The first thing to do is change your posture, and start breathing deeply. Oxygen is a rich source of *Life Force*. We can energize our bodies just by the breath. Try it now. Take a deep breath all the way in, and hold it for a second or two. Now exhale, and shout, "*Yes*" or, "*Woohoo!*" Clap your hands, or throw your fist in the air. Move your body, shake, dance and get funky.

When we short-circuit our old wiring, we create new possibilities. We open ourselves up to fresh ideas and new experiences. There is no way we can change our emotional state if we keep our head down and our shoulders slumped. The next time you feel sorry for yourself, STOP and stir up some shift. Look around and see what you can be grateful for. If all else fails, go to sleep. Karma can't affect us when we're sleeping. Clean the slate, tomorrow is a brand new day. We have to be careful that we don't keep everything inside. By allowing the pressure to build, you may blow a fuse. Unfortunately, we don't have a circuit breaker in our body. Overloading its circuits can lead to stress or cause a nervous breakdown. Get out of your old boring routines, and try new things. Be a child again. Don't let superstition, fear or laziness lock you into a routine. Life is gonna happen regardless—you can't control it. Embrace the moment, InJoy it.

Go for a run, or jog on the spot. Sing your favourite song, or play it loud. Meet your friends for some karaoke. Awaken your inner child, play hide and seek, buy an adult colouring book, jump on a swing, or play a new board game. Call your friends and have a guys/girls night out. Book a trip, ride a bike, lift some weights, or get a new haircut. Learn to cook new and exotic food. Try yoga, take an art class, anything. The list is endless. *What can you think of?* If you try any of these, you'll inevitably feel a little, or even a lot better instantly.

CLEANING HOUSE

Did you know that presently, the U.S. has a twenty-two billion dollar a year industry that caters to the storing of unused junk? Why do we believe that having more is better? Freedom and success isn't defined by how much crap one has. We horde scraps of the Earth and deny ourselves the riches of the Universe. Before you can move into a new house, you have to first empty the contents of your current home. One strategy that helps entice new home buyers is called staging. This is where clutter is removed to reveal a more inviting space. We don't need extra stuff, all it does is block energy from flowing. A busy external landscape leads to a busy and conflicted mind. Non-energetically speaking, plain aesthetics makes visual sense, too. Out of sight, calmer mind.

If you haven't used something in the last year, chances are you won't any time soon. I invite you to clean your house or living space of things you don't use anymore. There will be items, of course, that are seasonal, personal, and valuable which are best kept. Throwing away things that carry sentimental value can be very difficult. What these items do is keep active the memories they represent. If these echoes prevent you from living your life fully in the present moment, they aren't adding value to your life. Sell or donate them to those who can benefit. You can also call the junk removal companies. Chuck the junk. Besides being visually oppressive, clutter blocks energy.

Areas in your home to consider purging include: the basement, storage and locker, garage, shed, backyard, closets, drawers, cupboards, boxes, attic, guest room, bathrooms, kitchen, bedroom, and anything that holds stuff. In your *kitchen*, clear old spices, cookbooks, appliances, miracle gadgets that don't work, worn out dishware, pots, pans, glasses and cutlery. Reorganize the drawers and cupboards, remove old vitamins, expired drugs, empty the freezer and fridge of old food and condiments. Consider buying new items.

In your *closet*, clear out old clothes, drawers and filing cabinets with ten-year-old pay stubs. In your *bathroom* and *shower* throw away any old products like shampoo, deodorant and toiletries; if you need, buy new bath towels. Clear your home of half-used paint cans and toxic cleaning products. Donate books and trinkets that may be crowding your shelves and TV stand. Recycle and shred mail and documents that are out of date. In your *foyer* clear away old shoes, jackets, gloves, hats, scarves and so on. Clean your car, and garage. Pick one room at a time, rearrange the furniture, paint or clean walls, smudge, spray essential oils, shake area rugs, pillows, wash blankets towels, and so forth. If it's not too cold outside, open the windows and let the sun and fresh air in. This process can get addictive; you may get carried away and even want to renovate. Whichever you choose, make it visually streamline and pleasant to look at.

WHITE ELEPHANTS

Your *bedroom* should be clear both visually and electromagnetically. You don't want your bedroom to be a toxic wasteland overgrown with technology. Remove everything that is plugged in. This means WiFi routers, computers, televisions, clock radios and so forth. You'll feel so much better—not to mention getting quality sleep. While you're at it, detox your tech devices. Delete useless emails, texts, photos, and apps you no longer need.

Stagnant thoughts and emotions also keep you stuck in the past. These patterns and endless loops tie us to our previous hurts and stories. This is why it's good to burn old love letters and photos from former lovers. What are you hanging on to? If you feel they still serve you, then keep them. Declutter everything that's taxing your well-being, make no excuses. This includes unfollowing negative people, fear mongers and depressing news, movies, on and off social media. Remove self-limiting words and beliefs, gossip, mental chatter, verbal diarrhea, worry and overthinking. Discard your need for approval and victim identity. Stop watching horror, violent and pornographic movies. Drop the drugs and alcohol, stay away from their triggers. Let go of the past. Set new goals and intents. Tell a new story. Simplify your life.

If it's toxic, dump it. Pay attention to your thoughts and use empowering words.

Take a permanent vacation from negativity. Regardless of how tolerant you think you may be, you can only endure so much. Eventually and insidiously, these will start to affect you. Instead, infuse yourself with inspiring and empowering things. Have fun, watch comedies and enjoy your life. There is another way to clear limiting and stagnant energy from your life.

GRATITUDE

Why is it hard for most people to be grateful and appreciative? Deep in our psyche resides limiting ideas which are based on fear and myth. One is that of needing to suffer before earning the right to a reward. An other is not wanting to jinx whatever good is currently in our lives. Superstitious people can believe that showing happiness or contentment brings on the evil eye, and that by complaining (kvetching) wards it off. Our human psyche is so delicate that it will do anything to protect itself. Being ungrateful is a form of self-sabotage and must be eliminated if we are ever to succeed in any area of our life.

If we can't enjoy what we have now, we can never enjoy having more. Always be happy for an other's success. Instead, let them inspire you. We tend to look at what others have and compare it with what we don't. This reinforces our sense of not being good enough—we feel punished for it. Being jealous creates the vibration of lack and resistance. It's basically telling the Universe,

"No!" Being happy for an other's abundance is saying, "Yes to success." Abundance isn't exclusive. The nature of our mind is to equate our worth to things that we have or own. We think having more is better. This falsely creates a sense of separateness and superiority over those who have less. This is not the way to keep score on true success and happiness. Many want the new phone, or the latest fashion attire. Children are not shy showing they want something because all of their friends have it. Parents often respond by asking, "If Sally jumped in the lake, would you?" We can lose sight of all the abundance that is around us, blinded by our first world problems. It's all about perspective. The Physical Quality of Life Index (PQLI) is a way to measure the quality of life of a country. This is calculated by averaging the rates of literacy, infant mortality and life expectancy within the first year of birth. Presently, many in North America are considered winners of the geographical lottery.

Gratitude is one of the best ways to raise our vibration. Complaining lowers it. When we're grateful we are open to receive more. It acknowledges our worth, and shows self-respect. When you give a gift to someone who is unappreciative, it doesn't inspire you to give them more. We may feel that we have nothing to be grateful for and that there is no good in our life. Before you throw your next "poor me" party consider these facts: If you haven't fought in a war, been in prison or tortured, you are not a part of the half-billion people who are or have been. If you can talk freely about your religious beliefs and go to church without being harassed or tortured, you are not one of the billions of people who can't. Do you have food in your fridge, clothes in your closet, a bed to sleep in, and a roof over your head? Congratulations, you're richer than seventy-five percent of the people in the world. If you have extra money that you can donate, and are able to buy things you want, you're in the top eight percent of the wealthiest in the world.

Be thankful that you are alive and can breathe—for the warm water that magically comes out of the pipes—and to being stuck in traffic because you can afford a car. The fact that you can read these words means that you're more fortunate than two billion people who can't. It seems that those who have considerably more seem to be the most unhappy. Be grateful for whatever arises, regardless of whether we think it's good, or bad. Make it a practice to appreciate even the littlest of things. Don't let an unfortunate event be what makes you realize what you had and didn't appreciate. Be grateful for everyone and everything in your life, your health, family, and friends. Be thankful for whatever is in your pocket, even if it's just a tissue. With a little gratitude, we can drastically change our lives.

Unfortunately, many of us are not able to receive. The majority can't even take a compliment without trying to downplay it. Some feel indebted and obligated to give back when they do receive a gift. This also applies when giving; many do so with a motive attached, even if it's subconscious. This often boils down to low self-worth and can be remedied by Self-Love. Those with low confidence often attempt to offset these feelings by overcompensating. Many healers and empaths suffer from giving others too much while neglecting themselves. Also, accepting a compliment or gift without showing excessive humility can make a person appear conceited or entitled. Some say that the more insecure a person is, the more they will tip their server. We have to learn how to properly give and receive without feeling liable for how we come across. Gratitude when we receive, and unconditional when we give. This keeps our vibration high and aligned to abundance.

RISE AND SHINE

Just before we fall asleep, and as soon as we wake are the times when our minds are most open and easily impressed upon. The moment we wake, our mind is a clear canvas, a dry sponge ready to absorb new thoughts. When sleep comes, our thoughts and consciousness drift, all resistance dissolves… This is why it's a good idea to remove televisions, tablets, and smartphones from your bedroom, even your clock radio. The last thing we need is negative news and information entering our subconscious. Whatever we last see and hear we take to bed with us. I suggest meditating or reading an inspirational book before going to sleep. Waking up with a loud obnoxious alarm isn't the best way to usher in a peaceful day. Avoid checking your social media, emails and newsfeed upon awakening as this also sets the tone. These events put us in a reactive state. We want to start our day proactively. Take the time to program your mind with your own empowering content. Later, if you do indulge in social media, change your Likes, follows and subscriptions on your newsfeeds that reflect positive and uplifting content.

Each day when you wake up, declare with absolute resolution that, "Today is going to be the best day ever!" Stop looking for conditions to validate what a great day entails. No matter what happens, be grateful for whatever unfolds—anticipation without expectation. This way there can never be any disappointments. Decide to have the best day, don't wait for it to happen. Begin with gratitude, place your feet on the floor as you get out of bed and say, "Thank you," for being alive and for the great day that will unfold. Bring not yesterday's worries into today—instead, direct your thoughts to abundance, joy and empowerment. Sadly, the majority of our thoughts are negative and are usually recycled from our past. We have 86,400 seconds available to us each day to invest in. Every second is valuable. Negative thinking and emotions are like thieves that creep into the present that steal our happiness. Arm your mental security system, and protect your subconscious.

THE THREE THINGS JOURNAL

You'll need a notebook, blank or lined. Choose your favourite pen or writing tool of choice. On the cover you'll write, "Things That I Am Grateful For." Place it by your bedside table. *Make sure you can see it*—out of sight, out of mind. Every morning jot three things that you're grateful for. Make sure they are different each day. They can be about anything—your body, what you have accomplished, the people in your life, and so on. Read them aloud before you start your day. Each night before going to bed, write underneath your morning's entry three things that went right for that day. Explain how and why they did. Re-read your morning's gratitudes along with your new entry before you fall asleep. Carry this out for a minimum of thirty days, and watch your life magically change. Aim for a daily practice. Sometimes you'll forget to make an entry, or won't be able to. Whatever the case is, don't be hard on yourself. Take the notebook with you, or make Post-It notes and read them throughout the day. You are building a new habit, so don't worry if you forget sometimes. A powerful exercise is to write down three things that you value about yourself. Make note of how you added value to an other today. Strive to enrich the lives of the people you interact with every day. Give them a smile when they don't have one, or give them a genuine compliment. Pay it forward, buy someone lunch, just because. Gratitude redirects our mind to think and feel thoughts in a more positive way, and raises our vibration.

PRACTICE FEELING GOOD

Have you ever noticed that when you're doing something and are upset or angry that everything seems to go wrong? The more our temper flares and patience lessens, the worse it gets. Have you noticed that when you have a good day, you barely give it a second thought, but when even the smallest thing goes wrong, it's all you focus on? Feeling good raises your vibration and charges your electromagnet of attraction. The opposite is true, and this is why you need to keep your emotional state in high spirits. Ride the wave of awesomeness, or of destruction, it's your choice. You can choose to have fun with whatever it is you're doing, attaching no conditions to validate it. The now moment contains everything that you'll ever need to feel happy.

Wherever you are, look around and start being grateful for whatever is at hand. Even if it's not the most ideal, you can always reframe it. Emotionally, grab the next best feeling you can, then another, and stack them. Eventually you will climb the emotional ladder and raise your vibration to awesomeness. Jumping straight from anger to happiness is quite a feat and is highly improbable. If, however, you raise from anger to frustration, you'll get closer to pessimism and find it easier to feel hope. Then, you'll be well on your way to feel happiness, and then joy. As we adjust our emotional thermostat, our feelings (temperature) gradually rise. Once we begin to raise our vibration, we start aligning to people and opportunities that have the same resonance. We won't attract high vibrational people or events with a crappy frequency. By raising our energy to what we desire we become a match to it. Gratitude is the doorway for inviting joy and abundance into our lives. We are a product of our environment which is a byproduct of our thoughts and emotions. We attract the quality and level of what we vibrate. You have the tools.

15

BELIEFS

Before you can ask the Universe what you want, you have to believe that it's possible. Otherwise you're only fooling yourself and setting yourself up for disappointment.

Many Law of Attraction teachings state that all you have to do is focus on what you want, and you'll get it. You can keep repeating all the affirmations you want, but if you don't believe them, you will become disillusioned. This can be dangerous as it leaves people worse off than before they started. Law of Attraction does work—unfortunately for most of us, we end up manifesting more of what we don't want. *Many neglect the important step of removing their old programming before they begin the process.* This chapter will help you identify and change your limiting beliefs, and help you replace them with empowering ones.

When we are born we are a clean slate; an empty sponge. As we pass through events, our internal and external experiences of these form our beliefs. Those who rear us are responsible for most of what is programmed in our psyche; our inherent nature accounts for the rest. These beliefs create the foundation of who we are. Unfortunately, most of what we have been taught to believe are limiting and fearful ways of thinking. Beliefs are what help generate our feelings and emotions, they govern our actions. As we move through more events and gain more knowledge, our early opinions change. When these filters adjust, so does our behaviour and perceptions regarding life.

A *belief* is an internal feeling that something is true, no matter how unproven or irrational it appears to be. How many of you are willing to walk under a ladder without worrying about inviting bad luck into your life? Do you believe that you need to suffer before you get the reward? A *value* is a measure of the importance we attach to something. Our values are reflected in the way we live our lives. *An attitude* is the way we express our beliefs and values through our words and behaviour. Beliefs can be considered facts until proven wrong. *They are nothing but thoughts we repeat until they are ingrained into our subconscious mind.* When they are charged with feeling they become stronger. If doubt still remains, the belief hasn't formed fully.

Absolute knowing occurs when all uncertainty is absent. Affirmation is a way to imbed new beliefs into our subconscious mind, and is done by repeating a word, or words. This is referred to as a *mantra*. Imprinted thoughts are like a silent program running automatically in the background of our consciousness.

We need to inquire if there are any corrupted files, or viruses in our programming? The most powerful limiting beliefs are the ones we have no conscious awareness of. Notice the three middle letters in be*lie*ve. It's time to switch off the autopilot.

CHANGING BELIEFS

If you believe that you can or can't do something, you are absolutely correct.
We don't know what's possible. Sadly, we focus on what isn't. Just look back at the last twenty-five years and all the amazing technical advancements that have been invented. If you weren't a fan of *Star Trek* would you have ever conceived the possibility that over fifty years ago we'd have wireless phones and video chat capabilities that could fit in the palm of our hand? Soon there may be a Scotty, or another to beam us up. Imagine transporting in seconds to Italy's Amalfi Coast for an hour lunch. There will be technological evolution well beyond what we can conceive today. By this assumption, I invite you to imagine and believe whatever the hell you want to...because one day it will be possible.

The difference between success and failure is simply what we believe about them. By changing what we conceive as possible, we *make it so*. It would be easy if we could simply cut and paste a new, empowering belief over an old limiting one. As experience shows, this isn't so easy. When we know how a belief is constructed, we can change it. In order to believe something it has to be proven and supported by experience. Until Santa is proven unreal, he is real to a young mind. The more knowledge we gain, the more we can support or oppose a belief. The first step in changing any theory—limiting or not—is to identify it. Then we need to realize what is holding us to it. In other words, what is stopping us from believing otherwise. The next step is to become aware of how it is negatively affecting our life. Then we need to look for evidence that can deconstruct it. The next step is to replace it with a new empowering belief—*but not until we're fully convinced that the old one no longer serves us.* When we forge a new way of thinking we need to focus on things that will prove and support it. Eventually, the new belief will become fully integrated without question, or doubt. I have coined this process: *identify-deconstruct-replace and support (I.D.R.S).*

Just because a belief may have made sense before, doesn't mean that it still does. Look beyond your past conditioning. Training wheels may have helped you ride a bicycle, but can be a hindrance as you excel. Since we live in duality there really isn't a right or wrong way to do things. Life is about creating experiences. Granted, there are ethical and moral implications for every action we take. We are free to make any choice, but we are not exempt from their consequences. There are empowering and disempowering beliefs that affect the quality of our life. The question is, "How do you want to live it?"

THE PROCESS

You will need a pen and three sheets of paper for each topic. The following will address the most important areas in your life.

Before reading each section, I ask that you write down everything you believe about the subject on the first sheet of paper. Title this "Beliefs". Include both positive and negative, what you heard from your parents, family, friends and school teachers. You are finished only when you can't think of anything more. Take your time and really dig into your memories. I've provided common limiting beliefs that you may have not thought of. These may be the silent programs which are restricting you. If they resonate, add them to your list. Then on the second piece of paper titled "Limiting Beliefs", transfer all the restricting beliefs from the first page. For each belief that you have identified, write down how it has limited you, or let you down. When you're done, continue reading the rest of the section. With this information, you can find more unsupportive facts for further deconstruction. Take your time.

Get out the third piece of paper and title it, "Empowering Beliefs". Again transfer all the positive beliefs you wrote down on the first sheet. You can add to the list by using what resonates with you from the added suggestions. Next, find an empowering belief that will be installed in place of the old one. Following that, find facts and experiences that will support this new view—the more, the merrier. Once we have established a new belief we will find so many ways to validate it. When we first start out, all we may have available is faith that something is possible. When we keep trusting, things will begin to show up to support it. Keep debunking the negative patterns as they arise. When old doubts appear say, "No thanks, not my reality." Initially, if you don't believe the new statements affirm, "I can,

I am in the process of... I'm excited that... It feels good to have this," and so on. Get excited about the new experiences that will come to support this new way of believing. You won't believe it when you see it—you'll see it when you believe it.

At the end of this chapter, place all the negative/limiting beliefs of each category in an envelope and burn them in another fire ritual. Full moons are a great time to do this.

CATEGORIES

Money

You can start off your list by asking, "Money is_____. I like money because_____. I am not financially free because_____." I'd love to have more money but_____." Or you can just point-form each belief as it comes.

Here are some examples of common limiting beliefs to help you awaken unconscious ones:

Having lots of money is not spiritual, money is the root of all evil, money is not that important—it's only money, the rich get richer and the poor get poorer, money is a limited resource, I don't deserve money, you have to work really hard to make money, my family has never been rich, it's my destiny to be poor, it's selfish to want a lot of money, having enough is all we need, if we want more than we need we are being greedy, having less money is a virtue, money tends to corrupt people, having too much money is stupid and makes no sense, take care of the pennies and the dollars will look after themselves, it takes money to make money, a dollar down dollar a week, another day another dollar, a penny saved is a penny earned, money doesn't grow on trees, money can't buy happiness, more money more problems, rich prick rich bitch, by having lots of money I won't be able to trust people and their motives, rich people are selfish and take their money for granted, I don't deserve it, afraid to try and fail, afraid to lose it, look like a failure, it may change my personality, friends won't like me, people will try to get charity from me, charities will bug me, people will find out and break into my house, people will judge me, I'll look greedy and selfish, if I'm rich then that will make others poor, people will only like me for my money, it's hard to make lots of money. *If you know of others I may have missed, then please add them.*

Everyone has a different perspective and relationship with money. Learn which kind you have. Some people earn lots of it but cannot seem to save it. Others may not earn as much yet seem to be able to save and stretch it further than can higher income earners. There are those who buy the best or nothing at all. Ones who only buy new, others who never buy new. Some exaggerate when asked how much they make, while others refuse to talk about it altogether. There are people who use money to keep score, for status, power and safety. Some are happy with enough, others are never happy and it's never enough. The following are more examples: it's extravagant to spend money on myself, money is there to be spent, I'm not good with money, I let other people take care of me financially, I'm a failure if I don't provide, how much I make is tied to my confidence, I'm uncomfortable talking about how much money I have, money will make everything better and solve all my problems, I always look for deals, I'll never overpay for anything, people should work hard for their money not like the CEOs who make a year's salary in one month, money is power, people that don't have money are lazy and undeserving or too stupid. Unfortunately for many, success is measured only through the amount they earn.

WHAT IS MONEY?

Once upon a time we used to exchange items of value as currency. Eventually one form was collectively agreed on. On its own it's nothing—it's just plastic, or the material that it's created on. Money is simply an exchange of value and represents the energy of worth we give it. Everything is energy. The value we give matches our sense of self-worth. If we feel poor energetically, then that's what we will manifest. How often do we take less for our services for approval?

Initially, money seems like the answer to everything, but eventually we realize that material things don't bring lasting peace and happiness. We live in a world built on the use of currency, so we need it. Cash is energy and should reflect the feeling of abundance that we have within ourselves. The only thing that money can truly buy is time, and freedom. Do you know why you want to be financially abundant? It's usually not the money that we are after, but what it affords us. Freedom gives us more time to do the things we love. Like spending more time with family, travelling and eating at fine restaurants. Money doesn't change who you are. If you're an asshole without it, you'll be a bigger asshole with lots of it. Money just amplifies what you are. It allows you to live with your dysfunctions in more comfort. Money is an effective way to help others that need it. If you really want to help them financially, you can only do so when you have the resources. You can't be a philanthropist if you have nothing to give.

Interestingly, wealthy people have the belief that money is easy to acquire. They don't get caught up in the negativity of getting it. There is no conflict, it just comes to them. Those who struggle with their finances have subconscious barriers which cause them to self-sabotage. When you are passionate about what you do, the money usually follows.

Selling out for a quick buck usually leads to unfulfillment and unhappiness. Your job, or career should add value to you and others—it shouldn't deplete you. Every time you ask, "Why Am I broke, why can't I ever get a break?" the Universe will show you. This is not to punish, but to reveal what limiting beliefs you need to clear. When more evidence appears instead of complaining, address it. The more we sulk the more we perpetuate the *poor* pattern. We have a river of unlimited abundance flowing to us but we block it by dams of limiting and competing beliefs.

Affirm: "Abundance is flowing to me now. I remove all blocks with love and gratitude."

You can ask the Universal Wisdom (Higher Self) where your blocks are, and what you need to do to clear them.

Do you realize that billions of dollars are flowing through you right at this moment? Electronic money transfers, and peer-to-peer sharing are filling the ether with more money than you can imagine. Visualize yourself energetically attracting all the money you'll ever need. What type of signals are you sending out, and where is your thermostat set to? Ask, "When did I cap myself off from this flow?" If our vibrational set point is that of poverty, then no matter how much money we make, we will always be in debt. If someone has a millionaire mindset, they can lose millions but know how to make it back. A high average of lottery winners fail to keep their money and fall deeper into debt within a year of winning. This is *poor* programming.

Perceived value

An ad in a marketplace forum listed an item for one hundred dollars. Joe went to the seller and low-balled him fifty bucks. Mike, the seller, firmly refused, saying that the price was already low enough. Later, Joe had his two friends visit at separate times with even lower offers; twenty and thirty dollars respectively. Joe then went back and said to Mike, "Look, I've thought it over and I'm interested in buying, could we work out a deal?" The seller was more than happy to sell it for fifty bucks. A manufacturing plant was losing thousands of dollars a day because of an electrical issue. A service man was called in to fix the problem. The solution was simply a tripped circuit that needed to be turned back on. An invoice was later given to the plant manager at the cost of one thousand dollars. Furious he contested, "You charged me all this for turning on one lousy switch?" The technician replied, "You paid me for knowing which switch caused you the problem. How many thousands of dollars were you losing today before I fixed it?"

There is a deep seated belief in our psyche that we have to suffer to be spiritual. We make excuses why we aren't financially abundant. If you don't value your worth, no one will, and you can't exchange for it. You need to surround yourself with people that have money, those who will gladly pay you—people who value what you have to offer. Low confidence attracts and allows those looking for deals to bust your chops. We are usually underselling ourselves. I'm not suggesting to overcharge, either. People don't value cheap things. Do you really want to help? Then do charity work without charging a dime. You're not doing anyone a favour by people pleasing, and discounting your value.

Do you fear opening bills to the point of leaving it to the last minute? Does this lead to paying the interest penalty? *Pay* attention, don't let money be what is used to control you. Stop allowing the stress of paying bills, your mortgage, and the need of putting food on your table be what breaks you. This type of enslavement crushes your Spirit and stifles your creativity. Did you know that the government can print money whenever they want? They make you believe that it is scarce. If you make too much they'll just charge you more tax. This keeps you down. Religion preaches that money is evil, so why are they always asking for it? The Vatican is one, if not the, most richest establishment in the world.

We put conditions on our happiness through wealth. I'll be happy when… Stop this! You'll forever be postponing it. You need to be happy right now no matter how little you have, or you'll never be when you do have lots. Rewrite your list and complete the process. Write down what you feel positive and good about money. Use the other sheets of paper to gain clarity. Example: "Money gives me time to enjoy life and do the things that I want. I can spend more time with my loved ones. I have peace of mind knowing that I can pay my bills easily. I can help my children, go on trips, enjoy new experiences, etc."

Affirmation: "Money is energy, I am energy, as I raise my vibration more money flows to me with ease."

CAREER

You can start off your list by asking, "A career is_____. I like money because_____. I am not financially free because_____. I'd love to have more money but_____." Or you can just point form each belief as it comes.

Write down what you think a career should be. What do you love and hate about your current job? You are not your career; your Soul isn't defined by what you do for a living. One pitfall is to associate your identity to your job. In most cases a career is a means to an end. Many of us are stuck and feel trapped. If your career is something you love, then you have found true success. True wealth is achieved when our career is fuelled by passion and fulfilling a purpose. Most of the time we do whatever it takes to make ends meet at the expense of everything else.

The word "work" sounds like slave labour; an unhappy way to make a living. We are forced to go to a job that we hate for eight or more hours a day because we are caught in the slavery of debt to pay off "*The Man.*" This means time away from our loved ones, our creative pursuits, away from enjoying nature, or going on a nice trip. Sometimes it takes a health scare, or tragic event that wakes us from this hypnosis. Such an occurrence can force us to question everything. "What the hell am I doing? What's really important in life? Why did I waste all this time?"

Rewrite the script; one from waking up with dread and going to a hated job, to one with exhilaration and the passion to serve others in a way that empowers them. This is what I'm inviting you to explore. We shouldn't have a job, but a passion. It doesn't matter if it's sweeping floors as a custodian in a school, or being the principal. Making the school spotless for the children to learn in a pristine environment is adding value to their lives. Who would it serve if that same janitor cursed under their breath for the mess everyone made? You are here to grow and expand, not to complain. Misery loves company, so avoid other complainers. Changing perspective will give you joy. In reality, you are not only doing it for others, but for yourself. This is not selfish, because it comes from your heart and not from a need to impress others. Deep down we all want to be appreciated, loved and respected. This cannot be forced or demanded, it results by the authenticity of one's actions. We can't be everything to everyone, nor should we. Be you and express your gifts to the best of your ability. There are always people that need what you offer.

CHEAPSKATES AND ASSHOLES

Stop minimizing your worth by lowering your value. You won't impress anyone who is unable to appreciate what you have to offer. In many cases, those that accuse you of being too expensive do not value you, nor do they themselves. If they can't afford you, that's not your fault. If you do a job for an exchange of money, and you feel angry or resentful, it's time to charge more. If what you do has stopped nourishing you, then it's time to stop doing it altogether. There has to be a fair exchange. If you don't value yourself or what you offer, no one will. You will be taken advantage of, and attract those who clip coupons.

Before asking for a promotion or raise, make sure that you have given more than what you're currently being compensated for. Don't expect a higher pay scale because of a timetable or seniority. Always contribute more than you charge. Those that respect and recognize your merit will gladly pay you. Cater to those that can afford your services. Unless you work on volume, you can't be financially successful on the backs of the poor. This doesn't mean being greedy, nor helping those in need. I believe in giving back, I believe in charity. Your time is valuable, so give it to those that need it. Gifting your time and service is worth more than giving out discounts. Ultimately people don't need charity, they need inspiration. Be the one who inspires them to become the best they can be.

Contrary to popular belief, you don't need to be an asshole to make lots of money. There are two ways to make it, one requires more moral investment and integrity than the other. Many of us are programmed to believe that all rich people are greedy and immoral. Our parents, society and television have all contributed to this. *The Simpsons* television program alludes to this; Homer Simpson vs. the insidious Mr. Burns.

It has been said that a sociopath is more likely to become a leader and CEO and will succeed over those who are more caring. Does it take a lack of guilt, empathy and remorse to make one successful? Do nice people finish last? The answer is *no*. There is a conscious way of becoming financially successful that doesn't involve gaining from an other's loss. Give value, and do not manipulate anyone against their will. If they want what you offer, there is no moral conflict. Treat every customer like they were your mother.

Successful attitudes: get up an hour or so earlier than you usually do to get a head start on your day; remove all the negative complainers from your life; align with successful ones that find solutions, not problems; realize that wealth is unlimited; there is not one pie to divide from, but many; the Universe provides endless resources; never compete with anyone, nor prosper at an other's expense; the exchange should benefit all involved; always be happy for an other's success; don't be just another replica of the norm; be unique, offer something different; give more worth than your fees while maintaining your value; inspire those you hire, let them offer their talents and strengths; there is no need to devalue or slave-drive anyone. Free yourself of debt and stop using credit cards, live within your means. Find three hobbies: one that makes you money, one that keeps you in shape, and one that keeps you creative. In the next chapter we will address how to find your career—your calling.

RELATIONSHIPS AND LOVE

You can start off your list by asking, "Love is_____. I like money because_____. I am not able to love because_____." Or you can just point form each belief as it comes.

Write down every thought and belief you have around love, and another on relationships. What do they mean to you? Don't hold back, write down everything—all the positive and negative aspects.

LOVE

Here are some common beliefs on love:
Why would anyone ever love me? I'm not good enough, worthy, or successful enough for someone to love me. Why open up, it will only leave me exposed to be taken advantage of and get hurt. Love equals pain. I don't deserve it. I don't love myself, why would another? I'm not lovable. I'm broken. I will hold out until Mr. or Mrs. Right comes along (unicorn). To show/feel

love is weakness. God will send me love when I've earned it or suffered enough. I will never find love. No one ever really loved me in the past, why should they now? If they did, it was only because they wanted something or had motives; I can't trust. (start trusting life—you). I'll only receive love if I show it back, or earn it. Love isn't real, it's for poets and dreamers.

RELATIONSHIPS

Typical Relationship beliefs:
Sharing my feelings will make me look vulnerable or weak; sharing my concerns will burden others, or they may use my weakness against me. Don't fight or rock the boat because it's not worth it, rather, keep the peace; believing that talking doesn't solve problems, only actions do. *You may falsely believe that those in relationships aren't lonely;* that being single or being alone makes one lonely. *Why are you seeking a relationship?* A relationship will make me happy, fulfill me, make me feel complete or have a sense of self-worth (that's why I try to fix what's broken in the other, instead of seeing what they're mirroring back of what's broken inside of me). Once you fall out of love, you can't get it back; it's over! My past experience means that it will be the same again.

My partner has to do something different in order for our relationship to work. I can't improve my relationship, it takes two (a lie). If I only had more money, a better job, was skinnier, hotter... I can't change my life. Love takes too much work, it should be easy.

Love equals pain. I've never been in a long-term relationship, something always screws up. This probably won't last, either (sabotage). Men/Women can't be trusted. Good men and women don't exist (jaded) and if I find someone, they'll probably get bored, or won't be ready to receive. If I'm kind they'll think I'm too nice, or not fun enough. Women like the bad boys, men like bitches. Women have sex to be in a relationship, guys want a relationship to have sex. Love is pain, I'll lose myself, I'm not worthy or deserving of a real relationship, dating is scary and takes too much work, marriage is the number one cause of divorce, I'm afraid of getting divorced and losing everything, marriage jokes are true, I overlook red flags because I don't think I'll do better, I have to find someone before I'm fifty, expectations and timeline, and hanging on to an old flame.

Men:
I'm not good looking enough, not a stud or Alpha. I don't measure up, not rich enough, inexperienced, too fat, too short, bald, too old, it's too late, women want assholes, nice guys finish last; women are too emotional, drama queens, gold diggers, she'll take everything I own, I'll lose my man cave, my identity, and so on.

Women:
I'm not good enough or pretty enough, too fat, too thin, small boobs, I have kids, all men cheat, men only want what they can't have; all the good guys are ugly, married or gay; there are no good ones left, I am too strong, I intimidate men, they can't handle a strong woman, they get clingy and insecure, men like

drama bitches, all they want is sex, if they get to know who I really am they won't like me, all men bail when the going gets tough, they can't understand me emotionally, and so on.

LOVE AND RELATIONSHIPS

In Chapter 13, I explained the difference between conditional and Unconditional Love. Our very nature is Unconditional Love.

Since we've been disconnected from this realization, we mistakenly attempt to reclaim this by seeking it outward. As a result, what we end up experiencing is conditional love. We often seek another's affection in the hope that it completes us.

We can only love another person at the depth of how we love ourselves. Conversely, the love we withhold from others is equal to the love we withhold from ourselves. The only one who is going to love you fully is yourself, yet it's one of the hardest things for us to do. How can we be truly intimate with another if we can't be with ourselves? We can only share what we have. When our garden is abundant we can then offer to others. Are you tending to another's garden and neglecting your own? Real love is not a false house of cards that's built on a fault line of uncertainty. This is how trust issues arise.

A healthy relationship embodies two emotionally mature adults.

The majority are underdeveloped that constitute an adult and child dynamic. In some cases, reside children. Adults know how to communicate and express their thoughts and feelings in ways that do not put blame on the other, unlike children who are self-identified and attack when a wound is exposed. In a good relationship, the woman doesn't want a man-child to take care of, nor does the man want a daughter type. There is no sexual attraction in a healthy parent-child relationship. Whether we have learned to be a victim or a bully, we can thank our parents. We will attract similar traits in our partners until we finally work through them. If we continue blaming our partner instead of self-analysis, we'll keep repeating this pattern. Maybe it's not them after our fourth failed marriage. Unfulfilled aspects need to be addressed internally and cannot be nourished by another. A deep seated belief is that if we can fix this behaviour in our partner, then we can undo the damage and prove that we can be loved.

There are those who are looking for their soulmate, Twin Flame, Life Partner or whatever their romantic notion is. Ultimately, your Twin Flame is you. We already embody both the Divine Feminine and the Divine Masculine. The primary reason we seek relationships is for the other person to help coax that dormant aspect out in us. Male energy persuades the female energy to move from the emotional end of the spectrum closer to the reasoning end of it. Conversely, the female energy seduces the male energy to move closer to the emotionally intelligent end. The result is the balancing of both energies which are hidden subconsciously within each gender. The feminine principle is receiving, the masculine one is action. In the early stages of an awakening conscious union, there appears to be contrasting feminine and masculine energies. Unless both are awake, similar energies may cause conflict and a power struggle. A conscious union is one where both can share and experience love as balanced energies.

There is a saying, "We meet someone for a reason, a season or a lifetime." The true reason is to season us so we can be with our lifetime. Along the way we will meet many soulmates, who will help us innerstand and realize our own completeness. Each relationship is designed to mirror hidden inner aspects which we need to reflect on. Instead, we try to change the reflection we see rather than grow from it.

Don't expect more from an other who is unable to offer it. You attracted them into your life for a reason. Stop trying to fix and change them—figure out why they are in your life now. Instead we blame them for not completing us and get defensive when they show us what we need to learn. We threaten, bargain and try to manipulate them to cater to our needs. The relationship becomes conditional by the demands imposed to prove our lovability. We place requirements on our partners to validate that they love us. "If you loved me you'd do this, or you wouldn't do that." Initially, if they are also insecure and in need of approval, they will comply. Often times, we may feel that they aren't doing enough, leading us to believe that they don't care. We compare by how much they do with their contributions. Most of us overcompensate and do too much to please our partners.

We get angry when they don't reciprocate (or feel that they do). Eventually, this leads to resentment, defensive behaviour and/or tuning out. This isn't fair as it burdens the other. Why do we think that everyone is a mind reader and should just know what we need? We all have different languages and ways to show and communicate love.

Some people grow faster than others, or in different directions. If you've grown apart from your companion, accept it. Don't feel that because you invested in them that they owe you. Or that you don't want another to reap your hard work. We both learn from each other, it's not exclusive. We tend to forget that our partners were strangers before we met them and may become strangers again after the relationship is over. There is an alarming rate of divorce happening. Conversely, there are many unhappy couples who feel stuck and stay together for: financial reasons, children, self-worth issues, extended family, or for whatever rationale. Some bear through it, others have affairs, etc. If you have grown apart to the point of not having enough to keep you together, or if there aren't enough commonalities, then part ways.

This doesn't mean to bail at the first sight of conflict. Worthwhile things need investment such as nurturing, patience, communication, and persistence. If you're both committed and want to make it work, then fully immerse in the process. Instead of focusing on what's wrong in your relationship pay attention to what's right. Be grateful that your partner is showing you where you need to grow, and for refining what it is you truly desire. It takes two, if one isn't on board you can forget it. A bird can't fly with only one wing. How many couples are mailing it in, not wanting to rock the boat—safer to let things be rather than facing and fixing the conflicts? Most often communication is lacking or one partner gets defensive when approached. We've been conditioned to treat relationships as fair-weather endeavours. We're plagued with too many options, always wondering if there is something better.

Single people: decide why you want a relationship. What kind do you want? Do you find yourself attracting people that need to be fixed? Why do you feel the need to? Do you enjoy having sex without the commitment? Will you settle for half best or wait until you find the one? Stop looking for what you desire and become it first. Be the looked, not the looker. When you're ready, what you seek will seek you. Ironically, when you stop looking and when you fully love yourself, your Life Partner will walk into your life unexpectedly. When we seek in need, we attract the needy. Stop chasing love. If you try to get a cat's attention, it will ignore you. When you go about your business and stop engaging, it will suddenly sit on your lap.

Are you in love or in need? Have you ever considered instead of complaining why you aren't with your Life Partner, to just enjoy the process of finding them? Sometimes the goal is in the journey, to have fun attracting your Life Partner.

There will never be one person to offer you everything, only you can do that. Until you realize this, you will be forever searching for a unicorn. If you did find a close enough match, you'd most likely burden them with the responsibility of saving you, which would push them away. To attract a healthy partner you need to be in a non-needy state. How will you know you are there? When you stop looking. You won't feel that you need anyone. You'll be perfectly fine with the fact that you may never find them. When you meet someone new, trust your intuition and notice any red flags. This doesn't mean holding a reject stamp anticipating any sign of failing your requirement list. Look at the bigger picture objectively. You will be able to communicate with them transparently without taking anything personally. There is a famous quote, "How aware are you of your traumas and suppressed emotions? Can you tell me how you are actively working to heal them before you project them on me?" The best marriage vow would sound something like this, "I promise to never hold you responsible for my state of well-being."

Affirmation: "I am falling in Love with myself more every day. I am having fun learning about myself through everyone I meet. I am enjoying the adventure of finding my Life Partner."

HEALTH

You can start off your list by asking, "Health is_____. I am not healthy because_____. I'd love to be healthier because_____." Or you can just point form each belief as it comes.

I'm an emotional eater; I eat for comfort, when I'm sad or happy. I'm addicted to sugar, my life is too busy and I have no time to prepare good food. Life is too stressful, I need my wine.

I gain weight just by looking at food. I can't lose weight. It's too hard. I have big bones. I have a slow metabolism. Can't fight genetics, it's my hormones. I'm so tired all the time, don't have the energy to exercise. Life is too stressful. I'm going to die anyway, so I'll eat what I want. Life is too short.

Is health a matter of luck? Is it predisposed? A healthy and vibrant body is a result of a healthy and vibrant mental and emotional state. You can't address this from the outside in. Even if we sculpted a perfect body, if our self image is that of a fat person we will continue seeing that person in the mirror. As a result, we will sabotage our efforts. Before long our body will reflect what we believe at a core level. If we love ourselves we will love our body and take care of it. If we have self-hate, we will slowly try to kill ourselves by destructive habits. Don't be duped into believing Self-Love is being conceited, there is a difference. Some hate the mirror, others can't stop checking themselves out. We not only use food as a drug, but as a mechanism to create a defence system. A trauma can cause one to become obese as a way to protect themselves against being desirable. Self-deprecation is a way to flaunt, "I beat you to it, now leave me alone." Likewise, flexing big muscles cries for attention; this depends on the motive of either seeking approval, being safe against vulnerability, or, having a sense of confidence to be able to reject an other.

Those who feel too much tend to gain weight much easier than non-emotional people. Additionally, worry warts tend to carry high levels of stress which create elevated cortisol. There is a myth that being overweight can be blamed on having bigger bones. Actually, a bigger frame will only account for a couple of pounds; only fifteen percent of the population has so-called bigger bones. Obviously a taller person will be heavier due to their height. Genetics dictate about ten percent of how much someone weighs. The intake of food accounts for up to eighty percent of how much one will gain or lose. Resistance training and exercise contribute for only ten to fifteen percent. Like the saying goes, you can never work off a bad diet. When your hormones are out of whack, they will cause havoc with your health. As you know, they can be stabilized.

The weight scale can be downright evil—aside from the mirror, it has to be one of the most sinister devices ever invented. It can lead us to binge eat regardless of the reading of gaining or losing. When it shows we've gained or stalled, we can get depressed. This can lead us to emotional eating. Conversely, when it tells us that we have lost there can be a false sense of confidence which may lead to thoughts of a well-deserved indulgence. Furthermore, the scale can't tell you if you just lost water, or more importantly—precious muscle. Aside from tracking general progress, don't trust something that gives you fluctuating readings. Go by what your clothes tell you, they don't lie. There are many reasons that contribute to weight gain. One of them is emotional eating. Apart from being enslaved by our hormonal chemistry, our feelings are what can trigger our hunger for emotional nourishment. Create a food journal, record when and why you eat poorly; notice which emotional state you're in.

Sometimes our health deteriorates not only by what we eat, but by running our body too hard. There is a saying, "Focus solely on your health, you lose your wealth; focus only on your wealth, you lose your health." Misinformation is another cause of ill health. There are so many contradicting theories that it is hard to believe which ones are true. Become your own scientist and experiment. Research as much as you can and listen to both sides. Eventually, you will find the food that your body will flourish on. Our bodies thrived for millions of years, during this time they've accumulated infinite wisdom. The majority of us eat unconsciously, which is often influenced by our cravings and addictions to certain foods. By calming the mind and connecting with our body, we can feel what it needs. Sometimes it will want food the scientific community deems unhealthy, yet this is exactly what it needs. Your body will tell you through its heightened senses of taste and smell.

As you know, health is an attitude upheld by nourishing thoughts and emotions. When a dis-ease does show up, it's a manifestation of an imbalance. This may include an accumulation of toxins, too much stress and the wrong food; or a combination of each. There are many energy healers that say that a disease takes two to five years to manifest from its energetic form in the aura, to revealing itself in the physical cells. Our body is constantly rejuvenating, old cells are removed and new ones are created. There may be at any given time diseases and cancerous growth arising and subsiding within the body.

This process occurs to help heal it—it's the same when we get a cold or a flu.

If we took a snapshot of our biological environment we may find a disease. What may be just a minor temporary affliction can be interpreted as a serious disease—it's believed that cancer arises and subsides often within us.

What can result is an unnecessary medical assault on a healthy body.

Furthermore, modern medical approaches address the symptom and not the cause. Allopathy tends to the branches and leaves instead of the root cause of a disease, much like we use the weed-killer to eradicate the weeds. Granted, being hit by a car is much better dealt with by Western medicine than would with an herbalist. There needs to be balance.

Your health will improve as every other area of your life does. This entire book will help you achieve this. Become aware of your emotional state when you reach for *comfort* food. We use excuses for not taking responsibility. Food is a big one. As you have already learned in the food section, the relationship between health and food is significant. Greater still is the quality of our thoughts, emotions, lifestyle and belief systems. Your death style is determined by your lifestyle. At the very core level, Life Force is what keeps us alive, not food. Again, try putting food into a dead body.

Affirmation: "My cells are vibrant and healthy."

Moderate during the day and for the coming weeks limiting thoughts, beliefs and emotions that arise. Pay attention to the words you use. At first this may be difficult, but just like working a muscle, the more you do it the more efficient you'll get. Ask, "Why am I doing/saying/eating this?" What words are you saying? "I can't, I'll try, I wish, with my luck." If you give yourself a choice, you can change unhealthy eating and behaviours. If you impose ultimatums, you'll feel instantly deprived. Doing so commits you, and you will most likely crack, and give in. Instead say, "I can eat or do whatever I want. I have the choice, I decide not to at this time." You can use this process for every entry in each category. You can rewrite your life story by the same process. Change your life's narrative because you decide to, not because you have to.

16

WHAT DO YOU WANT?

A mother asked her daughter what she wanted from Santa Claus for Christmas. Her response was priceless, "Mommy, I can't tell you, it's a secret between me and Santa." When you visit a restaurant and the server asks you what you'd like to eat, you have to tell them. If you don't, you won't get any food. How can the Universe give you what you want, when you don't know what it is?

How many of you have actually done something for yourself? Really, only for you? Just for a moment, try and forget the script you've been given. Drop the obligations and expectations that have been subtly imposed upon you by friends, family and society. Forget about looking selfish or self-centred. If money was no object, you had no debt, and I gave you five million dollars right now; could you tell me what you wanted? Some of you would tell me exactly what without any hesitation. Most of you however, wouldn't be so clear. Would you help out your loved ones, and give to charity? Would you stay with your current partner, or dump them on the spot? Some of you may use the money to buy your dream home or car, buy some nice clothes, or travel the world. There are two paths you could take: buy more things, or use the opportunity to explore your inner self. You have to be clear on which it is, it could be a combination of both.

WHAT ARE YOUR WHY'S?

Knowing what you want is one thing, realizing *why* is another. If you don't know why you want something, you'll forever be chasing fruitless pursuits. The objective behind every desire is to attain fulfillment in some capacity. Yet, the moment it's satisfied the satiation it promised eludes us. Experience shows us that obtaining things satisfies the hunger of our Soul for only a short time. Success on a material level typically fills our external needs while leaving our inner yearnings unnourished. True happiness is not found in stuff; its fulfillment cannot be measured materially. All things born in physical time and space are temporary. True success is an inside job, in the timeless state. I'm all for material success and encourage it, but never at the expense of one's integrity and inner joy. Success is multi-faceted, which includes not only money, but mental, emotional and physical health. We need to love, feel loved and respected, and have the freedom to express ourselves. Prosperity in one area doesn't prop the others up. Eventually, however, we will come to the conclusion that true happiness and abundance comes from within first.

When we ask new questions, we get different answers. With enough "why's" we can achieve anything. Take some time and figure out why you want what you do. What is your motivation behind the wanting? Do you want a relationship so that you won't be alone? So you can have continual sex? To have another help with the cost of living? These are just a few examples of what you can ask yourself. You may come to realize that what you thought you wanted may not be the best for you. I'm not suggesting becoming a Buddha and renouncing all material things. What fun is that?

The journey is not about the goal, it's about what you learn getting there—it's about having fun. When we align what we value to what we desire, the magic begins.

PURPOSE, THE REAL MOTIVATION

To quote the famous Mark Twain: "The two most important days in your life are the day you are born and the day you find out why." We are designed to live our life by realizing and fulfilling our purpose. When we find it we thrive, when we don't we whither, and begin to self-destruct. Our purpose is the ultimate motivation. When we know what we want and why we want it, success is a given. Find what you love to do and nourish it. Working hard on something that we don't *InJoy* leads to stress. Working hard on something we love is called passion.

We have to define what success is. Some interpret this to be making five million dollars a year. Others consider it waking up on the right side of the Earth, not six feet under it. When we're clear on what success is for us, we'll know when we get there. True prosperity is being grateful for each step along the way. We all want to have meaning, and make an impact on the world. Many of us want to make a difference in peoples' lives, including our own. We've been taught that wanting more than we have currently is selfish. When we are green we grow, when we ripen we rot. Sadly, most of us have outgrown our present condition. We're like the lobster being crushed by its old constrictive shell. It's time to shed our armour and grow. It takes courage and honesty to recognize this and take action.

How do you align with your purpose? You have to feel it, it's not something you approach intellectually. What inspires you? Where does your attention often wander to? Do you act on these inspirations, or do you quell them? "What gives you joy?" Or, "What used to give you joy?"

You can follow the script that society has set out for you, or explore what is beyond, waiting for you to seize it. As children we are more in alignment with our passions than we are later on in life. We were alive, fresh and didn't care what others thought. We explored and experimented. We coloured, painted, played, imagined adventures, and made forts. When did we stop playing? When did we start getting old? Remember who you were before the world told you who to be. What is your passion? If you can't remember what you loved doing as a child, how do you find out? Maybe you think that kid's stuff can't make you money. Fact is, any passion can generate abundance for you. Brainstorm all the activities that you enjoyed doing as a child. What did you want to be when you grew up? Why? There may be a kernel of truth to whatever arises. If you're still totally stumped then you have two choices: first is to keep living life exactly as you have been until you eventually figure it out. I'm guessing that if this were true, you would have done so by now. Unfortunately, there is a good chance that you will live your whole life without ever finding out what it is. If you do, it may be too late. The second which I'll soon share, is much easier and faster than having to go through more potential hardship and disappointment. Unless that's safer for you?

CLARITY

This may sound counterintuitive, but I invite you to create a list of what you dislike about your life. Get out a piece of paper, create a title at the top of the page, "What I hate about my life now." If this sounds negative then even better. You want your emotions to fuel this list. In point form, write down everything that you don't like about it. Describe how it sucks right now. Don't spare any detail. Leave a space beside or underneath each point. I suggest you do this before reading any further.

The next step is to flip your reasons upside down. You are going to reverse engineer your list. Many of us need to go through life stuff to gain clarity on what we don't like. There comes a point when enough is enough already. How much more learning do we have to endure? Apparently forever, but it no longer has to be painful. Consider this an ongoing refinement process. Up until now, all of your life experiences have allowed you to know your likes and dislikes. This is why I've asked you to write them down. The next step is what I call the *contradistinction process*, or as some call it, clarity through contrast. It's time to go in the closet and dig up your skeletons. Thank the bogeyman for doing a great job. On a separate sheet of paper and for each limiting/what's wrong statement, write down a corresponding empowering desire like we did with beliefs. Please take your time and don't mail this in. The benefits will only be as good as your investment. Continue this process until you gain enough clarity. Here are a few examples of what you can write down: "I hate that I don't have enough money," becomes, "I desire an abundance of money." "I always attract toxic people," becomes, "I desire healthy and stable relationships," and so forth.

"I hate working in a small cubical," becomes, "I love working outside, or in spacious environments." "I hate my boss, I don't feel appreciated," becomes, "I have a grateful boss that values my contributions." You can revisit the beliefs chapter and integrate this process.

If you can't find out what it is you want at this point, then you're not ready. Go back to the moping and excuses. If you're on board, place your hate list into an envelope and save this for later. (Yes, you're going to burn it).

Ask yourself, "If today was my last day on Earth, What would I want to do now?"

PATIENCE ~ TRUST
Divine time

Imagine that the Universe is your personal baker, and chef. You ask for a cake. Have you considered that the wheat has to first be grown, harvested and then milled into flour? Then the eggs have to form, hatch, and so on. Just as the water gets added, you decide to change your mind because you lost your patience. You ask for scrambled eggs instead. The chef has to stop preparing the ingredients for the cake, and get on with the eggs. But before the eggs are done, you change your mind again and ask for a cheeseburger. Can you see the problem?

When you do finally decide on what you want, ask, and then leave it. You don't keep asking the server for your order. The most exquisite meal takes time to prepare, it has to be cooked to perfection. Patience is more than just waiting, it's about your attitude while you do. Forget about a timeline and enjoy the process. Just because what you want is not here yet doesn't mean that it's not happening. Relax, what you desire is on route. The most empowering action is trusting the process.

Before renovating a room in your house, the old structure has to be torn down before the newer one can be made. Have you considered that when we ask the Universe for something that our old structures and patterning also needs to go through this same process? Unfortunately, when this task begins we freak out. Additionally, when we don't see anything happening we may change our vibration before any physical evidence appears. The harder we hold on to what was, the more pain and suffering we feel. We can't have it both ways. So when it looks like your whole world is falling apart, instead of panicking and resisting it, bow in gratitude. What we think we want may not be what's best for us. If you don't get what you want, you may not be emotionally, or intellectually ready for it yet. You may still need some seasoning, otherwise in most cases the timing is off. Whatever is yours will be yours. If something moves away from you, let it go, it's not for you. Your Higher Self has your back, always. Trust that everything is working for your greatest benefit. All is well.

Be grateful for what you have now. We get what we need when we need it. If we always got what we wanted all the time, what fun would it be? There won't be anything left to look forward to. When we are in want of something, we're declaring that we don't have it. Complaining about our lack pushes it away, causing it to be absent in our current reality. Instead of asking the Universe for something say, "Thank you," as if you already have it. Learn the ultimate art of seduction, the cosmic foreplay. Enjoy the excitement and anticipation. The Universe is a classy lady, she won't give it up right away. Remember the old saying, "Careful what you wish for, you just may get it."

STOP TRYING SO HARD, LET IT HAPPEN

Animals are able to sense fear by a person's body language. They can also smell the change in pheromones. Ask any attractive woman who's constantly approached by men if they can sense their fear and desperation. They will tell you that the needy guys don't have a chance to get their number. Don't confuse persistence with desperation; there is a big difference. In the sport of hockey, there is a term called *holding the stick too tight*. This is when a player puts too much pressure on themselves to perform. The result is poor play, and is what causes them to miss an empty net.

When we try to control the outcome of an action, we actually lose our influence. Likewise, seeking power is forceful, selfish, harmful and manipulative. Self-confidence is true power that isn't forced, it is magnetic and draws toward itself. Being fully in the moment without the mind getting in the way puts us in an allowing state. It places us in the *flow zone*, and this is where the magic happens. Don't have any specific expectations, just know that an awesome adventure is waiting, let it happen. Expecting a certain outcome leads to disappointment. Making the best of whatever unfolds puts you in a playful mood, which draws in more fun. Stop trying to make things happen, and start letting them happen. Get out of your way. We take this life way too seriously. Life is short, and no one gets out alive. Somewhere down the line, an experience caused us to start resisting, and make up stupid rules. We lost sight of what's really important. Start having some fun.

EMOTIONAL BAROMETER

Our emotions act as indicators. They tell us whether or not we are aligned with our Higher Self. When our mind and heart are on the same page, we're on track, we feel good. When we aren't we feel upset, or irritable. When things start going wrong, it's a signal that we're going off course. Our natural instinct is to fight through it and resist. Doing so will only bring on more conflict and obstacles. Feeling good means that we are in a state of allowance, which helps us make better decisions. We are plugged in to a higher energy source and are in flow. When we are happy, the current moves quickly. Being angry slows everything down, and causes problems.

Some highways and roads have notches cut out on their shoulder. This signals the driver that they are veering off of the lane. Driving over these ruts causes an uncomfortable vibration. This safety measure forces the driver to centre back on the lane. If this would happen to you, would you get angry and keep driving over them? Or, would you simply recenter? Emotions perform the same function. Instead of reacting with another negative emotion, take pause and adjust. A negative emotion is like the cut in the road. You are not the emotion, nor does it define you. Let it pass. The next time an uncooperative emotion arises, ask yourself, "What am I resisting against? What do I really want, here?" Take in a deep breath and find something to be grateful about. Thank your emotion for showing up. Next, grab the best feeling you can and start climbing up the emotional ladder. Which ever the feeling, reach for the next best one above it. We can't go from zero to sixty in five seconds, especially when driving over those perforations.

"To be a great champion you must believe you are the best. If you're not, pretend you are." —Muhammad Ali.

We can use our thoughts and emotions to set the stage of attracting what we want. You have to believe it before you become it. Practice feeling good; feel the emotion of what you want, and what it will give you. Focus less on the object, or the feeling of not having it.

Gradually, you'll become an energetic match to it. Be happy without any conditions attached. Complaining about something keeps that vibration active. Your current vibration dictates what you attract. This also affects your decisions. When you are happy naturally, you will attract a vibrational match from that authentic emotion. Attaining happiness artificially by stimulants and numbing agents won't work. You may fool others and yourself, but you can never deceive energy. For this reason, you should never make promises or important decisions when you're angry, or drunk. This also applies when you're extremely ecstatic, or sad. You need to be grounded. When your heart and mind are aligned, you become a powerful magnet. Emotions are your best friend. Pay attention to them.

CONSISTENCY ~ DETERMINATION ~ PERSISTENCE

Consistency is what shows authenticity. This can be compared to a statistical average in sports. Faking authenticity is difficult to sustain—sooner or later cracks will appear. Great things take time to build, they are never a matter of intense strength, or by one great feat. They are accomplished by persistence and consistency. If you want to lose twenty pounds, you can't do it in one day—even if you stopped eating and worked out for eight hours.

Nor can one fall in love after a single act of kindness. It's the little things done daily over time that creates change. Determination is the focus *on* the purpose. Persistence is the continuation of the action *around* that purpose—not giving up. Consistency is the doing of the action daily over a long period of time. In *The Ultimate Journey*, I wrote about two frogs falling into a bucket of fresh cream. One gave up treading and died. The other that was determined to stay alive continued paddling. Eventually, he churned the cream into butter and used it to jump out. If you really want something, and your desire is predominate, you'll find a way to get it. If not, you'll find excuses.

How many give up after attempting a new challenge and fail? We may not succeed with the first try, but this doesn't mean we're a failure. How many times did you fall when you first learned to walk? Did you stop trying? We only fail when we give up. Each failure offers us a new lesson on what not to do. It's that simple. When we remove the emotional investment and the judgment, failure isn't possible. Accomplishing goals is not always about incessant action. Once we recalibrate our vibrational set point by establishing successful patterns and habits, it gets easier. Getting up to speed takes the most effort. Then we can lay off the gas pedal and let the momentum move the car.

ROCCO AND HIS TRACTOR

There once was a man named Rocco. He dug holes for a reputable excavation company. He was a simple man, hyper, lacking etiquette, and had little social skills. Some believed he may have been illiterate as well. Rocco wasn't the sharpest tool in the shed, but what he did do well was dig holes. One day a friend asked him to use his company's tractor to dig out his backyard for a pool. Rocco agreed, and naively asked his boss to borrow the company's shovel. "Are you crazy?" his bossed barked back, "I can't let you use the shovel!" "Why not?" Rocco responded, a bit confused. "Man you've got balls, I can't lend you my machine for a side job. Do you know how much they cost? Do you have any clue how insurance and liability works?" "I won't break it boss, come on." The boss was in utter shock and couldn't believe his employee didn't get it. He retorted, "If you want one, then go buy one yourself!" "OK, I will, then." His boss, shaking his head, said, "Good luck Rock, I hope you've got one hundred and fifty-thousand dollars lying around."

At this point Rocco goes back to tell his friend what had happened. His friend said, "Go to the bank and get a loan so you can buy a tractor." "Uh, how do I do that?" All Rocco wanted was a shovel, and knew little else. After some professional coaching offered by his friends, he was given a sound proposal to show the bank. He got the loan. Fast-forward, in just a few short years he became a very wealthy man by digging out pools. Rocco was only thirty-two years old. What can we learn from this?

When a computer programmer writes code for a new program, he inputs commands to execute a certain action. There is no negotiation, there are no thoughts or emotions that interfere. If *(a)* is programmed to be greater than *(b)*, then it must perform *(y)*. If a program has two opposing commands, it will most likely crash. Conflicting beliefs do the same thing. Most of us are driving around in our car with one foot on the gas pedal, and the other on the brake. We are overthinking. Do we really need to know how to split the atom to power the lightbulb? No, we only need to hit the switch. Similarly, when we want to manifest something we simply tell the Universe what that is. Let the Universal Intelligence figure it out, it's not our job to know how. You see, Rocco didn't concern himself with the how, he just focused on the what.

Many of us would feel embarrassed to ask our boss for the company tractor. We'd be worried about not getting approved by the bank. We'd stress over how to pay back the loan. What if we lost our job? What if this, what if that?

REPROGRAM

Do you ever wonder how people like Rocco find success? This can be very frustrating especially for those who are smart and work their ass off, yet have nothing to show for it. No matter how hard one tries to become successful, if we aren't programmed for it, it won't happen. Our childhood indoctrination is a big factor. Zero to seven years of age is considered our programming years. In this timeframe our brains are mainly in theta, which is when we're in meditative and hypnotic states. We absorb everything that happens around us. This is why we can learn a new language in no time. Children are full of imagination and actually believe what they create. The majority of our life is governed subconsciously by what has been impregnated during these short years. The rest is tweaking. When what we want is supported by our programming, there is ease in achieving it. Struggle is the evidence that we're trying to overwrite a limiting program. No matter one's level of intelligence, it's all about how our subconscious was imprinted.

In the last chapter you learned how to recode and change the reference point of old beliefs. Now they have to be embedded into your psyche. You can't relive your younger years, so you need to use either hypnosis, or unwavering repetition to achieve this. This doesn't mean reading casual suggestions on Post-It notes. New commands need to be repeated until they become habits. Once your subconscious gets it, it's locked and loaded. Affirmations alone are bullshit, especially if you don't believe them and have conflicting limiting beliefs.

The only time I suggest dwelling in the past is to extract the memories of previous accomplishments. Stack these impressions together to build momentum. As long as you did something better than yesterday you're excelling. You can reframe yesterday's failures into positive perspectives. There are two sides to everything, so any viewpoint can be repositioned.

What is one of the first things you do when you get up? Go to the bathroom? Eventually, you'll look in the mirror. This is the perfect opportunity to instil powerful affirmations. At this time, you are in a highly suggestive state—before you start filling your mind with yesterday's memories, and the day's potential worries. Get yourself a dry erase marker and write empowering words on the mirror. These are not recommendations that you will say only once or twice. These will be your daily mantras which you'll repeat as often as you can during the day. Vision boards are a great way to imprint on our subconscious, and are good reminders of what you need to instil. They alone won't magically manifest your intentions. The mind forgets and is easily distracted. By placing prompts around your home, car and office, they will keep your mind engaged. Surround yourself with people who are inspiring and support your goals. Write down motivating affirmations on Post-It notes, cue cards, or wherever you can. Affirm them many times during the day. It's not enough to memorize them, you have to feel them and believe them. Without a burning desire, you'll forget and easily become distracted. Use positive words that speak in the present tense. Feel as you have them already. Thank the Universe for them now. Get excited.

SETTING GOALS

Setting goals seems like an old paradigm, however this process is still important. We don't know what we don't know. This may seem like a feeble attempt to undermine and micromanage Source's wisdom. Yet, there is a magic that happens when you set a goal with a target date. The timeline should be realistic and doable. Committing to eat better and start exercising for a week is more realistic than expecting to lose twenty pounds during the same time. Having a goal creates a point of attraction, like a polestar. The star serves as a magnet, drawing toward it things and conditions that will make it happen. Goals set the tone, engages the mind, and makes you accountable. Circumstances may delay or sway you off course, but you're always in its trajectory. Intense passion, and consistent persistence will overcome any obstacle.

The purpose of goal setting is to create a template or map. However, you must be open to whatever unfolds. Whatever is yours will come to pass. Your Soul has your best interests. Get out of the way and don't get hung up on specifics. Careful what you ask for, because usually you'll get it. Many times what we think we wanted, we don't. We may get more than we bargained for, extras, loaded with unforeseen obstacles and challenges. Whatever you intend, always desire it to be for the highest benefit of everyone involved—never at the expense of another. You are not responsible for what others choose to create, it's their reality and experience—not for you to impose on.

Affirmation: "I receive this under grace and in the perfect time, and a benefit to all."

REALITY

Besides our belief systems and early programming, we have real life obstacles to contend with. The way life is currently set up, we are forced to work to pay the bills. This restricts many of us from living our lives how we want. It doesn't have to be this way. We can hack the system, and I'm not suggesting leading a life of crime. Initially, we have to stick it out until we figure out what we are destined for. In the meantime, continue doing what you are doing, making sure you do the best job possible. Use your current job to support your passion, until that flourishes to the point that it can support you. Sometimes you have to take chances and make that leap of faith. Either way, you have to get out of your comfort zone. I suggest getting *out of debt* as your first goal. This is what keeps us slaves to the system.

If you are unhappy in your profession, is it truly because you don't like it? Is it the environment of your workplace, clients or customers? Follow your passion—forget about what you think you should be doing. We're under the weight of others' obligations and expectations. Do your best to put bread on the table. Find others who will support you and your vision. Forget about what has happened in the past—your canvas is clear now. It's not too late, you are not too old and there is enough time. Focus on your strengths, not your weakness.

CAN I TAKE YOUR ORDER?

Give the Universe an offer it can't refuse. Now it's time to make your desire list. Grab a fresh sheet of paper, and write down what comes to you. Take some time with this and write down what you can. What do you want and why do you want it? Remember there are no rules here, except for the ones you create that limit you. Your list doesn't have to be perfect; in fact, it won't be. The beauty is that you can change it, and you most likely will. You will want to refine it as time goes on. The more you learn the clearer you'll be. You have all the tools to make this happen.

17

PUTTING IT ALL TOGETHER

Congratulations, you've made it all the way here. If you have fast-forwarded to this point and have not yet completed the exercises presented, it is my hope that you'll re-read, and do so. Nothing of worth is found on Easy Street. I understand that looking for the quick fix is human nature. If creating the life you desired was easy, then everyone would have done it by now. Ask yourself if you have ever achieved anything meaningful in your life. If you haven't, why not?

Some readers will go directly to the last page or chapter of a book before they begin reading it from the start. They want to know how it ends. Fortunately, the story never ends. The ending is actually the beginning, and the start to another adventure. We forget that this life is a journey. We all want to get to the finish line quickly like the rabbit did in *The Tortoise and the*

Hare story. The process of getting there is the most important thing. You don't run a marathon simply for the medal at the end. The medal represents the hard work and sacrifice invested in the race—eating healthy, getting up early, training hard, and so forth. Once we cross the finish line, the race is over. Then what?

There will be waiting, another goal, desire and challenge. You see, it never ends, there is no getting *there*; it's not a destination. There is no tomorrow, because it's always right now. There is no merit in living in past glories. The journey is the goal, it's who you become in the process.

You are the master of your story. No one else can tell it for you, nor live it on your behalf—only you can. Standing in your truth means having the mental and emotional discipline not to fall into your old patterns of behaviour. It means taking responsibility for your words and actions when you fall. Life is about growing and expanding your awareness with integrity and transparency. It's not about judging and finding fault with yourself or others when you screw up. It takes strength to live your truth in a world where everyone wants to be accepted, and is literally dying to fit in. Love yourself, reclaim your power, and make no apologies.

YOU'RE ALREADY A MASTER

Regardless of what you believe, you are already a master creator. You are an alchemist and have been since the beginning. What ever you have materializing in your life right now, you are responsible for creating. Whether you think it's good or bad, it took effort to bring about. The difference now, is that you will begin to create consciously. The alchemy that I'm presenting here is not based on converting metals into gold. I'm speaking about the transformation of energy into matter to create our reality. No one knows the ratio between how much free will one has to what is predestined.

Either way, without Source Energy, nothing is possible. Instead of being a passenger in God's plan, why not be an active player, and a co-creator.

We may have come here to learn preordained lessons and to achieve pivotal milestones, but it's up to us how we choose to respond and influence what unfolds. Until you awaken and gain mastery over this reality's illusion, you will be at the mercy of outside influences. These include cultural, religious, educational, governmental, and even the planetary influences that reside in the heavens. Bow to no one, only to your creator. The time has come to realize the magnificence that resides within you.

Realize that you are Spirit, unlimited and eternal, with infinite potential. You are pure Love. You have taken on a body to experience this reality. Social, cultural and religious influences have conditioned you into believing that you are a mortal, and powerless. There is a force here on Earth that is based in fear and chaos that's designed to keep you from Self-Realizing. You are hypnotized into believing that this current reality is the absolute truth—it's not. This is all part of the Cosmic Game to help you awaken. The verity is that you have the power and wisdom to achieve anything you want. Awaken like Neo in the movie, *The Matrix*.

ASK AND GET OUT OF THE WAY

Figure out what you want, and ask for it. Focus on what you desire, not on why and what you don't have. Allow it in, offering no resistance, and no excuses. Hold on to that intention and know that it's coming. Feel excited until it appears. Matter follows thought through intention. Your thoughts direct the energy, emotions are what amplify it, and action increases its momentum. The doing helps you to enjoy the experience, or the process. Intention is the beam of energy you create, and attention is where you aim it. Manifesting is a simple process if we allow it to be. Sadly, we get in the way. When the experience is fun and easy, we're on the right path, and guided by Spirit. When it's complicated it's from our ego, indicating that we're veering off course. Fear and doubt will surface due to our past conditioning. They will cause us to give up and disbelieve that success is possible. Have none of it—don't succumb to the old patterns and programs.

If we keep attracting the same people and situations, it just shows that we need to adjust our vibrational output. We have to stop blaming others for what we are manifesting, it's on us. The more we experience the clearer we get on what we want—thus refining our intentions. When we keep our focus steady, it will come—eye on the prize. Keep this process simple. Still your

mind and senses, clear the space of worry and impatient expectation. Be ready and learn how to receive, this allows it in. Let your inspirations and feel good emotions guide your actions. We are Divine extensions of Source Energy, we have already become and experienced everything energetically. We only need to pass through them in the physical. Feel the feeling of already having what you desire. How would it feel to have it right now? Feel it. Whatever manifests, be grateful for it. If it's not exactly what you wanted it's OK. It's getting closer, it's coming.
Let that closeness of the match be what motivates you.

We are not here to compete against anyone. Life is not a competition or a race—it's the freedom to create and express yourself fully and authentically.

You have all the tools you need to create the life you desire. You have learned about what real motivation is, and how it's not about working harder, but smarter. The story that you've bought and invested in isn't who you really are. Narratives have been imposed on you, you don't need to accept them. Life can be created any way you want it to be. You write the script. Intense experiences can create scars and lead to many limitations. However, these can be released and healed by forgiveness and taking responsibility. When you can identify, understand and express your emotions, all your past hurts and emotional wounds can be addressed and nourished. When you learn what keeps you stuck in your comfort zone, and why you commit self-sabotage, you can release their hold on you. No more will you use excuses, and let fear immobilize you. Through Self-Love you'll develop courage, and empower yourself from within. Your confidence will be independent, and without the need for any external validation.

By understanding your physiology, biology, internal rhythms and chemistry, you can use them to your advantage—no longer will you be their slave. You know how important exercise, meditation, proper rest and food can be and how they're used to achieve optimal health. Understanding which foods cause your body harm, and which ones benefit it is vital for performing at your highest capacity. By learning how to focus and discipline your mind, you can begin to take command of your body and have control over your senses. Without the respect for others, especially to our Earth Mother, one cannot achieve greatness in its purest sense. All living life is interdependent, all with symbiotic relationships. When we understand how energy works, and how it flows, we can harness its power and direct it how we wish.

When we are clear about what we want, when our beliefs are aligned, in gratitude, we can then use the power of our thoughts and emotions to *create the life* we desire.

18

THE END OF THE BEGINNING

Welcome to the beginning of your new life. This isn't the final chapter, it's a brand new one. The book of life is eternal, and you are its everlasting author. You are the writer, director and producer. You've been awarded a lifetime book deal, and the exclusive rights to all the movies and theatrical productions. You also have permission to co-author and help produce with an other's story.

I invite you to make a promise to yourself: That you will commit to be the best possible version of you. What you hold in your hands is a mirror capable of reflecting the potential power that's laying dormant within you.

I _____, commit to be the best version of me that I can become.

Signature _____ Date _____

Imagine living your life fully knowing that fear doesn't exist, and that you are Unlimited Potential. What would you do right now knowing that you could never fail?

You are deserving.
You are loved.

www.ingramcontent.com/pod-product-compliance
Lightning Source LLC
Chambersburg PA
CBHW070757020526
44118CB00036B/1822